What Workers Say

What Workers Say

Employee Voice in the Anglo-American Workplace

EDITED BY

Richard B. Freeman, Peter Boxall, and Peter Haynes

ILR Press
An imprint of Cornell University Press
Ithaca and London

First published 2007 by Cornell University Press
First printing, Cornell Paperbacks, 2007

Printed in the United States of America

Library of Congress Cataloging-in-Publication Data

What workers say : employee voice in the Anglo-American workplace / edited by Richard B. Freeman, Peter Boxall, and Peter Haynes.
        p. cm.
    Includes bibliographical references and index.
    ISBN 978-0-8014-4445-6 (cloth : alk. paper) —
ISBN 978-0-8014-7281-7 (pbk. : alk. paper)
    1. Management—Employee participation.   2. Communication in industrial relations.   3. Comparative industrial relations.
I. Freeman, Richard B. (Richard Barry), 1943–   II. Boxall, Peter F.
III. Haynes, Peter, 1955–

HD5650.W47 2007
338.6′9—dc22

                                            2007003486

Cornell University Press strives to use environmentally responsible suppliers and materials to the fullest extent possible in the publishing of its books. Such materials include vegetable-based, low-VOC inks and acid-free papers that are recycled, totally chlorine-free, or partly composed of nonwood fibers. For further information, visit our website at www.cornellpress.cornell.edu.

Cloth printing   10 9 8 7 6 5 4 3 2 1
Paperback printing   10 9 8 7 6 5 4 3 2 1

Contents

Acknowledgments

Many people contributed to this book. We thank first of all the country-level contributors: Alex Bryson, Mike Campolieti, Brian Cooper, John Geary, Rafael Gomez, Morley Gunderson, Peter Holland, Keith Macky, Amanda Pyman, and Julian Teicher. We approached leading industrial relations specialists in six countries. Because this work is based on major surveys, the chapters written by the country authors reflect an enormous amount of work by them in survey design, data gathering, and data analysis as well as in drafting their chapters. We are very grateful to them for this work. Similarly, we are grateful to the analysts who drew the implications of the study for unions, employers and the state across the Anglo-American world: Ann Frost, Konstantinos Georgiadis, Tom Kochan, David Peetz, and John Purcell. We thank the Labor and Employment Relations Association Conference, which held a special workshop in Philadelphia in January 2005, convened by Paula Voos, for the analysts to present their implications to a wider academic audience.

In terms of getting this project off the ground, we acknowledge a particular debt to the University of Auckland, which provided a special research grant to Peter Boxall while he was head of the Department of Management and Employment Relations. We thank John Hood, then vice chancellor, and Barry Spicer, dean of business and economics, for a policy of improving support to heads of departments and for its implementation. The University of Auckland's support enabled visits by Richard Freeman to New Zealand, which were critical in planning this project, and helped with the costs of the workshop we convened with most of the research team in Auckland in September 2004. We are very grateful to Thia Mouton, who ensured that the workshop was superbly organized and very much enjoyed. We are also grateful for administrative assistance to Peter Haynes provided by Marijke Oed and to Richard Freeman provided by Jennifer Amadeo-Holl.

At Cornell University Press, we are particularly grateful to Fran Benson for her backing of this project, to the independent reviewers of the manuscript for their helpful suggestions, and to the team at the Press who have worked on the book, including Karen Laun, Cameron Cooper, and Katy Meigs. Finally, we thank our partners and families for their ongoing support and interest in our work. Special thanks go to Marijanne, Sophie, and Alida.

What Workers Say

Introduction

The Anglo-American Economies
and Employee Voice

RICHARD B. FREEMAN, PETER BOXALL, AND PETER HAYNES

This book is about employee voice in the workplaces of the highly developed Anglo-American economies: the United States, Canada, the United Kingdom, Ireland, Australia, and New Zealand. These are among the most economically successful countries in the world. Despite being located in three different geographic areas, the Anglo-American countries have a common language and legal tradition, have close economic and political ties, and are linked by flows of people, goods, and capital. Many of the same firms operate in each country. The unions in each pay more attention to their counterparts within the group than to unions in other countries. The Anglo-American brand of capitalism—market oriented and open to competition, with modest welfare states and income transfer systems—differentiates the countries from countries in the "social dialogue" model of the European Union (although the United Kingdom and Ireland are part of the Union) and from the highly unionized labor system of Scandinavia.

Similarities among the Anglo-American countries notwithstanding, analysts rarely consider them as representatives of a broad class of capitalist economies. Many studies compare the other Anglo-American countries to the United States, which directs attention to differences among the countries rather than to commonalities. In this book we argue that the six countries are sufficiently alike to make them a distinct capitalist model while also evincing sufficient variety to enable us to derive useful lessons from comparisons among them. Were Darwin to return as a social scientist and journey to the Anglo-American countries to observe their labor relations, he would note the familial similarities and common descent from the United Kingdom. He would ponder the different adaptations to the economic and social environment, just as he noted the varieties among plants and animals in various parts of the world during his journey aboard the *Beagle*. At the turn of the twenty-first century, he would also note that the traditional institution for worker voice and power, the trade union, is facing substantial pressures in all of the Anglo-American countries. In the United States and Australia, the union movements are in deep crisis. In the other four countries, unions are also struggling to respond to challenges from employers, globalization, and neoliberal economic policies.

What Workers Say: Goals, Terms, and Methodology

Although trade unions are invariably a central concern in any study of employee voice, this book goes further in considering nonunion as well as union voice in the six advanced Anglo-American countries. Our aim is to identify the voice workers have in those countries and compare it with the voice they want. Workers are the main "consumers" of the institutions that govern workplaces, which makes it incumbent on government, unions, and business to pay close attention to the views of workers in constructing or reforming those institutions. We designed *What Workers Say* to assess employee attitudes with minimal prompting from researchers. As much as survey methodology permits, we have let workers in the Anglo-American world speak for themselves about their employment institutions and experiences—and about the reforms that might improve employee representation and participation.

To examine employee voice in the six countries in a way that facilitates comparison, we organized a team of country experts in labor relations and labor markets. We coordinated their work through the Internet and then through a workshop at the University of Auckland in September 2004. Our team of researchers adopted a common research methodology: to examine employee views from a linked set of surveys based broadly on the 1994–95 *Worker Representation and Participation Survey* in the United States (Freeman and Rogers 1999) and the 2001 *British Worker Representation and Participation Survey* (Diamond and Freeman 2002).[1] Although the surveys drew their inspiration from this common base, researchers modified questions to suit their country context, to follow up on their particular interests, and, in some cases, to draw on other representative surveys. The original U.S. survey sampled 2,408 adult

---

[1] In terms of specific methods, all but the United Kingdom survey gathered data by telephone interview using standard computer-assisted telephone interviewing (CATI) techniques.

workers in private-sector firms with more than twenty-five employees. The other surveys included all groups of workers. The British study involved face-to-face interviews with some thirteen hundred randomly chosen workers. The Canadian survey used the 1996 *Canada-U.S. Labor Attitudes Survey* by Lipset and Meltz (1997, 2004), which drew many items from Freeman and Rogers (1999). This survey sampled 1,495 workers. The Australian and New Zealand surveys randomly drew 1,000 workers from residential telephone directories. The Irish survey randomly sampled 1,420 workers.

In addition to these country studies, we recruited experts to consider the implications for the institutional parties across the whole set. Thus, the book incorporates analyses of the implications for unions, employers, and government.

While the surveys ask questions in different ways to fit the particular institutional and demographic context of the country under study, they all seek to compare the voice workers have in their workplaces with the voice they want to have. But what do we mean by "voice"? We understand employee voice as incorporating representative voice and various forms of participation developed directly between management and workers. Trade unionism has been the historical vehicle for formal representation of worker interests, but, outside the United States, workers can legitimately have formal voice regarding their working conditions through structures such as joint consultative committees and works councils. The role of unions in nonunion committees and councils varies. In some cases, union representatives are deeply involved in these organizations, while, in other cases, the committees or councils operate in workplaces that are not unionized. Representation thus traverses both union and nonunion institutions.

Participation covers an array of activities in which managers engage workers in work-related decisions, either on the job or off it, and through which workers can exercise some kind of influence in how their work is organized or their workplaces are run. These vary across the Anglo-American world from the "town hall" meetings seen in the United States to the team briefing processes used in the United Kingdom to the employee involvement groups, problem-solving teams, and more autonomous jobs now found, to some extent, not only in the Anglo-American countries but throughout the world.

Although it is common to draw a distinction between representation of employee interests and employee participation in management, we note that there is considerable overlap between representation and participation and the institutions designed to foster them. Managers, for example, often design consultative structures with participation in mind—to inform and to get worker support for management proposals but to stop well short of negotiation of interests. On the other hand, structures starting life as top-down channels may "morph" into forums in which management listens to, and then acts on, employee concerns about their interests. Similarly, unions that represent workers in collective bargaining may also facilitate employee involvement in production decisions. Rather than assuming we know what is going on in the different forms, we ask workers to tell us what is happening and whether they find it effective. Collectively, the *What Workers Say* surveys enable us to address four core sets of questions about the representation and participation of Anglo-American workers at their workplaces:

1. *Union representation gaps:* To what extent, if at all, do workers want greater union representation than they have at their workplaces? Are some groups of workers more frustrated in their inability to gain union representation than others? Are some workplaces or sectors more prone to frustrated union demand?

2. *Worker attitudes toward representation generally:* In the broadest possible terms, how do workers feel about the different ways their interests are represented in their firm? What can unions, in particular, learn from worker desires for representation and assessment of the effectiveness of institutions to meet those desires?

3. *Worker attitudes toward participation and styles of voice:* How do workers feel about employer-driven forms of influence? Are these forms more effective when complementary with unionism? How well do they work independent of unionism? What styles of engagement with employers do workers seek?

4. *Employee voice and public policy reform:* Are there "institutional rigidities" that render public policy on employee voice ineffective in some Anglo-American countries? What institutional models are more successful in giving workers the voice they seek at workplaces?

The first of these questions, focused on the union representation gap, carries forward a key concern in the work of Freeman and Rogers (1999). We know that a large number of workers in the United States want union representation but cannot obtain it. How large is this unfilled demand for unionism in other Anglo-American countries, and what can we say about where it occurs?

The second question is a more general one, examining how workers feel about representation more broadly, including their assessment of the relative costs and benefits of unionism. Better understanding of contemporary worker attitudes toward representative voice is important for all parties but is critical for unions if they wish to modernize their operations to provide more workers what they want from a workplace organization.

The third question is the natural companion to the second one. Throughout the Anglo-American world, the decline of unions has occurred in parallel with the rise of management-driven forms of participation, often concentrated on individual rather than collective voice. To what extent do management-led voice systems fill a role that workers consider valuable? How are management-led systems connected to union voice? Given a choice, what style of engagement do workers want with their employers?

Finally, we assess implications for public policy. Which countries have developed institutions that are worth emulating and in what ways? Which prevent workers from obtaining the voice that they seek? Our overriding goal here is to provide the information so that decision makers in these societies can find ways to improve their voice regimes for the benefit of workers, employers, unions, and society as a whole.

Although the personal predilections of researchers invariably influence the tone and direction of their work, we and the chapter authors have tried to minimize a priori views and theoretical preconceptions to focus on the empirics of the representative surveys. We want to report what workers say, not what we as researchers think they ought to say. In this introduction, we set the stage for the rest of the book by focusing on the Anglo-American economies as a distinct group in comparative labor relations. We examine the commonalities among the six countries that distinguish them from other advanced countries and highlight some of the key differences within the group. We explain how the book is organized and outline what lies ahead.

Classifying Economies: Common Descent and Common Characteristics

Do the economies and labor systems of the United States, Canada, the United Kingdom, Ireland, Australia, and New Zealand constitute a single family or type of capitalist labor institutions that merit analysis as an economic model comparable to the "Nordic" model of the Scandinavian countries or the EU "social dialogue" model that represents the advanced continental EU countries? We argue that they do, in two stages. First, we define the attributes that economies should have in common to be classified as a single group. Then we show that the Anglo-American economies have these attributes. We reach our conclusion that the Anglo-American economies are a single family on the basis of their British heritage; the similarities in the rules they use to govern labor market and other economic transactions; the similarities in the de facto operation of their economic and labor institutions; and their pattern of decline in collective bargaining compared to other advanced countries. We further show that adjacent countries—the United States/Canada, the United Kingdom/Ireland, Australia/New Zealand—have particularly close institutional arrangements, which justifies treating them as pairs in some analyses.

Economists classify economies largely on the basis of the extent to which they rely on private property and competitive markets to allocate resources and distribute income. At one end is the "invisible hand" capitalist economy, where private property predominates and almost everything operates through markets. With the collapse of Communist planned economies, where the state owns productive property and almost everything operates through government decisions, we are left at the other end of the spectrum with more institution-driven market economies, which rely extensively on social dialogue between business and labor in decision making (Freeman 2006). The "war of the models" among advanced capitalist economies is between economies where market forces determine wages and employment with little role for institutions to affect outcomes and those where institutions—unions, centralized or coordinated bargaining, government regulations—also affect the outcomes.

Most studies use observable laws or practices to assess how much a given labor market or economy relies on markets as opposed to institutions. Does the country have employment protection legislation? Do employer federations bargain with centralized union groups? Are minimum wages important? And so on. Some classifications focus on the similarity in de jure labor (and other) codes and regulations among countries (Botero et al. 2003). Others deal with observable procedures such as the centralization of collective bargaining (OECD 2004). Since de jure regulations may be weakly enforced and observable institutions may operate differently in different countries, other classifications are based on surveys that ask respondents to report on actual practices on the ground (Chor and Freeman 2005).

Biology, where classification is more important in analysis than it is in economics, initially grouped animals and plants according to their observable or phenotypic similarity. Since then biologists have used the principle of common descent to classify creatures by their family tree or evolutionary history. Cladistics, which relies extensively on statistical analysis of family trees, has morphed into molecular systematics based on genomic DNA analysis. Approaching the classification problem from a different perspective, economists have come to recognize the value of historical lineage in analyzing economies. They have begun to use the lineage of institutions as an instrument to estimate the independent effect of those institutions on outcomes (Acemoglu, Johnson, and Robinson 2001; Botero et al. 2003).

To assess whether the Anglo-American economies are sufficiently alike to form a separate family among advanced economies, we consider their lineage/common descent from Great Britain and their observable characteristics.

Historic Lineage/Common Descent

The United States, the United Kingdom, Australia, Canada, New Zealand, and Ireland are countries where English is spoken (primarily) and are democracies with a heritage of British concepts of law and contract. In the Botero et al. (2003) classification of countries by legal tradition, they fit into the "Anglo common law" category, though French Canada embodies a French legal tradition. There is one reason for these similarities. All of the countries were colonized by Great Britain. All but the United States and Ireland are members of the British Commonwealth.

The lineage similarities go further. They include similar national origins of the populations. The countries have large British-ancestry populations. The North American countries and Australia and New Zealand have large Irish-origin populations, as well. This is because they offered Irish peasants opportunity to escape a poor rural society when Ireland was a British colony. The United Kingdom and Ireland have an open border, so that the United Kingdom also has a large Irish immigrant population; and New Zealand and Australia have relatively open borders, which allow persons from one country to migrate and work in the other. Finally, there are other substantive people flows among the Anglo-American countries. The United Kingdom hosts large numbers of immigrants from the United States, Australia, Canada, and New Zealand. Persons born in Canada and Britain make up the largest proportion of advanced country immigrants to the United States. Persons born in Australia and New Zealand often work in the United Kingdom for some years, and many move to the United Kingdom permanently.

The flow of people affects the nature of unions and of business. Important union leaders in particular countries were immigrants or the children of immigrants from other Anglo-American countries. Samuel Gompers, founder of the American Federation of Labor, came to the United States from the United Kingdom. John L. Lewis, president of the United Mine Workers of America, who helped found the Congress of Industrial Organizations (CIO) in the United States, was of Welsh descent. James Larkin, the founder of the Irish Transport and General Workers' Union, was born in Liverpool. The labor links are particularly strong between adjacent countries. Some Canadian unions are part of U.S. "internationals," and Canadians have attained the presidency of some of those unions: for instance, Lynn Williams and, later, Leo Gerard headed the United Steelworkers (USW). The Irish Congress of Trade Unions has close ties with the British Trades Union Congress (TUC).

Business ownership patterns also overlap considerably. The United States is the largest investor in Canada. The United Kingdom has the largest foreign direct investment position in the United States. The 1983 Australia New Zealand

Closer Economic Relations Trade Agreement (ANZCERTA) makes it relatively easy for firms from either country to invest in the other.

The Anglo-American economies also share common characteristics in financial markets and corporate governance structures, which has important implications for labor management. Strong emphasis on property rights and shareholder value, along with deep equity markets in the Anglo-American economies, buttresses more dispersed and less committed corporate ownership than in many other advanced economies. In their survey of the ownership of large and medium companies in twenty-seven countries, La Porta, Lopez-de-Silanes, and Shleifer (1999, 512) found that "the United States shares relatively high ownership dispersion with other countries with good shareholder protection, particularly the other rich common law countries," the latter composed for the most part of other Anglo-American countries.[2] Equity markets play a greater role in determining business ownership in the Anglo-American economies than in other economies. In 1997, for example, the value of the stock market in the United States and United Kingdom accounted for 100.9 and 154.4 percent of GDP compared to no more than 31.4, 40.6, and 58.1 percent in Germany, France, and Japan, respectively (Deutsches Aktieninstitut 1998, cited in Jurgens, Naumann, and Rupp 2000).

Some analysts have argued that the shareholder-centered liberal model of corporate governance in the Anglo-American economies encourages short-term thinking among corporate managers, resulting in significant underinvestment (Porter 1992; Shleifer and Vishny 1990; Stein 1988, 1989). While surveys of managers give some support to these arguments (Poterba and Summers 1995; Segelod 2000), the performance of the U.S. economy in the 1990s through the mid-2000s has muted such criticisms. Indeed, the tone of recent analysis of the liberal model has tended to the triumphalist: "The rest of the world seems to be following the U.S. lead" (Holmstrom and Kaplan 2003, 19).[3] Whichever point of view is correct, financial and governance structures do seem to be related to labor-management practices. Comparing the United States and the United Kingdom with Japan and Germany, Gospel and Pendleton (2003) argue that the Anglo-American finance and governance system leads to greater emphasis on the interests of capital vis-à-vis labor, short-term

[2] Surveying investor protection laws in forty-nine nonsocialist countries, La Porta et al. (1998) found that the common law countries had significantly higher protections for investors than the various civil law countries. For shareholder protections there was less variation among the Anglo-American countries than across the common law group as a whole, and the mean scores for the Anglo-American countries were higher than that for the common law group as a whole. Although the common law countries scored below their Scandinavian civil law counterparts for strength of legal enforcement of investor rights, further calculation shows that the differences between the Anglo-American countries taken alone and the Scandinavian group were not significant at the .05 level for five of the six factors tested.

[3] For a more balanced analysis, see Jacoby (2000) and Jurgens, Naumann, and Rupp (2000).

time frames, and financial objectives and measures, which in turn creates less secure employment, less in-house skills training, and more market-based methods to secure worker commitment as opposed to employee voice.

Finally, in the area of economic thinking, there is a powerful, English-speaking liberal economic tradition stemming from Adam Smith and Alfred Marshall that differs in many respects from the economics tradition in continental Europe. And, while all union movements have some socialist leanings, the unions in the Anglo-American world have been more business-oriented than unions in many other advanced capitalist economies (Hyman 2001; Streeck and Hassel 2002).

In sum, common descent and lineage suggest that the six English-speaking economies in this book constitute a single model or family of economies, comparable to families in biological taxonomy. Common lineage and descent does not, however, mean that economies operate according to the same rules or that, in the context of this book, their labor markets produce similar problems of worker representation and participation, much less solutions to those problems. We consider next whether the Anglo-American economies also meet the test of comparable economic and labor market institutions and performance.

General Market Orientation

The most widely used measures of the overall operation of economies are indices of economic freedom. Since the 1980s, the Fraser Institute in Canada has produced the most extensive index of economic freedom based on metrics for "personal choice, voluntary exchange, freedom to compete, and protection of person and property" (Gwartney and Lawson 2002, 5). The Fraser index scales economies from 1 to 10, where higher scores reflect greater dependence of outcomes on markets as opposed to institutions. Since 1995, the Heritage Foundation/Wall Street Journal (Heritage/WSJ) has provided the competing Index of Economic Freedom that scores countries on a different list of variables.

The conservative orientation of the Fraser Institute and of the Heritage/WSJ affects how they define economic freedom. Both code protection of property as a positive factor in economic freedom but code protection of labor as reducing economic freedom on the grounds that it restricts the ability of businesses to make decisions. Both score government regulations and welfare state spending as lowering economic freedom, although these institutions arguably limit monopoly power and expand the economic freedom of disadvantaged groups. Issues of nomenclature and of the specific ways the foundations code variables aside, the indices provide a reasonably valid picture of the market orientation of economies.

Columns 1 and 2 of table intro.1 give the Fraser and Heritage/WSJ rankings of the Anglo-American economies, of other advanced Organisation for Eco-

TABLE INTRO.1
Advanced economies ranked by the market orientation of the overall economy, the labor market, and the government share in economic activity

	Overall economy		Labor market		Government role	
					Gov't spending as % of GDP, 2003	Social expenditure as % of GDP, 2001
	Fraser, 2003 EFA	Heritage, 2005 EFA	Fraser, 2003 Labor	GLS, 2005		
United States	3	12	10	6	35.9	14.7
United Kingdom	6	7	19	13	42.8	21.8
New Zealand	3	5	38	16	39.8	18.5
Ireland	8	5	47	17	35.2	13.8
Australia	9	10	32	17	36.2	18.0
Canada	7	16	25	15	40.1	17.8
Mean (SD) AA	6 (2.5)	9.2 (4.4)	28.5 (13.3)	14 (4.2)	38.3 (3.0)	17 (3.0)
Mean (SD) others less Asian Tigers	23.1 (13)	23.5 (14.8)	66.5 (27.6)	25 (3.8)	49.0 (5.7)	24.2 (3.8)
t-statistic for difference	5.18	3.56	4.42	5.42	5.63	4.71
Switzerland	3	12	34	19	—	26.4
Netherlands	13	17	52	29	48.6	21.8
Finland	17	15	90	26	51	24.8
Iceland	13	8	12	—	46.5	19.8
Denmark	13	8	71	26	56.6	29.2
Luxembourg	9	3	33	—	—	20.8
Austria	13	19	83	25	51.6	26
Belgium	20	21	63	29	49.7	27.2
Germany	19	18	101	23	49.4	27.4
Portugal	34	37	77	—	46.8	21.1
Sweden	24	14	96	29	59	29.8
Japan	30	39	28	17	38.3	16.7
Norway	24	29	89	27	48.4	23.9
Spain	30	31	54	—	39.3	19.6
Italy	54	26	95	24	48.5	24.5
France	38	44	58	26	54.4	28.5
Greece	38	59	94	—	46.7	24.3
Asian tigers						
Hong Kong	1	1	5	—	—	—
Singapore	2	2	42	9	—	—
Taiwan	24	27	61	7	—	—
Korea	35	45	81	10	—	—

Sources: Heritage Foundation (2005) *2005 Index of Economic Freedom;* Gwartney and Lawson, with Gartzke (2005) *Economic Freedom of the World: 2005 Annual Report;* Global Labor Survey (2005); Chor and Freeman (2005); U.S. Bureau of the Census (2005) *Statistical Abstract,* table 1344 using government expenditures; OECD Social Expenditure Database: Total public social expenditure (1980–2001) by main category, as a percentage of total GDP (http://www.oecd.org/dataoecd/56/37/31613113.xls). Note that the OECD provides other estimates in *Factbook 2006* and in Adema and Ladaique (2005).

nomic Co-operation and Development (OECD) countries, and of the four 'Asian Tiger' economies (Hong Kong, Singapore, Taiwan, and South Korea), respectively. The numbers in the ranking exceed the numbers in the table because the rankings include developing economies that we do not report in the table. The summary statistics give the average unweighted scores and standard deviations for the scores for the Anglo-American economies and for the other advanced economies exclusive of the Asian Tiger economies, and the t-statistics for the differences between those means.

The Anglo-American economies rank higher in their market orientation than do the other advanced (non–Asian Tiger) economies. The standard deviations of the scores for the Anglo-American economies in the Fraser Institute rankings are extremely low. This shows that they have very similar market-oriented economic institutions. Using a t-test to measure the difference between the mean Fraser Institute rating in economic freedom for the Anglo-American economies and other advanced economies (again, exclusive of the Asian Tigers), gives a statistically significant 5.18. We treat the Asian Tiger economies, listed at the bottom of the table, separately because they vary so much in their market orientation. Singapore and Hong Kong, which have the English common law tradition, place at the top of the overall economy indices, while Taiwan and Korea, whose histories are quite different, score considerably lower on the free market scale.

The Heritage/WSJ index shows greater variability in the rankings of the Anglo-American economies and smaller differences between them and the other advanced economies. It gives a lower ranking for the United States and Canada, and higher ranks for some of the EU countries. Some of this seems due to the way the Heritage/WSJ index treats the labor market. For instance, the Heritage/WSJ index gives Sweden the same free market score on wages and prices as the United States, despite Sweden's greater dependence on institutions in wage setting.[4] Still, this index also shows that the Anglo-American economies form a distinct group closer to the free market ideal than the other advanced economies. The t-statistic for the difference in means is a statistically significant 3.56.

Disaggregating the Fraser index of economic freedom into its basic components reveals the reasons for the differences in freedom indices among the advanced countries. The Fraser index gives all advanced economies comparable high scores in several indicators of market orientation: protection of property rights, independent legal systems, sound monetary policies, free trade. The advanced countries score closer to an "invisible hand" ideal than do developing countries in all of these measures. This produces the positive correlations between economic freedom indices and levels of GDP that analysts find in studies of the economic freedom indices (Gwartney and Lawson, with Gartzke 2005; Heritage Foundation 2005). The differences among advanced economies occur in two areas: labor market institutions, which are more significant in advanced countries than in developing countries, and which play a bigger role in determining wages and working conditions in EU countries than in the Anglo-

---

[4] Apparently Sweden's reliance on the market to set product prices dominates Sweden's use of collective bargaining to determine wages.

American countries; and the government share of GDP, which tends to be high in countries with extensive welfare states such as the Nordic countries.

Column 3 records the rankings of economies in the Fraser Institute subindex for the market orientation of labor markets.[5] Until 2001, the Fraser index dealt only cursorily with labor institutions. In its 2001 report, however, the institute presented a more comprehensive freedom index for fifty-eight countries that included six indicators of labor institutions. By 2003, it had extended these measures to 103 countries. The rankings of countries by labor market status gives high scores to countries with little or no labor protection, such as Uganda, the United Arab Emirates, Zambia, and Haiti (the top four countries in the Fraser labor market freedom subindex for 2003), while giving low scores to countries that have well-developed legal systems of protecting workers, such as Germany and Sweden. This scoring creates some odd differences and produces a negative relation between "economic freedom" in the labor market and GDP per capita (Freeman 2004). Still, the subindex gives a sensible ranking of the advanced countries. It rates the Anglo-American economies higher on reliance on the labor market to determine labor outcomes than other advanced economies.[6]

Column 4 of table intro.1 records the rankings of countries in the market orientation of their labor market from a different source—the 2004 Global Labor Survey (GLS) (Chor and Freeman 2005). The GLS is an internet-based survey that asked selected union leaders, labor relations professors, government officials, company labor relations executives, and other experts to report on the *actual situation* of labor in their country. The sample consisted disproportionately of respondents favorable to labor institutions (Chor and Freeman 2005). This contrasts with the market orientation of the analysts who construct the economic freedom indices of the Fraser Institute and the Heritage/WSJ. The GLS index shows, however, a similar country pattern to the Fraser labor index: Anglo-American economies depend more on the labor market and less on institutions to determine labor outcomes than do the other advanced economies. Once again, the t-statistic for the difference in means is significant. That the rankings of countries by labor practices are similar in the GLS and Fraser measures indicates that the orientation of analysts did not noticeably affect their reporting of country labor practices.

Turning to the role of the government in the economy, column 5 of table intro.1 records the proportion of GDP that consists of government expenditures. It shows that government plays a smaller role in the Anglo-American economies than in others. Column 6 gives the proportion of GDP that the OECD

---

[5] As the Swedish-U.S. comparison in the text indicates, the Heritage/WSJ index does not delve in depth into labor market issues. Its subindex treats price and wage setting together.

[6] Because the Heritage/WSJ measure of economic freedom does not treat the labor market with the same attention, we do not report its subindex in table intro.1.

categorizes as social expenditures.[7] It shows that much of the difference in the government share of GDP takes the form of smaller welfare state interventions designed to buttress the living standards of lower-income groups in the Anglo-American countries than in others. As before, the differences in the means for these two statistical measures are significant. The Anglo-American country with the highest government and social expenditures' share of GDP is the United Kingdom, whose spending falls below all but two of the non-Anglo-American countries (Japan and Spain in column 5 and Japan and Iceland in column 6).

It seems, then, that common descent among the Anglo-American countries has manifested itself in some common economic behaviors. The Anglo-American economies are, in general, more market friendly with relatively smaller governments than other advanced capitalist economies.

Labor Market Outcomes and Institutional Patterns

Data on labor market outcomes and institutions strengthen our contention that the Anglo-American economies constitute a distinct group for analysis. With respect to outcomes, perhaps no aspect of the economic performance of the Anglo-American economies has attracted as much attention as the low unemployment rate and high employment rates that they generated in the 1990s to mid-2000s. On the basis of the better employment and unemployment record of the Anglo-American economies (figure intro.1), many policy-makers and analysts in the EU have come to believe that Anglo-American labor institutions are superior to EU labor institutions in creating full employment. Whether this claim is empirically justifiable or not (Freeman 2005), there is no gainsaying that the labor institutions as well as labor market outcomes differ greatly between the United States, the United Kingdom, Australia, Ireland, Canada, and New Zealand, and most other advanced countries.

The first and, arguably, most important institutional difference between the Anglo-American and other advanced economies is found in the extent of unionization and use of collective bargaining to determine wages. In 2000, union density in the Anglo-American economies averaged 26 percent while density in the other countries averaged 38 percent.[8] But the bigger difference is in the percentage of workers covered by collective bargaining. In many EU countries, mandatory extension of collective bargaining contracts brings many workers and firms who were not part of the agreement under its terms. In the United States, the United Kingdom, and Canada, this was never the case. In New Zealand and Australia, wages and conditions were historically set by a cen-

---

[7] The OECD defines this to measure "the extent to which governments assume responsibility for supporting the standard of living of disadvantaged or vulnerable groups."

[8] Based on data from the OECD (2004, table 3.3).

Unemployment rate

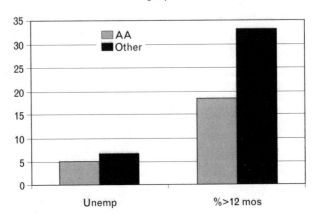

Employment rate

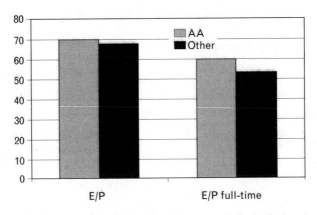

Figure intro.1: Unemployment and employment/population rates in the Anglo-American (AA) economies and other advanced economies (other)

Source: Tabulated from OECD (2005).

tralized award system, in which courts effectively extended agreements to the entire economy. But New Zealand ended its centralized system in 1991 and Australia began moving away from its award system in the mid-1990s. Collective bargaining coverage fell hugely in New Zealand and began to decline in Australia in the 2000s, following a significant decentralization of bargaining to the plant and company level. The exception to this pattern is Ireland, which in 1987 developed a Social Pact for wage-setting to help the country escape from a major recession. Consistent with the Anglo-American traditions of decen-

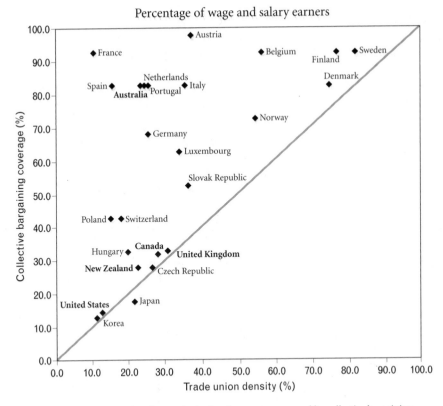

Figure intro.2: Percentage of workers unionized and percentage covered by collective bargaining, 2000

Source: OECD Employment Outlook 2004. Copyright OECD, 2004. Data for Ireland are not available.

tralized decision-making, however, the unions balloted members over potential settlements as part of their involvement in the Pact.[9]

Figure intro.2 shows how the Anglo-American economies compare to other advanced countries in the rate of unionization and collective bargaining coverage in 2000. The 45 degree line represents the situation where the rate of collective bargaining equals the rate of unionization and thus where there is no

[9] In their classification of countries according to "patterns of bargaining coordination," Ebbinghaus and Kittel (2005) emphasize the diversity within the Anglo-American camp over the period 1971–98 because of the New Zealand, Australian, and Irish cases. We would argue that since 1998 the Anglo-American countries have become significantly less "mixed" in terms of bargaining coordination patterns: there is no evidence that the regulatory changes in New Zealand in 2000 have moved New Zealand away from the "flexible uncoordinated bargaining" pattern that Ebbinghaus and Kittel ascribe to the United States, Canada and the United Kingdom; and Australia has moved firmly into this camp (chapter 5 in this book).

extension of contracts. Points above the line reflect some form of extension. Four of the six Anglo-American countries lie along line. Ireland lies above it.[10] In 2000, Australia was considerably above the line, but Australian collective bargaining coverage has fallen since then toward the line.

Collective bargaining is the critical institution in wage setting, leading to many categorizations of wage-setting systems in advanced countries in terms of the extent and nature of such bargaining (OECD 1997). The most recent analysis by the OECD (OECD 2004, table 3.5) used two related categorizations—one which divided collective bargaining arrangements into five groups based on centralization of bargaining and one which divided the arrangements to allow for coordinated bargaining. The centralization grouping ranged from economies where wages were predominantly determined at the company and plant level (scored as 1) to economies where central-level agreements were of over-riding importance (scored as 5). This categorization placed four of the Anglo-American countries in the most market determined group, put Australia into the second most market determined wage group and put Ireland into the second most centralized wage-setting group (OECD 2004, table 3.5). Taken as a whole, the Anglo-American economies averaged 1.8 on the wage-setting institution scale while the other advanced OECD countries averaged 2.8.

When countries determine pay by collective bargaining or other institutions, they almost invariably compress the distribution of earnings. Given the reliance of the Anglo-American countries on markets for setting wages, we expect that these countries would have greater dispersion of wages than other advanced countries. The horizontal axis of figure intro.3 records one widely used indicator of pay dispersion, the ratio of the pay of persons in the ninetieth percentile of wages and salaries relative to the pay of persons in the tenth percentile. The United States has the highest dispersion; Norway has the lowest. The mean for the Anglo-American countries is 3.65, statistically significantly higher than the 2.85 mean for the other countries.

Another institutional difference between Anglo-American economies and most other advanced country economies relates to employment protection given to workers on the job. In the Anglo-American economies, employers "own" jobs and can lay off workers with little legal restriction. In other advanced countries, workers tend to have greater employment protection. This often takes the form of requiring that firms negotiate with a works council on a "social plan" for retraining before they lay off workers; and of paying legally mandated severance pay when the firm chooses to lay them off. Such regulations have the potential for increasing employment by making it more expensive to lay off workers. But they also have the potential to decrease employment

---

[10] Although comparable data are not available for Ireland, expert opinion places Ireland above the line (see Ochel [2001] and Visser [2000] for the mid-1990s and European Commission [2003] for 2000).

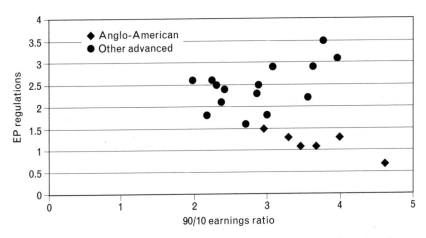

Figure intro.3: The Anglo-American economies and other advanced economies, dispersion of pay and employment policy regulations)

Source: EP regulations: OECD (2004), table 2.A2.4, version 2; wage dispersion: OECD (2004), table 3.2. Note that data are from 1995 through 1999 with figures from Austria, Belgium, Denmark, Portugal for 1990—1994, and data for Spain and Greece from Martins and Pereira (2004), table 1.

by making hiring more expensive, since firms recognize that if they have to lay off workers, it will cost more. In theory, the regulations or collective bargaining could set just the right severance pay to shift income from employers to workers without having an effect on employment. Empirical studies suggest that the regulations have little effect on the overall rate of unemployment but shift unemployment from older workers to younger job seekers (OECD 2004).

The vertical axis of figure intro.3 measures employment protection legislation (EPL), as indexed by the OECD. There is no overlap between Anglo-American economies and the other advanced economies. The Anglo-American economy with the strongest EPL regulations, Australia, had markedly weaker EPL regulations than the countries with the weakest protection outside of the Anglo-American group, Denmark and Switzerland. And the labor market legislation adopted by the Australian Government in 2006 will increase the space between the Anglo-American countries and others since it will considerably reduce Australian workers' employment protections. By displaying the dispersion of earnings and the difference in employment protection legislation together, figure intro.3 shows starkly the difference between the operation of the labor markets in Anglo-American economies and those in other advanced economies.

Labor laws and regulations help determine the way in which a country divides the responsibility for labor market outcomes between market forces, largely operating through the behavior of firms, and institutions, largely operating through unions. To measure the strength of regulations, Botero et al. (2003) coded the laws regulating employment contracts, industrial relations, and social security regulations in 85 countries. Higher values indicate greater labor regulations. The Anglo-American countries have lower scores than the other advanced (non-Asian Tiger) countries in all three areas but the magnitude of the differences between the Anglo-American countries and other advanced countries varies greatly. Using a t-statistic to measure the difference between the means, the greatest difference is for industrial relations laws, followed by employment laws, with no statistically significant difference for social security regulations.

The laws governing labor are likely to influence how the labor markets function and workplace practices, but they are unlikely to be determinative. De jure rulings do not inevitably produce de facto practices on the ground. One way to see how country labor systems differ in practice is to ask business and labor practitioners about the ways in which the labor markets in their country operate.

For the business view, we rely on the global competitiveness reports of the World Economic Forum (WEF). The WEF asks executives annually how their country performs in diverse areas, including some aspects of labor market performance (World Economic Forum 2003). Table intro.2 gives the average ranking of the Anglo-American countries and other (non-Asian Tiger) advanced countries in four dimensions of labor market decision-making for 2003.

Column 1 shows that executives in the Anglo-American countries reported that their country relied less on wage-setting institutions than the executives in other countries, though the mean difference is not huge. The differences are not huge because Ireland had a highly centralized wage-setting system while Australian wage setting was moderately centralized in 2002–03. Column 2 gives the average ranking of countries by the extent to which management can relate pay to productivity. On this dimension, Ireland and Australia are closer to the other Anglo-American countries, producing a higher t-statistic for the difference between the Anglo-American economies and the other advanced economies. Column 3 turns to hiring and firing practices—the employment protection laws described earlier. Executives in the Anglo-American countries give their country a more market-oriented ranking on this dimension because, as we have already seen, those countries have weaker protections for workers. The United States, which has the strongest "employment at will" rules among the Anglo-American economies, and where firms are free to replace workers who go on strike, is the Anglo-American country with the highest market score (World Economic Forum 2003, table 10.18).

TABLE INTRO.2
Mean values of ranks of Anglo-American and other advanced economies in executive reports on labor institutions (low value = market oriented)

Mean, t-test	Wage flexibility	Pay linked to productivity	Hiring and firing	Delegation of authority	Cooperative labor-mgmt relations
Mean, AA	26	11	27	11	25
Mean, other	60	39	53	18	25
t-test	2.60	5.09	2.72	1.40	0.08
	AA firms have more control over wages	AA firms link pay to productivity more than others	AA firms have greater power to hire and fire	AA firms slightly more likely to delegate authority	No difference perceived in labor-mgmt cooperation

Source: Computed from World Economic Forum (2003).

Finally, columns 4 and 5 of table intro.2 show the average rankings of the Anglo-American countries and other advanced countries by the extent to which management delegates authority, and cooperation between labor and management. Here, the executives surveyed by WEF do not see marked differences between the Anglo-American countries and others. Five of the EU countries included in the non-Anglo-American advanced country group score better in the measure of delegation than the Anglo-American countries (the five are Denmark, Sweden, Finland, Netherlands, and Switzerland). The column 5 data shows no difference in the extent of cooperation in labor-management relations between the Anglo-American countries and other advanced countries.

For the labor-oriented view, we report the ranking of countries from the Global Labor Survey of labor practitioners (table intro.3). The survey rank order is in terms of how favorable respondents judged the country toward labor interests as opposed to business interests in 33 countries, so the rankings are from 1 to 33. For consistency, we have reverse coded the rankings so that countries with practices more favorable to business are ranked higher.[11] The five columns in the table give indices of conditions for overall labor market performance, freedom of association/collective bargaining, labor disputes, regulations and working conditions, and employee benefits. In each case, the Anglo-American countries are rated as more favorable to business than to labor interests by statistically significant amounts.

Both sets of reports, then, from executives and labor practitioners, give a consistent picture of the differences between the Anglo-American economies and other advanced economies in actual labor practices: the Anglo-American

[11] Specifically we subtracted the score from 34, so that the country ranked 1 (most labor friendly) obtained a rank of 33, and the country ranked 33 obtained a rank of 1, and so on.

TABLE INTRO.3
Mean values of ranks of Anglo-American and other advanced economies in labor practitioner reports
on practices (low value = market oriented)

Mean, t-test	Labor market conditions	Freedom of association/ collective bargaining	Labor disputes	Regulations and working conditions	Employee benefits
Mean, AA	16	15	12	13	13
Mean, other	26	26	22	25	26
t-test	4.13	5.03	3.34	3.29	5.67
	Labor market is more business-friendly in AA countries	AA countries make freedom of association and collective bargaining more difficult	AA countries have a more pro-business stance in disputes	Labor regulations are more pro-business in AA countries	Workers in AA countries have fewer benefits than in other advanced countries

Source: Computed from Global Labor Survey (Chor and Freeman 2005)

economies are relatively more business friendly than labor friendly in most domains.

Variation in the Anglo-American Family

> There is a tendency in nature to the continued progression of certain classes
> of varieties further and further from the original type.
> ALFRED RUSSELL WALLACE (1858)

Just as animals and plants evolve in different environments from the "parent form," so too have the Anglo-American countries diverged over time from their British traditions. Developments in one country have also spilled over to the parent country and to others. For instance, in 2000, the United Kingdom introduced labor laws that created a secret ballot election process to resolve situations in which firms refused to recognize unions that claimed to be representative of workers, following the principle of the National Labor Relations Act (Wagner Act) in the Unites States. But it is the countries with close adjacency where institutional forms have evolved together most similarly.

The North American pair, the United States and Canada, has a common Wagner Act heritage. The United States enacted the Wagner Act in 1936 to move the battle over union recognition from the streets to the ballot box. Canada enacted its labor laws after the Wagner Act, with the federal government and provinces paying close attention to what the Wagner Act did and did not do. But Canadian labor law differs from U.S. labor law in two important respects. First, whereas the Wagner Act outlawed nonunion, company-sponsored institutions of voice, Canada decided against prohibiting groups of employees dealing directly with management independently of trade unions. Second, rather than centralizing labor law at the national level, Canada followed its strong federalist traditions and allowed provinces to determine the bulk of labor law. This has produced variation and experimentation in legal governance of labor relations within Canada, whereas the doctrine of federal preemption of private-sector labor law in the United States has led to stasis in the law, with unions and management exercising virtual veto power over potential experimental reforms.

The United Kingdom and Ireland share a voluntarist tradition. They have, however, parted company over the last twenty years. Instead of following the United Kingdom's path of restricting union power, including abolishing the closed shop, Irish governments have adopted a social partnership model in which central union and employer organizations reach national wage agreements. The United Kingdom–Ireland pairing is interesting in another sense: both countries are members of the European Union. They are thus subject to European directives and institutional diffusion, including the spread of works councils, although the scope to customize these institutions is considerable.

The Antipodeans, Australia and New Zealand, have a shared heritage of compulsory state-provided arbitration of labor disputes, created in the late 1890s and early twentieth century when there was widespread concern over the "labor question." The arbitral structure was completely dismantled in New Zealand in 1991, and it is in the process of being interred in Australia in favor of individual contracting and collective bargaining. The switch from the arbitration and awards' system to a decentralized system provides social science with a powerful before/after natural experiment on how changing labor regulation affects labor practices.

Summary and Outline of What Lies Ahead

In sum, the Anglo-American economies share a common descent and similar economic orientation and structure and have evinced similar labor market behaviors and governmental regulatory stances, which distinguish them from other advanced countries and justify studying them as a group, as we do in this book. The variations within the Anglo-American set also create possibilities for the countries to learn from the experiences of the other countries in the group. To be sure, any country can learn from experiences in other countries, but countries with similar lineages and traditions, such as those in the Anglo-American group, are more likely to be able to adapt the experiences of one another than the experiences of countries with different institutional lineages and practices. For the same reason, while countries outside of the Anglo-American group can learn from the experiences of the Anglo-American countries, they will have to consider how what works or does not work inside the Anglo-American model fits in their own institutional frame.

The remainder of this book is organized into two main parts. Chapters 1 to 6 present detailed investigations of employee voice in each country, organized into the three sets of geographic pairs, beginning in each case with the larger country. In chapter 1, Richard B. Freeman asks whether the United States can clear the market for representation and participation. He builds on, and extends, the analysis contained in *What Workers Want* (Freeman and Rogers 1999), updating information on the degree of frustrated demand for unionism in the United States, examining the relationship between the extent of the problems in a workplace and the desire for unionization, and exploring alternative hypotheses regarding union decline. Freeman emphasizes the preference of U.S. workers for voice institutions that enjoy management cooperation and reviews recent attempts by U.S. unions to find ways of attracting workers that do not depend on gaining collective bargaining at particular work sites. In chapter 2, Michele Campolieti, Rafael Gomez, and Morley Gunderson examine worker attitudes to union and nonunion voice in Canada. As they emphasize, Canada is a case of decentralized bargaining in which union density has *not* fallen dramatically. They review the key institutional differences with the United States, including the way in which the Canadian versions of the Wagner model allow for nonunion representative voice. The chapter profiles the kind of workers most likely to have access to formal collective voice and those most likely to want it. It also analyses worker preference for direct voice in Canada and explores ways in which government, unions, and employers are evolving their strategies for worker voice.

Diversity of voice practices increases as we travel north in North America and more so as we cross the Atlantic. In chapter 3, Alex Bryson and Richard B. Freeman consider the voice that British workers want. They trace the history of voice institutions in the United Kingdom: from a society in which employee voice was synonymous with trade unions to one in which voice practices incorporate management-driven ones, such as team briefing and joint consultation, and most recently, European-inspired state-mandated works councils. They analyze worker preferences for voice institutions across this mix. Among other things, they show that, as in the United States, workers with a high number of problems at their workplace have a stronger desire for union voice than others and document a high preference among workers for cooperative styles of voice. John Geary analyses employee voice in the Irish workplace in chapter 4. This chapter describes how workers feel about their representation and participation in a society in which unions are "social partners" and wage bargaining is centralized, a rarity in the Anglo-American world. Geary examines the profile of union members, attitudes toward union activities, reasons for joining and not joining unions, and worker attitudes toward direct voice. As the analysis unfolds, the chapter shows that there is more conflict in Ireland among the institutional parties than in the United Kingdom over the shape of employee voice at workplace level.

The country studies are completed by the Antipodeans. In chapter 5, Julian Teicher, Amanda Pyman, Peter Holland, and Brian Cooper ask whether Australian workers are finding their voice; while in chapter 6, Peter Boxall, Peter Haynes, and Keith Macky examine employee voice and voicelessness in New Zealand. The surveys in these countries were closely coordinated and the two chapters traverse the heritage of voice institutions; the extent and contours of the representation gap; attitudes toward unions and nonunion voice; and the implications of the findings for unions, employers, and government. While the attitudes of workers toward unions, toward nonunion voice, and toward labor-management cooperation are remarkably similar, the voice regime in New Zealand has been evolving into a more stable, more consensual model than in Australia, which has headed into a serious crisis over the shape of its voice institutions.

In the second part, the book turns to cross-country analysis. David Peetz and Ann Frost examine the implications of the country studies for unions in chapter 7. While recognizing declining union density and the difficulties that unions face, they see positive signs for unions in employee attitudes and explore ways in which unions might build more collectivist behavior and enhance their internal responsiveness to worker needs. John Purcell and Konstantinos Georgiadis examine the implications for employers in chapter 8, asking why employers should bother with worker voice. Their answer considers evidence on the performance impacts of voice practices, looks at their role as ways of handling employee problems, considers the possible use of voice practices as ways of substituting for unions, and concludes with a discussion of the role of voice institutions in enhancing the social legitimacy of firms. Then, in chapter 9, Tom Kochan discusses why governments should care about employee voice and identifies a series of principles for government policy designed to support worker voice and representation.

In the concluding chapter we summarize the overall picture of the country studies and, building on those studies and the cross-country analyses, offer our answers to the four key questions we identified in the early part of this introduction. In a nutshell, we contend:

- Many more workers want traditional, union-based representation than are organized; unfilled demand for unionism is greatest among workers who are vulnerable or who have severe workplace problems.

- Worker needs for representation vary in important ways; no single mode of employee voice, such as unionism, can fit the needs of all workers.

- By and large, workers endorse the growth of management-driven forms of involvement and show a strong preference for the expansion of more co-operative styles of voice.

- Compared with the other countries, the United States has a rigid, outmoded system of employee voice that does not protect workers' right to choose the voice options they want and that restricts firms and workers from developing nonunion modes of voice. The Australian government's effort to weaken unions and push workers and firms into individual contracts could potentially create similar problems. The more successful labor regulatory regimes are those that foster diversity and complementarity among the various institutions of voice.

Our argument is that public policy should ensure that workers can choose the voice options they want. Without privileging them as the sole or exclusive voice of workers, it should ensure that unions can operate as normal institutions in a capitalist democracy. Flexibility and innovation in employee voice is to be encouraged, not least in the United States.

We invite readers to consider the evidence and analysis underpinning these conclusions.

Chapter 1

Can the United States Clear the Market for Representation and Participation?

RICHARD B. FREEMAN

"O Trade Union, Trade Union! Wherefore art thou, Trade Union?"
(paraphrased from SHAKESPEARE's *Romeo and Juliet*)

Union density in the United States has been on a seemingly endless down-ward trajectory. In 2005, union membership in the private sector was 7.8 per-cent of employed wage and salary workers—comparable to the level a hundred years earlier. Density in the public sector was 36.5 percent—nearly five times private sector density; but the public sector accounts for just 15 percent of the U.S. workforce.[1] As a result, economywide density was 12.5 percent in 2005, a drop from 14.3 percent in 2000 and from 23.8 percent in 1990. Total density may eventually stabilize at a rate higher than the 10 percent that Freeman and Medoff projected in *What Do Unions Do?* (1984, 241), but it could fall even fur-ther. In the state with the lowest rate of unionization, North Carolina, density fell from 5.3 percent in 1990 to 2.7 percent in 2005.[2]

In contrast to other Anglo-American countries, which have alternative forms of collective voice for workers—employee-initiated staff associations, mandated works councils, employer initiated committees—the United States has developed no new institutions to close the gap in representation and par-ticipation created by declining unionism. Section 8(a)(2) of the National Labor Relations Act outlaws company unions, which rules out the company-sponsored labor committees that cover 14 percent of the workforce (and 20

[1] http://www.bls.gov/news.release/union2.t03.htm
[2] See Hirsch and Macpherson (2003).

percent of the nonunion workforce) in Canada (see chapter 2). U.S. management has instituted employee involvement (EI) committees, quality circles, and teams that focus on productivity and quality of output, but these groups cannot legally discuss issues relating to labor-management relations or worker well-being. Labor law protects concerted action by workers, be they union or nonunion, but de facto the only way workers gain representation is when a majority votes to unionize in a government-sponsored election and has enough bargaining clout to win a collective bargaining contract.

Some analysts (Flanagan 2005; McLennan 2006; Farber 1989; Farber and Krueger 1992) have interpreted declining density as evidence that U.S. workers increasingly reject trade unionism as their institution of voice. Perhaps employee involvement committees, human resource departments, and open door policies, which give individual workers access to management, and employment laws that protect individuals suffice to meet workers' expressed desires for voice and due process at the workplace. Perhaps the college graduates, professional, technical, and managerial workers, service-sector workers, and women and immigrants, whose share of the workforce have risen, do not want union representation and participation. Perhaps . . .

But the 1994–95 Workplace Representation and Participation Survey (WRPS), which was the basis for *What Workers Want* (Freeman and Rogers 1999), found that 32 percent of nonunion private-sector workers would vote for a trade union at their workplace, and that larger numbers wanted some worker-based organization to discuss issues with management absent collective bargaining. Surveys in the 1990s and 2000s suggest that the proportion of nonunion workers who want a trade union has come to exceed the WRPS estimate, but they also show that most workers prefer some form of workplace committee to meet with management to discuss issues.

Why has the United States generated such a large unfilled demand for unionism? Why has the country failed to develop alternative institutions for collective voice? What, if anything, can the United States do to "clear the market for representation and participation" per this chapter's title question?

To answer these questions, I examine the 1994–95 Workplace Representation and Participation Survey ; the U.S. module of the Lipset and Meltz survey of Canadian and U.S. workers that followed the WPRS; opinion polls on unionism and worker representation, and Current Population Survey (CPS) data on the locus of union membership. The first wave of the WRPS asked some twenty-four hundred randomly chosen workers in the private and not-for-profit sectors about their situation at work and their attitudes toward unions and other labor institutions. The second wave covered eight hundred workers and focused on specific policy reforms. The Lipset and Meltz survey asked some one thousand Americans (as well as about the same number of Canadians). about their attitudes toward unions and labor institutions. Polling groups, such as Peter D. Hart and Associates, Gallup, and Harris, regularly ask samples of workers ranging from six hundred to twelve hundred what they think about unions and union leaders.

My analysis yields four findings:

1. The United States has a large representation and participation gap at workplaces. Given the dichotomous majority-status union or nothing choice that the U.S. labor relations system offers workers, this gap shows up in unfilled demand for unionism. But most workers prefer modes of collective voice beyond traditional collective bargaining, such as workplace-based committees to discuss problems with management.

2. Many workers have few needs/problems at their workplace and thus have limited desire for collective voice to resolve problems. But some workers have many needs/problems. The greater the number of workplace needs, the more likely workers are to favor unions or other forms of worker organization independent of management.

3. Company open door policies and employee involvement committees reduce employee needs for representation and participation and their desire for unionism. Management attitudes toward unionism, which generally take the form of resisting unionism, affect worker decisions about whether to organize or not.

4. Union experiments with new community and Internet-based organizations that operate outside of collective bargaining offer the best chance to meet unfilled demand for representation and participation. Existing labor law would have to be significantly reformed for firms to develop nonunion voice initiatives like those found in other Anglo-American countries.

What Workers Have

Data on density by industry and occupation from the Current Population Survey shows that the decline in unionization in the United States has been ubiquitous across occupations and industries, save for the largely public sector or nonprofit areas of health and education. From 1983 to 2005, density has fallen in durable manufacturing, transportation, mining, utilities, nondurable manufacturing, and construction.[3] The ubiquity of the decline gainsays any explanation of falling density in terms of shifts in the composition of the workforce

---

[3] Data on unionization by industry and occupation are from CPS data given on www.trinity.edu/bhirsch/unionstats.

from mining and manufacturing, where unions had great strength, to the historically nonunion service sectors.[4] Since unions have grown in the United States through spurts in which unions organize traditional nonunion sectors or occupations (less skilled factory workers in mass production industries in the 1930s–1940s; public-sector workers in the 1960s–1970s [Freeman 1998]), the critical issue in understanding the decline in density is not the shifting composition of the workforce but why unions have failed to organize new and growing nonunion private-sector industries or occupations. Where is the new "spurt" in high tech, finance, or services?

The CPS data also show large changes in the demographic mix of union membership. The historically greater union density among men than women has ended as union membership held up better in the more female-intensive public sector than in the male-intensive private sector.[5] But the biggest change in union density by workers' characteristics is by education. In 1983, union density did not vary by education. The rate of union membership was the same for high school dropouts as it was for persons with postcollege education. In 2005, by contrast, the less educated had lower rates of unionization than the more educated. Persons with postcollege education had over two-and-a-half times the union density of persons with less than high school education. Unionized workers in the United States are disproportionately teachers, nurses, airline pilots, entertainers, machinists, police, firefighters, craft workers, and other highly skilled workers.

The Inflow of New Members

Union density depends critically on the inflow of new members into unions. In any given year, the number of union members equals the number of newly organized workers plus the number who were in unions in the previous year less the attrition in membership due to the closure or shrinkage of unionized workplaces. Density changes from one year to the next as the size of the workforce changes as well. When the workforce grows, as it has in the United States, unions must organize more workers to maintain density even if there is no attrition of members.

Since enactment of the National Labor Relations Act in 1936, government-sponsored secret ballot elections have been a major source of new members into unions. The United States chose this mode of union recognition to avoid the costly recognition strikes that characterized union drives in the 1930s and earlier decades. In the mid-1950s through the mid-1960s unions organized

---

[4] Riddell and Riddell (2004) find that at most 20 percent of the drop in union density from 1984 to 1998 was associated with shifts in the composition of employment by industry or occupation.

[5] Data on unionization by demographic characteristics are tabulated from the CPS MORG files available at the National Bureau of Economic Research (http://www.nber.org/data/morg.html).

from 0.5 percent to 0.7 percent of the workforce annually through the election procedure. In the 1970s and 1980s, the proportion of the workforce organized annually in union electoral victories fell to less than 0.2 percent (Freeman 1985). In the 1990s and early 2000s it fell below 0.1 percent—barely one hundred thousand workers unionized per year through National Labor Relations Board (NLRB) elections. Given that about one-quarter of those workers never gain a collective bargaining contract and eventually lose their union status, the inflow of new members through the electoral process is negligible relative to a workforce of over 120 million (as of 2005). On the other side of the equation, even in years of rapidly growing employment, some existing union firms go out of business or reduce employment. Attrition of union density is on the order of 2–3 percent per year, so that if union density was 20 percent, density would fall by 0.4 to 0.6 percentage points per year; while if union density was 10 percent, density would fall by 0.2 to 0.3 points per year. With a 2 percent rate of attrition and an organizing rate of 0.1 percent of the workforce, union density will fall until it reaches 5 percent of the workforce.[6] Taking the attrition as exogenous, the critical factor in the decline in unionism in the United States has been on the inflow side—union failure to organize new workers through NLRB elections or other modes of organization.[7]

Unions were slow to appreciate that inability to gain new members meant a loss of union strength and influence. In 1972, when AFL-CIO head George Meany was asked about union problems in organizing new workers he replied, "I don't know, I don't care. . . . Why should we worry about organizing groups of people who do not appear to want to be organized? . . . I used to worry about . . . the size of the membership . . . I stopped worrying because to me it doesn't make any difference. . . . The organized fellow is the fellow that counts" (see Buhle 1999, 196).

Still, each time the Democrats controlled the House, Senate, and presidency, the AFL-CIO sought to change labor law to make organizing easier. In 1976, unions pressed the Carter administration and Congress to enact a labor law reform bill that would give unions equal time to speak at so-called captive audience meetings where management orders workers to attend antiunion meetings on company time, that would strengthen the remedies for employer violations of the law, and that would speed up the enforcement of the laws. A filibuster in the Senate led by Orin Hatch of Utah defeated the bill.

In the early 1990s, unions pressed the Clinton administration to enact labor

---

[6] Let Ut be the union density in t, ORGt be the ratio of newly organized workers to the workforce and λ be the rate of attrition of density. Then the equilibrium rate of unionization will be ORGt/λ. At 2 percent attrition, a 0.1 value of ORG would lead to an equilibrium rate of unionization of 5 percent.

[7] Unions win around 50 percent of NLRB elections. What have fallen are the number of elections and number of workers in elections relative to the growing U.S. workforce. Unions lack the resources to run enough NLRB election campaigns to organize huge numbers of workers.

law reform. The administration established the Commission on the Future of Worker-Management Relations (known as the Dunlop Commission after its chair, John Dunlop) "to recommend ways to improve labor-management cooperation and productivity." Making the charge to the committee about cooperation and productivity rather than workers' rights to organize showed a retreat from the 1976 effort to reform labor law. The commission endorsed quick NLRB elections to establish legal union status rather than the card checks that unions favored. The Republican victory in the congressional elections in 1994 made the commission recommendations moot, but even had the Democrats maintained their House majority, Congress was unlikely to have changed labor law as unions wanted. The union share of the workforce had fallen so much that unions could not pressure Congress to support legislation favoring them.

In the mid-1990s union leaders turned inward in assessing the decline in density. Many blamed the decline on the failure of unions to devote enough resources to organizing. In 1995, national union leaders forced AFL-CIO head Lane Kirkland to resign and elected John Sweeney to invigorate organizing efforts (Dark 1999). Sweeney's New Voice team called for unions to spend larger shares of their revenues on organizing. Some unions did so. Some unions elected organizing directors to head the union. But many internationals and locals did not increase organizing budgets, while others could not find fruitful campaigns on which to spend the money they had. Union density continued to fall.

In 2005 several major unions, led by the Service Employees International Union (SEIU) and the Teamsters, withdrew from the AFL-CIO because they believed the central federation was incapable of reversing the decline in density. They set up the Change to Win coalition to increase union resources for organizing and to jumpstart a turnaround in union density. Perhaps competition among unions would spur more successful organizing than the unified house of labor.

Where Are the Alternatives?

The decline of unionism does not mean that U.S. workers have no institutions for voice at their workplaces. Many firms have advanced human resource practices ranging from grievance systems that deal with workplace problems to employee involvement committees to improve worker participation in decision making. But U.S. labor law restricts companies in what they can do to substitute nonunion collective voice for independent unionism. Section 8(a)(2) of the NLRA outlaws the strongest form of firm-sponsored organization—the company union—and uses a broad definition of union, so that it

TABLE 1.1
Percentage of workers with policies or institutions at workplace

Dealing with workers individually	
Open door for individual problems	85%
Personnel or HR department	68
Grievance system with arbitration	32
Dealing with workers as a group	
Survey opinion of workers	38%
Open door for group problems	63
Regular town meetings	47
Committee of employees discusses problems on regular basis	37
Production issues	
Employee involvement program	52%
Participated in program	31
Committees/teams for	
Productivity or quality	36
Autonomous work teams	20
Collective bargaining	14%

Source: Tabulated from Worker Representation and Participation Survey, downloadable from NBER. Note that workers in the private and not-for-profit sectors only were surveyed.

is difficult for firms to develop nonunion worker organizations. As a result, the United States lacks the staff associations found in many establishments in the United Kingdom and the employer-formed committees found in Canada. Employee involvement committees cannot legally discuss changes in wages and work conditions.

Workers at workplaces with human resource policies or firm-based institutions for dealing with employee representation and participation issues can be arranged into three sets (see table 1.1 for percentages in each set). The first set of policies relates to problems that workers are likely to face as individuals. The most common practice is an open door policy by which workers bring problems to management, while grievance/arbitration systems are the least common form of dealing with individual problems. Some large firms require workers to use company-formed alternative dispute resolution (ADR) systems for workplace problems, including those protected by labor law, instead of going to court. ADR guarantees that workers get a low-cost hearing on their problems, but firms determine the rules and appoint and pay the arbitrators.

The second set of policies relates to modes of dealing with problems that workers face as a group. The most common practice is again the open door, but fewer workers report open door policies for group problems than for individual problems. Nearly half of workers report that their firm holds regular town meetings and many are covered by employee attitude surveys. Committees of employees that discuss problems on a *regular* basis are the least common practice.

The third set of policies involves worker participation in production activities. Half of workers report that their firm has an employee involvement program and nearly a third said they participate in the program.

Overall, the most common policies and institutions are those that management can most readily control, while the least frequent are those that give workers greater autonomy or power. But even the least common of these systems covered a much larger proportion of workers than the 14 percent that were unionized in this data set.

Why Workers Want Voice: Workplace Problems and Needs

Worker desires for voice at their workplace are rooted in problems that arise at workplaces. Almost all managements make some errors in decisions regarding workers. Some managers may use their authority summarily and treat workers with little respect. Some may make poor decisions because they lack information on the actual circumstances at a workplace. On the worker side, some workers will create problems through their behavior. And management and workers invariably differ over the division of returns to their joint activity. At workplaces with good labor practices, the number of problems of these kinds should be infrequent relative to those at workplaces with bad practices.

To examine the nature and frequency with which workplace problems/needs arise, I aggregated the responses to WRPS questions about the problems workers face at their workplace and the needs workers have for representation and participation into a single "workers needs" variable. This variable has the virtue of any broad index. It captures general patterns in the data about worker attitudes rather than relying on a single question or wording of a question to assess how workers view their workplace. This is particularly useful in analyzing the WRPS since it used a split sample design that asked questions on similar issues differently to different parts of the sample. To the extent that we view individual survey items as efforts to obtain information on an underlying latent variable such as the "labor relations climate" at a workplace, the needs variable provides a valuable scalar measure of that latent variable.

The two waves of the WRPS asked different numbers of questions about workplace problems/needs, which are easily compared using the needs measure. The main wave of the WRPS asked employees about the influence workers had in workplace decisions and the influence they wanted in those decisions. The difference between the influence workers had and the influence they wanted is Freeman and Rogers's (1999) "representation/participation gap." The main wave also asked about general workplace climate, such as trust in management, security of employment, pleasantness of jobs, employee-management relations, and the like. To form the aggregate workplace needs variable, I coded responses to each question 0 or 1, where 0 means the worker had no need for representation or participation or reported no serious workplace problem and where 1 means that they reported a need or problem. For instance, when workers said that they wanted "a lot" of influence in an area and also said that they did not have "a lot" of influence, I counted this as 1, indicating a need or problem. Similarly, when workers said labor-management relations were poor or very poor, I coded this as 1.

The second wave of the WRPS had five additional questions that asked workers to grade management in dealing with workplace issues using a school grade scale from A to F. Given two waves and the split sample design of the survey, each worker on the WRPS answered thirteen (sometimes different) questions about needs in the first wave and an additional five questions on the second wave. From these data, I constructed two measures of worker needs, one of which could vary from 0 (no needs) to 13 (needs for every item) for the main wave; and one which could vary from 0 to 18 for the second wave.

The distributions of the number of needs for nonmanagerial workers in the WRPS in the two waves have the same shape (figure 1.1). They show a substantial bunching of needs at 0—many workers report no problems at their workplace—and a declining proportion of workers with increasing numbers of needs, so that only a small proportion of workers report many needs. The distribution of needs in the figure diverges from the distribution that would arise if worker needs were randomly drawn from an urn in which the probability of drawing a need depended on the mean number of needs divided by the number of items. In this case, the distribution would be binomial or Poisson-distributed and approach normal as the number of items increased. Responses would cluster symmetrically around the mean. The reason that the observed distributions do not follow these shapes is that the needs of workers on different items are highly correlated. Some workplaces (those with good labor practices) generate no needs while others (those with poor practices) generate many needs.[8]

---

[8] Power laws relate the frequency of events to their magnitude raised to a power, so that small events have a high frequency while large events have low probability. The result is a line linking the ln of the frequency and the ln size of the event. The exponential distribution also attaches more probability to a small event, but it attaches lower probability to large events. Measuring needs differently would produce a different distribution. For instance, a summated rating scale, which sums responses on a scale where the most extreme negative report on an item is a 4, and those who gave other responses 3, 2, and 1, gives a more normal-looking distribution but still shows a large tail of persons with high reports.

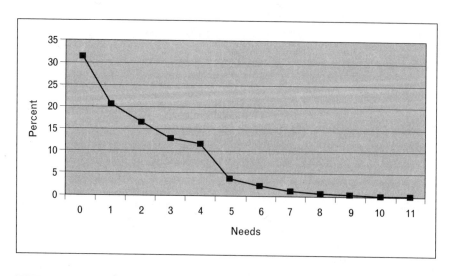

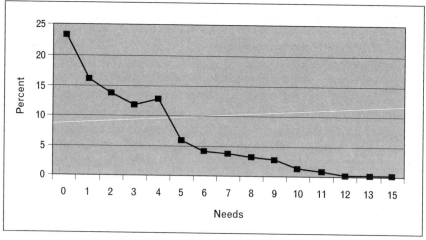

Figure 1.1: Distribution of needs for worker representation, non-managerial workers (WRPS)

Source: Tabulated from Workplace Representation and Participation Survey.

Determinants of Needs

What differentiates workers who report many needs from those who report few needs? To answer this question, I compared the number of needs for workers with different characteristics. These comparisons show:

1. Needs differ among workers by occupation and industry. Workers in managerial and professional occupations report 22 percent fewer needs

than laborers or semiskilled workers; and workers in retail trade report fewer needs than those in manufacturing or mining or wholesale trade.

2. Needs differs by demography. Whites report 25 percent fewer needs than blacks; workers aged 45–54 report 22 percent more needs than workers aged 24 or younger and 9 percent more than those aged 25–34.

3. Needs do *not* differ noticeably by earnings. Dividing the earnings distribution into quartiles and calculating the average number of needs in the quartiles gives: 1.82 (lowest quartile); 1.88 (2nd lowest); 1.93 (3rd lowest); 1.73 (highest).

4. Needs differ by human resource policies. Workplaces with open door policies to deal with group problems have 30 percent fewer needs compared to workplaces without such policies. Workplaces with EI committees also have fewer needs. By contrast, the presence of a human resource department raises the number of problems modestly, possibly because it allows workers to voice their complaints without directly confronting management.

Desired Institutional Solutions

So, what institutions do workers want to resolve the problems they have at their workplace and improve their well-being more generally?

Since preferences among institutions are more complex than, say, preferences between chocolate and spinach, the WRPS asked workers their views of institutions in different ways.

First, it asked the standard question of how workers would vote in an NLRB election. It allowed for three possible responses: for the union; against the union; or uncertain. Nearly a third of nonunion workers said they would vote for the union; 55 percent said they would vote against the union; and 13 percent were uncertain how they would vote. Two years later the Lipset and Meltz survey asked workers how they would vote, allowing for four responses: definitely for the union, probably for the union, definitely against the union, and probably against the union. Sixteen percent said they would definitely vote union, and 32 percent said they would probably vote union, giving 48 percent for the union.

Surveys from Peter Hart and Associates, which also allow for four responses, show a rising trend in the proportion of nonunion workers that say they would vote union. In 2003, for the first time in the history of the poll, over half of nonmanagerial nonunion respondents said they would vote union in an NLRB election. In 2004, the percentage fell to 47 percent, but in 2005 it rose to 53 percent. Still, survey responses on the question vary: a Zogby survey (2005) reported that 35 percent of nonunion workers said they would vote union—almost the same as the WRPS estimate. The most conservative reading of these data is that, at the minimum, one-third of nonunion workers favor a union at their workplace—evidence of a huge failure to deliver what workers want.

The second WRPS question about preferences for institutional solutions asked workers to specify the attributes they wanted in a workplace institution. The attributes covered were the mode of selecting representatives for the group—volunteers, elected, or chosen by management; whether the workplace organization should be run jointly by employees and management or just by employees; whether it should include similarly situated workers or all but top management; whether management or an arbitrator should make decisions in cases of conflict; whether the organization should have access to confidential company information or not; whether it should draw on company budgets or its own budget (Freeman and Rogers 1999, exhibit 7.1). The vast majority of workers wanted some workplace institution. Forty-four percent chose an institution that would elect employee representatives and rely on an outside arbitrator to make final decisions in case of conflict; while 43 percent chose an institution that gave management greater power to select members or make final decisions. Most, including the vast majority of union members, wanted the organization to be "run jointly by employees and management."

The reason for this preference is that both union and nonunion workers believed that a workplace organization had to have management cooperation to be effective. Three-quarters of workers said that an employee organization could be effective only if it had management cooperation. Nearly two-thirds of workers said that they preferred an organization with little nominal power but that had management cooperation to an organization that had "more power, but [which] management opposed" (Freeman and Rogers 1999, exhibit 3.8).

Following up these results, Peter D. Hart and Associates asked workers in 1997, 1999, and 2001 to "suppose there was a proposal to form an employees' organization that was not a union in your workplace but that would represent the interests of employees and meet regularly with management to discuss important workplace issues" and found that 78 percent of workers said that they would definitely or probably vote for forming such an employees' association. The 2001 Hart poll compared the proportion of workers who would vote for an employee association with the proportion who would vote for a traditional collective bargaining union. Thirty-nine percent of workers said that they would vote for both. Thirty-five percent said that they would vote for an association but against a union, while just 2 percent said that they would vote for a union but against an association. As for the remaining workers, 14 percent were against both organizations and 10 percent were unsure on one or both organizations. In short, there is both unfilled demand for unions and even greater unfilled demand for workplace organizations that discuss issues with management outside of collective bargaining.

The third WRPS question about institutional choice offered workers several ways to deal with workplace problems: increased legal protection, workplace committees that meet with management, a union (asked of half the sample) or an elected group of workers who would bargain with management (asked of the other half), or nothing. Of those asked about unions, 24 percent made a union their first choice. Of those asked about a bargaining organization (a union in all but name), 33 percent of workers chose the bargaining organization as their choice—nine percentage points more than chose the union option. These data show that offering more options reduces the proportion of workers selecting unions and that the term "union" has a negative connotation so that a union in all but name appeals to more workers than an organization labeled union. Even so, given alternatives and using the union label, nearly one-in-four U.S. nonunion workers would choose to be represented by a trade union if they could.

The Relation between Needs and Preferences for Institutions

To what extent, if at all, is worker desire for unionism related to the number of needs or problems they perceive at the workplace? If workers view unions instrumentally, one would expect the proportion of workers favoring unions to rise with the number of needs or problems (shown to be the case in figure 1.2). It gives the relation between needs and worker desire for union voice from the first wave of the WRPS. Panel A shows that among workers with no needs, 26 percent say they would favor a union compared to 45 percent among those with four needs and 81 percent of those with seven or more needs. But the number of needs is not the only workplace-based factor that influences support for unionism. Conditional on the number of needs, "progressive" human resource practices, such as employee involvement programs and open door programs, are associated with lower worker desire for unions. Regression analysis shows that EI participants are ten percentage points less likely to say they would vote union in an NLRB election than workers in firms without EI programs, holding fixed the number of needs that workers report.[9]

Going beyond the dichotomous union choice, panel B of figure 1.2 also shows that the proportion of workers who desire forms of workplace organi-

---

[9] The regression of the 0/1 vote for union variable (VOTEUNION) to the number of needs reported (NEEDS) and participation on an EI Committee (EI) gave the following result:

VOTEUNION = 28 + .04 NEEDS -.10(EI) with n = 1767 nonunion nonmanagerial workers, with the coefficients on NEEDS and EI being highly statistically significant.

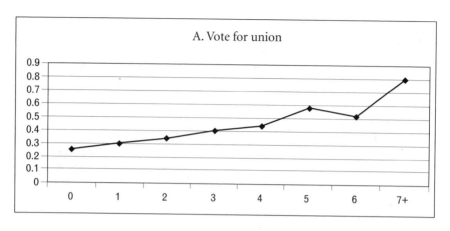

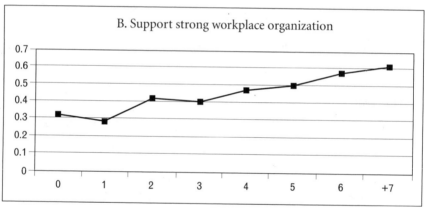

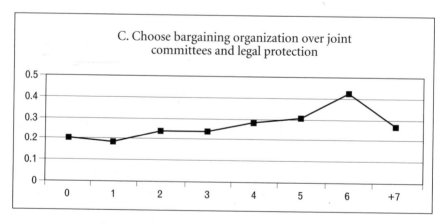

Figure 1.2: Worker needs and support for union or unionlike organizations—nonunion workers

zation that resemble unions also rises with number of needs, though less sharply; while Panel C shows that the number of needs has a more modest though positive effect on workers' choice of a collective bargaining organization over joint committees that discuss problems with management and legal protections. Giving workers more choices than the 0/1 union option decreases the tendency for those with more problems to choose a union.

The second wave of the WRPS asked workers to give management a school-mark grade on various issues. The relation between the grades workers gave management and desire for unionization underscores the strong link between how workers perceive the way management treats them and desire for union voice. Seventy-one percent of nonunion workers who give management an F grade for *concern for workers* said they would vote for the union, whereas barely a third of workers who gave higher grades so reported; 69 percent of those who give management an F grade for being *unwilling to share power* said they would vote for unions compared to 47 percent who gave management a D grade, 35 percent who gave management a C grade, and just 20 percent who gave management an A or B grade. In sum, the needs for representation and participation that their workplace generates and the options that firms provide for dealing with these needs go a long way in explaining worker desires for unions or other forms of voice.

Why the Great Divergence between What Workers Want and What They Have?

There are four plausible hypotheses for the divergence between what workers want and what they have in representation and participation in the United States: (1) that management is responsible; (2) that workers have lost interest in unions; (3) that lack of union organizing effort is responsible; and (4) that the restricted choice set that U.S. labor institutions give workers and firms is responsible. I consider each of these hypotheses in turn.

"It's management, stupid"

Unions blame the divergence on an unfair playing field in organizing through the NLRB process, which gives management leeway to conduct aggressive campaigns against unions. Management campaign tactics include captive audience speeches, in which management orders all employees to listen to antiunion messages while forbidding union supporters from making their case, carried out in 92 percent of elections; "forecasts" that unionization will lead to closure and job loss, carried out in 51 percent of elections; bombarding workers with company campaign material; denying unions access to workers on company property; ordering supervisors to hold one-on-one antiunion meetings with workers, subject to the firm having the right to fire supervisors who refuse to campaign against unionization (Bronfenbrenner 2000). In addition, employers can delay the NLRB election process for significant lengths of time, and end up without reaching a collective agreement with the newly elected union.

Going beyond legally permissible tactics, some managements fire or illegally discipline union activists in NLRB elections. Bronfenbrenner (2000) found that 25 percent of employers fire at least one worker for union activity. Particular tactics aside, the confrontational tone that management adopts when workers seek to unionize carries with it an implicit threat of an unpleasant workplace relation with a union that runs counter to the desire of workers for a cooperative relation with management and their belief that a workplace organization can succeed only if management is cooperative.

Since Freeman and Medoff's *What Do Unions Do?* identified management opposition as a factor in the decline of unionization in the United States, scholars have debated the magnitude and effectiveness of employer campaigns to defeat unions. Analysts agree that the high U.S. union wage premium gives firms a greater incentive to oppose unions than in almost any other country and that management responds to this incentive. The WRPS asked managers in nonunion firms how they would respond to a union organizing drive and found that 53 percent would oppose efforts by employees to unionize, while 27 percent said they wouldn't care, and 15 percent said they would welcome the effort. The large number of labor-management consulting firms that specialize in helping business maintain a "union-free environment" (Logan 2002) further shows that management intervenes extensively in the unionization process.

The debate is over how much management opposition matters. Noting that one indicator of management opposition—management unfair labor practices per NLRB election—stabilized from the mid-1980s to the 1990s, Flanagan (2005) has argued that whatever role management opposition had in deterring unionization in the 1960s and 1970s, by the 1980s it was no longer that important. Freeman (2005c) responded that once firms found the level of opposition that deterred unionization, they would maintain that level and not increase it further, and thus that stability in unfair practices per NLRB election does not imply that management opposition is ineffective.

To see whether management's attitude toward unionism affects how workers would vote in an NLRB election, the WRPS asked workers if they would change their vote if management were to change its views toward unionization. Some 12 percent of workers who said they would vote against a union reported they would vote for a union if management was not hostile and 8 percent of workers who said they would vote for a union said they would oppose the union if management were opposed. Swings of these magnitudes could readily shift most NLRB elections (Dickens 1983).

"It's the workers . . ."

While the survey evidence indicates that many workers want unionism but are unable to gain it, there is, as McLennan (2006, 615) notes, "considerable difference between a telephone answer to a hypothetical question . . . and the individual's binding decision to support a union." Perhaps workers who say they want a trade union on a survey do not realize how unions operate. By campaigning against unions, management assures that workers hear both sides of the union story, and thus reduce the desire to unionize. The divergence between what workers say on surveys and the actual level of union representation in the country is thus a divergence between ill-informed responses to survey questions and informed responses to real choices.[10]

However, there is no reason to believe that survey response bias has grown over time (which would account for the trend in the Hart results); differs among countries (which would account for the greater expressed desire for unions in the United States than elsewhere); or is so large as to make meaningless the huge numbers who say they want unionism. Still, there is only one way to lay to rest concerns about whether workers mean what they say: to see whether workers will join unions independent of management opposition at workplaces. In summer 2004, the AFL-CIO sent organizers to ten cities to ask people to join a non–collective bargaining AFL-CIO affiliate called Working America. This was not meant to test the validity of the survey findings of a huge unfilled desire for union voice—the AFL-CIO is not in the business of providing field experiments for social science—but it provided the needed test. If a large number of nonunion workers truly wanted to join a union organization, albeit in a different setting than voting in an NLRB election, they would presumably sign up for this organization. Consistent with the survey findings that many want union representation, union organizers quickly signed up hundreds of thousands of workers, so that by winter 2006, Working America had over 1.4 million members.

Taking the survey responses at face value, Farber and Krueger (1992) pointed out that if workers' desire for unionism was unchanged, the proportion of nonorganized workers who want unionism should rise as union den-

---

[10] In addition, workers who have bad experiences with unions in other workplaces may lead the opposition to the union (Penney 2004). The WRPS found that while a majority of ex-union members report favorably on their experiences with unions, 25 percent reported that their experiences were bad or very bad. If these workers speak out against unions, they may influence the votes of workers who otherwise would have favored the union solution.

sity falls. More prounion workers would find themselves in nonunion settings and add to the number saying they wanted union representation. Since desire for unionization among nonunion workers remained roughly constant between 1977 through the early 1990s while density fell, they argued that worker desire for unionism had fallen. The surge in worker support for union representation shown in figure 1.2 is inconsistent with the falling desire argument. It suggests that the queue for union jobs is long and lengthening.

"It's the unions . . ."

There are two ways in which unions and union leaders have potentially contributed to the decline in union density: by failing to deliver the services that workers want at workplaces; and/or by failing to invest in organizing new workplaces. On union delivery of services, Farber (1989) found declining perceptions of union instrumentality were one reason for the drop in nonunion workers' desire for unions in the late 1970s and early 1980s. The WRPS found that workers score their union high in gaining "monopoly" benefits for members and operating at the local level, but score them low in other areas (Freeman and Rogers 1999).

Surveys in the 2000s show that union workers have a positive but critical perspective on what unions do. A 2003 Peter D. Hart and Associates survey asked: "Overall, how effective do you think labor unions are these days in improving wages, benefits, and working conditions for their members?" Twenty-four percent responded "very effective," 36 percent responded "fairly effective," while 32 percent said just "somewhat effective" and 8 percent said "not effective." This gives a 60 percent to 40 percent split between the top two categories and the bottom two categories. Another Hart question asked: "Thinking now about the union you belong to, how would you rate the overall performance of your union in representing members like you?" Here, 72 percent gave responses in the top two categories (20 percent "excellent" and 52 percent "good") compared to 27 percent in the bottom two categories (20 percent "not so good," 7 percent "poor"). The Workforce Survey—conducted by the Survey Research Center at the University of California, Berkeley, between July 10, 2001 and January 27, 2002 and sponsored by the Institute for Labor and Employment at the University of California—asked about union effectiveness in getting members more say in workplace decisions and found that 70 percent of union members rated unions in the top two categories (22 percent, "very effective"; 48 percent, "somewhat effective") compared to 31 percent who put them in the bottom two categories ("not too effective," 22 percent; "not effective at all," 9 percent). This survey also reported that 79 percent rated their personal experiences with the union in their company in the top two categories (23 percent, "highly satisfactory"; 54 percent, "satisfactory") compared to 16 percent who said their experiences were "not so satisfactory" and 6 percent who said they were "very unsatisfactory." Finally, a Harris Poll (2005) that asked union members whether they got their money's worth for the dues they paid found that 26 percent strongly agreed that they did, 35 percent agreed somewhat, while 19 percent disagreed somewhat and 20 percent disagreed strongly. In short, on the order of 60 to 80 percent of union members have positive views of union efficacy.

Consistent with this, the vast majority of members favor maintaining union status. Ninety percent of unionized workers in the WRPS said that they would vote for the union in an NLRB election (Freeman and Rogers 1999); 90 percent of unionized workers in the Lipset-Meltz survey also said they would vote to keep their union, and 86 percent of unionized workers in the California Workforce Survey said they would keep their union.

Within the U.S. union movement, the debate over efficacy is about restructuring national unions to parallel economic markets and improve bargaining power (Lerner 2002), and about effectiveness in raising and using resources to organize new workers. The unions that left the federation in summer 2005 complained that the AFL-CIO had done too little to galvanize organizing efforts and spent too much dues money on Washington political activity. The problem goes beyond the allocation of resources to organizing, however. The cost of successful organizing campaigns has risen greatly as management contests union organizing drives, while union resources available per nonunion worker have diminished as density has fallen. Farber and Western (2002) and Freeman and Rogers (2002a) estimate that unions would have to devote the bulk of their budgets to organizing to win enough workers to maintain their present density, though it is possible that some great organizing triumph—such as organizing Wal-Mart or another giant nonunion firm—could spark a new wave of low-cost organizing success.

"It's the institutions . . ."

The view that the institutional structure associated with the National Labor Relations Act underlies the decline of unionism was once viewed as heretical. The act was passed to encourage collective bargaining. Historians refer to it as the Magna Carta of organized labor. In principle, the law protects any group of workers who take concerted action on their own behalf, whether as a minority or majority, and provides the most democratic way to determine the union status of workplaces imaginable, through secret ballot election. But the de facto choice facing workers and firms has been between a collective bargaining majority union and no worker organization, with nothing in between. This is partly due in part to Section 8(a)(2) of the National Labor Relations Act that outlaws the company-sponsored systems of collective voice that provide nonunion channels of collective voice in other Anglo-American countries. And it is partly due to the difficulty of workers organizing through the NRLB framework. The potential for experimentation and innovation at the state level is limited by court interpretation that the supremacy clause of the United States Constitution gives the federal government preemption over state modifications or enforcement of the act so that the states cannot alter or enforce the labor law themselves.[11]

The Majority Rules Fallacy

If the desire for unions were randomly distributed among workplaces, the need for a majority to vote union could readily explain virtually all of the divergence between what workers want and what they have in the form of union representation. Say that 40 percent of workers at every nonunion workplace want a union to represent them but that these workers were randomly distributed among workplaces. Unions would be found only at workplaces that happened to draw enough pro-union workers to constitute a majority. If the average workplace had one hundred workers, just 3 percent of workplaces would meet the majority condition. If the average workplace had one thousand workers, essentially no workers would be in a workplace that met the majority condition.

The flaw in the "majority rules" explanation of the unfilled demand for unionism is that workers who want unions are not randomly distributed among firms. Rather, they are concentrated in selected industries, occupations, and workplaces. To get a sense of how concentrated workers seeking unions might be, the WRPS asked how respondents thought the majority of workers at their workplace would vote in an NLRB election. Seventy-three percent of the 32 percent who said they would vote union believed that a majority at their workplace would vote union, which implies that 23 percent ($= .73 \times 32$ percent) of all workers were in workplaces where they and a majority of the workforce favor unions. By contrast, 29 percent of the 13 percent who were undecided/refused to answer whether they supported unions thought the majority at their workplace would favor a union. This adds another 3 percent ($= .29 \times 13$ percent) of all workers who said a majority at their workplace favored unions. Finally, just 11 percent of the 55 percent who opposed unions thought that a majority of workers at their workplace would vote union, giving another 6 percent ($= 0.11 \times 55$ percent) of all workers reporting that a majority at their

[11] The one exception is the Taft-Hartley Amendment that allows states to enact "right to work" laws that forbid union and management to sign union shop contracts that require all workers in an organized workplace to pay union dues.

workplace supported unions. The result is that 32 percent of workers reported that a majority of workers at their workplace supported unions—identical to the 32 percent who said they would personally vote union. So much for the majority rules story.

Efforts to Clear the Market

Given that the unfilled demand for unionism in the United States is real, generated by the institutional rules and behavior of the relevant parties, what efforts have the groups involved in labor relations taken to change behavior and close the market for representation or participation?

Government, Firms, and Nongovernmental Organizations

After the Dunlop Commission, the federal government has done little to reform the U.S. labor relations system. Republicans in the Congress have offered the Teamwork for Employees and Managers Act to make it easier for firms to set up employer-run committees of workers and managers, but they have run into opposition from unions. The Bush administration has ignored issues of worker representation/participation, while using administrative rulings to weaken unions of federal employees and to change the rules governing overtime pay.

Some nonunion organizations have tried to fill the gap created by the loss of union voice. Public-interest legal organizations have tried to help workers in the enforcement of employment laws (Jolls 2005). Human rights groups have campaigned for labor standards (Elliott and Freeman 2003). But since workers do not elect either of these groups, they are not intermediaries of worker voice. Membership-based organizations such as the Industrial Areas Foundation, which organizes low-income communities to give voice to workers (Osterman 2003), and workers' centers for immigrants (Fine 2003) have the potential for representing the views of those they seek to aid, but, in their review of nonunion institutions, Freeman and Hersch (2004) concluded that as of the early 2000s these organizations had not developed the scale to substitute community-based voice for worker representation and participation in the labor market.

Toward a New Unionism?

The major source of innovation in U.S. labor relations has come from unions, whose leaders recognize that they must radically change policies to survive in the twenty-first century.

The most innovative union effort has been to develop "open source" union forms (Freeman and Rogers 2002a, 2002b) that do not require NLRB votes or employer recognition for the union to represent workers. Open source unions use the Internet to connect workers and to deliver information and services at low cost, and use neighborhood or community resources to bring workers together in a geographic area rather than at workplaces. Three such unions are: www.alliance@ibm.org, an affiliate of the Communication Workers of America organized as a minority union within IBM; www.washtech.org/wt, another Communications Workers' affiliate based on information technology workers in northern California and Washington; and the National Writers Union, an affiliate of the United Automobile Workers that organizes freelance writers around the country (www.nwu.org) (Diamond and Freeman 2002). The Communication Workers has expanded its effort to connect IT workers (www.techs unite.org) and developed a five-city organizing campaign associated with this website. The Machinists have established Cyberlodge (www.cyberlodge.org,), an Internet-based union for information technology workers, which it describes as having a guildlike structure where workers retain their traditional employee-employer relationship while enjoying benefits normally reserved for employees with collective bargaining agreements. The Steelworkers have initiated a "new form of individual membership, open to anyone regardless of employment" that offers modest services at modest dues.

But the most radical innovation has been the AFL-CIO effort in 2004 to enroll nonunion workers into the noncollective bargaining "community affiliate to unionism": Working America (www.workingamerica.org), referred to earlier. In summer 2004, Working America sent out four hundred staff members to canvass neighborhoods with many union members whose nonunion neighbors could be expected to have prounion attitudes (Greenhouse 2004). Working America gathered the addresses and e-mails of workers and told members they would help determine policy through online ballots. When the Bush administration changed the administrative rules governing overtime in July 2004, Working America showed what it could do on the Web. Almost immediately, it added a page, "Is Your Overtime Pay at Risk?" to its website, with FAQ about the new regulations, and offered a lawyer, who posted responses to questions online. As a result, the organization began attracting over two thousand members per week via the Internet—a conversion rate of visitors to the site of 7 percent, which is about as high as any site can do.

Working America anticipates having two million members by the end of 2006, which will make it one of the fastest growing labor organizations in U.S. history. Whether Working America can develop a workplace presence and/or the sufficient support services for workers to meet the unfilled demand for unionism is highly uncertain at this writing. The split in the AFL-CIO may embolden the federation to pour more resources into Working America as its major entry into the market for representation and participation. Or the split may lead a financially strapped federation to use the membership list for political campaign purposes only. The Service Employees International Union, the leading union in the Change to Win coalition, has developed its own open source initiative.[12]

Historically, worker representation and participation has never developed smoothly. In virtually all advanced economies, union membership increases have occurred in great spurts, with new union forms and new groups of workers leading the way, while firms have developed nonunion forms either in response to the threat of unionization or under government mandates, as with the works councils in the European Union. The open source mode of organizing outside of collective-bargaining majority unionism seems to represent the best chance for U.S. unions to expand membership and fill the massive representation and participation gap in the country. Absent major changes in legislation and an imminent threat of unionism, U.S. firms are unlikely to invest much effort in trying to fulfill worker demands.

Looking to the Future

The analysis presented in this chapter shows that the U.S. system of labor relations is broken. The National Labor Relations Act was supposed to give workers access to unionism and collective bargaining if they wanted it. Instead it has produced a labor market in which tens of millions of workers who want unions have no viable way to obtain union representation and in which firms cannot set up the nonunion committees or councils for workers to meet and discuss issues with management that tens of millions of other workers would like at their workplace. The result is an enormous unfilled demand for voice at the workplace, both union and nonunion.

A major change in the U.S. labor relations system is needed if the country is to clear the market for representation and participation. The open source union movement offers one way for unions to sidestep management opposition to collective bargaining and connect with workers who seek union services. The organizing activity spurred by the Change to Win coalition may succeed in bringing collective bargaining to some low-paid workers in the service sector. But without a change in the entire system, huge levels of unfilled demand will continue. Given that the Congress is unlikely to reform the national labor law, perhaps the only way forward is to give the states greater leeway in regulating private-sector labor relations, as Canada does (Freeman 2005). States could then experiment with alternative labor policies. Some might enact legislation favored by business. Others might pass laws or seek to

---

[12] The SEIU announced in summer 2004 that it was forming its own open source union, www.purpleocean.org, with the goal of enlisting one million members (Strope 2004). The SEIU also created a site for unionists to debate the future of the movement.

enforce national laws in ways favored by unions. The competition between alternative modes of worker voice among the states would invigorate the entire labor scene and could potentially produce a better system that the bulk of the country might find attractive. While there are no guarantees, the results of transferring the law regulating private-sector labor relations and/or its enforcement to the states cannot be much worse than current outcomes. The catch in this reform is that for the states to have more leeway would require new national legislation or new court interpretation of federal law.

Chapter 2

Say What?
Employee Voice in Canada

MICHELE CAMPOLIETI, RAFAEL GOMEZ,
AND MORLEY GUNDERSON

Most people spend the bulk of their lives working, yet many of the rights normally afforded citizens in the political realm are unavailable once work clothes are donned and they become employees. As elsewhere in the Anglo-American world, the governance of the Canadian workplace is for the most part a private matter. It is management, largely free of third-party involvement, that decides the extent to which employees are afforded a "say at work." The lack of a guaranteed minimum level of workplace voice leaves the door open to a variety of employee representation schemes that require documentation, exploration, and understanding. In this regard, Canada is no different from the other countries discussed in this book.

Canada, however, is of particular interest for a number of reasons. It is one of the few countries in the Anglo-American world where decentralized bargaining prevails and where unionization has not plummeted. It is also unique among Anglo-American countries in that it houses both common and civil law traditions. This is due to the presence of Quebec within the federation. In fact, roughly 25 percent of Canada's population resides in Quebec with its own system of industrial relations. Quebec is closer to the North American than the Continental system, in that it maintains a Wagner Act model of labor relations, but departs from the rest of Canada in significant ways. In particular, the province supports greater state intervention, houses a neocorporatist political culture that enhances the capacity of labor organizations to influence governments, and maintains a more centralized collective bargaining environment between employers and unions through what is known as the decree system, which again yields considerable power to labor organizations in Quebec (Deom and Boivin 2005, 408).

Because Canada is a federal country, this means that not only is Quebec granted special leeway in designing its own labor laws, but ten separate provincial labor relations systems also coexist; though surprisingly this produces a more uniform set of employment relations outcomes than in the United States, with its single National Labor Relations Act. Drawing international attention to what Canadian workers want in terms of representation and voice, and whether they are getting what they want, provides unique insights for not only the Anglo-American world but for countries sharing similar national characteristics.

We begin by outlining Canada's labor market institutions, often drawing a contrast with Europe, and especially Canada's closest comparator, the United States. We then discuss the data and methods used in our analysis, briefly detailing how Canadian worker responses to questions concerning voice and representation were collected. We present a number of outcomes: employee influence at the workplace; the size and contour of union and nonunion representation in Canada; assessments of how well each type of voice is working; worker preferences for employee voice; and reasons for joining and leaving unions. We then discuss what (if anything) the three major actors (unions, employers, and government) are doing to remedy frustrated demand for alternative forms of voice representation at work. We conclude by highlighting the most relevant lessons to be learned from the Canadian experience for employee-relations policy and practice.

The Institutional Context: A Made-in-Canada Compromise?

The institutional environment in Canada is based on a parliamentary system, where the party (or coalition parties) with the majority of elected representatives forms the government. Unlike the United States, where a Democratic president can be rendered less effective by a Republican Congress, or vice versa, in Canada, a governing party has a greater chance of attaining its objectives. This makes it relatively easier for Canadian governments to change labor laws. The political environment for union-management relations in Canada has experienced swings during the past century, moving from laissez-faire and even promanagement to prounion, and then to lesser support for unions (Reid, Meltz, and Gomez 2005).

Unlike the European Union, there is no statutory system in place (e.g., works council system) to provide voice and representation (Frege 2002). Unions are therefore the primary channel for formal representative voice at the workplace. Like the United States, collective bargaining laws protect unions, but unlike the United States, nonunion systems are neither promoted nor banned.[1] In other words, there are no prohibitions against groups of employees dealing directly with management, absent union representation, regarding their terms of employment (Kaufman 1999; LeRoy 1999, 2006; Taras 1997a, 1997b, 2000, 2006). Canadian employers are free to innovate with a variety of nonunion mechanisms. A nonunion association may even ratify a lengthy written deal with management that resembles a collective agreement, although covered employees are considered to have individual contracts of employment with the employer, even though they are collectively applied (Taras 1997a). Such employees must seek redress in the ordinary court system for violations of such contracts.[2]

By contrast, a union agreement has the protection of collective bargaining laws, and aggrieved parties have recourse to their provincial labor board (MacNeil, Lynk, and Engelmann 2003; Adams 2004). Such boards operate in all ten provinces and three territories, whereas in the United States there is but one National Labor Relations Board. In Canada roughly 90 percent of employees are covered by provincial labor laws (Lipset and Meltz 2004, 128), with the rest subject to national labor laws that apply to the federal public sector and federally regulated industries such as transportation and communications. Yet, despite the potential de jure heterogeneity in labor laws across jurisdictions, there are not huge disparities in such laws across jurisdictions, in contrast to the United States, where state laws differ massively (Block, Roberts, and Clarke 2003). No jurisdiction in Canada, for example, has a "right to work" law. Rather, under the "Rand formula" that prevails in most provinces, Canadian employees represented by unions (which have a statutory obligation to provide all benefits and services to every worker who falls under a collective agreement) must pay union dues or the equivalent to a charity. In certain provinces lacking the Rand provision, such as Alberta, there is still an expressed recognition that in negotiated collective agreements there can exist provisions that require union membership and payment of dues. This stands in stark contrast to many U.S. states where the practice of mandatory due payments is expressly forbidden in labor acts.

---

[1] Kaufman and Taras (2000, 4–7) discuss Canada-U.S. differences in statutory treatment of nonunion representation systems. Taras (2000, 128–33) provides a comprehensive list of Canadian (including provincial) labor law provisions defining labor organizations and prohibiting management domination.

[2] Every so often, a nonunion plan may collide with a union organizing drive or a determined prounion employee, giving rise to difficult cases requiring labor boards or courts to determine employer intent. In a recent paper, Taras (2006) examines thirty cases arising in multiple Canadian jurisdictions between the 1960s and 2003, seeking patterns that have guided jurisprudence on employer intent regarding nonunion systems.

In all provinces, statutes specify unfair labor practices for both unions and management. Only one union can represent any group of employees, and generally speaking a simple majority will determine whether the union gains representation rights for the whole of the bargaining unit (including employees who opposed unionization). To maintain labor stability, Canadian law prevents raids by other unions during the life of the collective agreement.

Canada, as a consequence, fits comfortably within the Wagner Act model of industrial relations in that employees have the right to unionize, to bargain collectively, and to have protection through labor boards. Although there is some history of industrywide bargaining in certain sectors, the decision-making unit is almost always at the level of the workplace.

With respect to nonunion associations, Canadian legal decisions rarely describe the actual representation system in detail, using the term "association" to cover a broad range of structures. These "associations" may be highly structured and provide formal nonunion plans, or they may take amorphous forms such as town hall meetings or ad hoc committees. This is in sharp contrast to the United States, where the exact character of the nonunion plan is of vital importance to its legal status.

The Data

Our empirical analysis of the incidence and preferences for voice and representation at work utilizes data from the 1996 Canada-U.S. Labor Attitudes Survey conducted by Lipset and Meltz (1997, 2004). The survey characteristics match very closely the population characteristics as given by the Canadian Census (Gomez, Gunderson, and Meltz 2002). Many of the survey items were intentionally borrowed from the Freeman and Rogers (1999) Workplace Representation and Participation Survey to enhance comparability. Information was obtained on general values of workers, including views on individualism versus group or communitarian orientation, the appropriate role of governments, confidence in institutions, and perceptions of labor market outcomes such as expectations about layoffs.

What Workers Have and What They Say They Want

What Kind of Representation Do Workers Have Access To?

Given the freedom of Canadian employers to offer nonunion voice channels, how many Canadians have access to voice (union and nonunion) at their workplace? We define access to union voice as union membership or collective agreement coverage and/or whether a worker is employed in a unionized workplace. Nonunion voice is defined as those who respond yes to either or both of the following questions: "Are you a member of an organization other than a union that bargains on your behalf?" or "Are you covered by any non-union employee representation at your workplace?" Such forms of nonunion representational voice include professional and staff associations, but they generally do not include employee involvement programs, since they neither bargain for nor represent employees. Clearly, restricting the nonunion voice mechanism to membership or coverage in an employee bargaining or representation function misses many informal communication mechanisms, such as an open door policy, newsletters, briefings from management, or any other type of one-way communication. But this omission is deliberate, as we want to avoid any designation that does not provide meaningful two-way communication between employer and employee.

We find that 55.7 percent of Canadian workers have access to some form of representative voice at the workplace. Most have access only to union voice as measured by who is covered by collective agreements (42.1 percent), followed by nonunion voice exclusively (9.1 percent), and then dual channels (4.5 percent).[3] Despite the leeway granted Canadian firms to offer nonunion voice, unions still provide the bulk of representative voice in the country.

What type of worker is more likely to have access to voice? We find five variables to be significantly related to voice at work and the type of voice provided. To illustrate these relationships we present simple breakdowns of the difference in voice probability associated with these variables. The magnitudes are based on a logistic regression that controlled for other variables such as personal characteristics (age, gender), occupational and job-related characteristics (income, tenure, employment status), and finally characteristics related to the nature of the establishment where the worker is employed (type of organization, workplace size) (see table 2.1).

- *Age:* Young workers are much less likely to have access to voice overall and union-only voice in particular. A mature worker (aged 45–54), with all else equal, is 12.8 percent more likely to have access to some form of voice com-

---

[3] The percentage of workers who have access to union voice is perhaps higher than expected and differs from the even higher total of 55.9 used in column 1 of our regression in table 2.1. There are two reasons for this. The reason for the first outcome is that our definition of union voice refers to the broader measure of access to voice, based on the presence of a union in the workplace, rather than simply to membership and/or coverage. The reason for the second outcome is that in our multivariate estimations, we use the full sample of Canadian workers available in the data set, which includes an oversample of union workers. The 42.1 percent figure reported here refers to the representative portion of the data that excludes the oversampled portion of the survey.

TABLE 2.1
The incidence or probability of having formal voice by selected characteristics

	Covered by any formal voice at the workplace‡ [1] Mean = 0.695		Covered by union-only voice‡ [2] Mean = 0.559		Covered by dual voice [3] Mean = 0.045		Covered by nonunion voice [4] Mean = 0.091	
	Mean	Δ Prob	Mean	Δ Prob	Mean	Δ Prob	Mean	Δ Prob
1. By gender								
Female	0.446	—	0.446	—	0.443	—	0.446	—
Male	0.554	0.056	0.554	0.061	0.557	−0.005	0.554	−0.003
2. By age†								
18–24	0.096	—	0.096	—	0.099	—	0.096	—
25–34	0.249	0.044	0.249	0.114	0.255	−0.026**	0.249	0.055***
35–44	0.336	0.088	0.336	0.154**	0.332	−0.030**	0.336	−0.054**
45–55	0.242	0.128**	0.242	0.196***	0.239	−0.022*	0.242	−0.039
55+	0.077	0.028	0.077	0.081	0.075	0.025***	0.077	−0.051**
3. By education								
Less than high school	0.106	—	0.106	—	0.102	—	0.106	—
High school only	0.218	−0.036	0.218	−0.040	0.218	0.000	0.218	0.001
Some postsecondary	0.359	−0.061	0.359	−0.100	0.361	−0.020	0.359	−0.005
Postsecondary	0.317	−0.137	0.317	−0.191**	0.319	0.003	0.317	0.033
4. By tenure†								
Tenure low	0.245	—	0.245	—	0.248	—	0.245	—
Tenure mid	0.455	0.045	0.455	0.040	0.452	0.023**	0.455	0.033*
Tenure high	0.285	0.068	0.285	0.091*	0.285	−0.016*	0.285	−0.040**
5. By income†								
[<10,000]	0.066	—	0.066	—	0.068	—	0.066	—
10,000–29,999	0.317	0.026	0.317	−0.022	0.328	0.034	0.317	0.064
30,000–49,9999	0.366	0.151	0.366	0.181*	0.378	0.024	0.366	0.014
50,000–99,999	0.195	0.184**	0.195	0.197**	0.202	0.045	0.195	0.055
100,000+	0.023	0.007	0.023	−0.068	0.024	0.098	0.023	0.131

	Mean	ΔProb	Mean	ΔProb	Mean	ΔProb	Mean	ΔProb
6. By employment								
Part-time	0.186	—	0.183	—	0.186	—	0.186	—
Full-time	0.814	−0.045	0.817	−0.046	0.814	0.006	0.814	0.003
7. By workplace size†								
<25 employees	0.196	—	0.192	—	0.196	—	0.196	—
25–99 employees	0.086	0.226***	0.083	0.309***	0.086	0.026	0.086	0.021
100–499 employees	0.109	0.254***	0.110	0.362***	0.109	0.063	0.109	0.002
500+ employees	0.610	0.468***	0.616	0.599***	0.610	0.025	0.610	−0.028
8. By ownership/sector†								
Private firm	0.259	—	0.258	—	0.259	—	0.259	—
Public firm	0.206	−0.005	0.210	−0.007	0.206	0.012	0.206	0.016
Government	0.330	0.421***	0.334	0.473***	0.330	0.045*	0.330	0.032
Other	0.204	−0.093*	0.197	−0.054	0.204	−0.004	0.204	−0.039*
Observations	1,076	1,076	1,041	1,076	1,041	1,041	1,076	1,076
Pseudo R²	—	0.335	—	0.380	—	0.116	—	0.046

Notes: Numbers in Mean column refer to cell proportions, which may not add up to 1 due to rounding or missing response categories. Numbers in ΔProb column represent percentage point changes based on logit regression estimates (available upon request). Significance is denoted by *** at the 1% level, ** at the 5% level and * at the 10% level.

† Indicates that an explanatory variable with multiple regressors is jointly significant (i.e., the hypothesis that the coefficients of all its regressors are jointly zero is rejected).

‡ The percentage of workers who have access to all forms of voice and who are covered by union voice differs from the totals of 55.7 and 42.1 used in the text to describe the pattern of voice in Canada. The reason for this outcome is that in our multivariate estimations above, we use the full sample of Canadian workers available in the data set, which includes an oversample of union workers. The 42.1 percent figure reported for union only voice in the text (and the corresponding lower overall voice total) refers to the representative portion of the data set, which excludes the oversampled respondents of the survey.

pared to a young worker (aged 18–24; omitted reference category) with otherwise similar characteristics.[4] However, younger workers are more likely to have dual or nonunion-only voice than their older peers.

- *Tenure:* Controlling for age, workers with more tenure have an increased access to voice. Once again, this is particularly true of union voice but diminishes when we look at nonunion-only forms of voice. Highest tenured workers (15-plus years) are most likely to have union-only voice and least likely to have nonunion-only voice.

- *Income:* Higher-income workers generally have greater access to voice overall, and this extends to all forms of voice, including dual and nonunion only. The one exception is the highest-income earners ($100,000 or more), who have a lower likelihood of having union-only voice.

- *Workplace Size:* Size of establishment, as measured by number of employees, is the strongest determinant of overall voice, largely because the association with union voice rises steadily as workplace size rises. The relationship is weaker (albeit generally positive) for dual voice and seemingly nonexistent for nonunion voice. Workers employed in workplaces with twenty-five to ninety-nine employees are 22.6 percent more likely to have access to some form of voice compared to workers in workplaces with fewer than twenty-five employees. This difference increases steadily as workplace size rises, to 46.8 percent for workers in the largest workplaces (over five hundred).

- *Sector:* Compared to all forms of private sector organizations, public sector workers are 42 percent more likely to have one or more forms of voice. This major difference is due to higher access to union-only (47.3 percent more likely) and dual (4.5 percent more likely) voice in the public sector.

On balance it appears that older workers, those employed for a lengthy time, and those in large and public-sector establishments are the most likely to have some form of voice present at their workplace. These results are not surprising, as workers with more experience and presumably more bargaining power would be expected to have greater access to voice overall. Those workers with lower tenure and who are younger have less voice overall; exit presumably being their vehicle for demonstrating displeasure with working conditions. Younger workers, however, are more likely to have access to dual and nonunion forms of voice. Unfortunately, these voice channels are spread over too few workplaces to compensate for the lack of traditional union voice for these workers.

---

[4] In formal terms this is the percentage-point difference relative to the omitted reference category.

The Link between Voice and How Work Is Perceived

How well are the types of voice (or lack of) working? That is, what is the independent effect of voice in general, and different forms of voice in particular, on job satisfaction after controlling for the effect of other factors that can influence such satisfaction? Are certain forms of voice more likely to be associated with particular workplace practices (e.g., high-commitment workplace practices) and outcomes such as the extent of freedom and fair treatment at work?

To answer these questions we examine how worker responses to six positive aspects of the job and workplace vary by whether workers have any form of voice or not, and then separately by the particular type of voice in place (i.e., union voice, dual, nonunion only). The results again are based on a logistic regression that controls for a set of personal and workplace characteristics.[5]

The vast majority of Canadian workers, 86.4 percent, rate their level of job satisfaction as high. Relative to having no voice, workers with union-only or dual voice are only slightly more likely to be highly satisfied with their job, while those with nonunion-only voice are 6.8 percent more likely to be satisfied. These effects, however, are not statistically significant. When combined into the aggregate category of any form of voice, the effect is statistically significant, with such workers being 3.4 percent more likely to rate highly their satisfaction on the job, compared to those with no voice.

Around half (50.6 percent) of Canadian workers feel they have a high ability to express their opinions without fear of repercussions. Workers with voice are 5.1 percent more likely to feel confident in expressing their views than are workers in the no-voice category. There was little difference across voice regimes.

High-commitment workplace practices (reported by 52.2 percent of workers) are 11.7 percent more likely to be found for workers with access to voice, a common finding across Anglo-American workplaces such as the United Kingdom (Millward, Bryson, and Forth 2000) and United States (Freeman and Rogers 1999). This is especially so for workers with dual voice (21.3 percent), but it is not significant for union and nonunion voice.

Overall, 61.4 percent of Canadian workers report that they have high influence over workplace decisions. Workers with voice are only 2.8 percent more likely to rate highly their influence over workplace decisions. Workers with union voice are less likely than workers with dual and nonunion only voice to rate highly their influence over workplace decision making, and once again, workers with dual voice appear to rate their influence highest. In no case is the difference statistically significant.

Workers with union voice only are 33.5 percent, and workers with nonunion voice only are 10.8 percent, more likely to have a formal grievance procedure than are workers with no voice. In terms of ratings, however, workers with nonunion voice only appear most satisfied with their method for resolving grievances, being 21.7 percent more likely to rate highly their grievance procedures compared to workplaces with no voice. This is important, as it makes it clear that not all forms of voice are created equal, in that some do not appear to grant either the same access to grievance procedures or generate the same satisfaction among workers for those procedures. Union voice may be a victim of its own success, in that extending grievances procedures almost universally to all members increases the pool of users, and dissatisfaction is likely to be higher on average. Union members may also have higher expectations.

In summary, it appears that having some form of voice is not a hollow gesture. It generally produces better results in terms of overall job satisfaction, high commitment workplace practices, formal systems to solve grievances, and a high rating of problem-solving systems at work. Somewhat surprisingly, however, voice does not appear to provide greater influence over workplace decisions.

What Kind of Voice Do Workers Say They Want?

Next we turn to a set of questions based on whether the *actual observed* distribution of voice matches what workers want. That is, are worker preferences for voice being met? Or are workers without voice actually desirous of voice, and, similarly, are there sizeable numbers of workers who are currently part of a particular voice regime (i.e., workers covered by a collective agreement and paying union dues) but who would prefer to be nonunion? If a significant portion wants out of their current voice regime, why are they dissatisfied with their current status? And finally, what are worker preferences, in general, for how to deal with management (individually or collectively) over problems that may arise at work?

In general, workers who say they want voice may have differing preferences for individual (direct) versus collective (representative) forms of voice. The Lipset-Meltz survey contains several measures that capture part of this distinction. In one question, workers are asked, "How would you prefer to solve a workplace problem of your own? Would you feel more comfortable dealing directly with management yourself, or would you feel more comfortable having a group of your fellow employees help you deal with management?" A majority of Canadians (57.8 percent) prefer direct over collective forms of voice, at least in dealing with their own workplace problems. The propensity to prefer individual to collective forms of voice is significantly related to the following three variables, after using regression analysis to control for the effect of other determinants of such preferences (see table 2.2, column 1):

- *Age:* Older workers (twenty-five and older) are roughly 8 percent more likely than younger workers to want direct voice.

- *Union status:* The preference for direct voice is around 10 percent greater for workers who are not union members (slightly higher for past members than for never members).

- *Workplace size:* Not surprisingly, for workers employed in larger and presumably more impersonal work environments, the desire for direct voice is lower. Compared to the smallest establishments (<25 employees), workers in workplaces with 25–99 employees are 19.6 percent less likely, in workplaces with 100–499 employees 21.0 percent less likely, and in workplaces with more than 500 employees 13.3 percent less likely to want direct as opposed to representative voice.

Workers were also asked if they would be interested "in joining an organization that would engage in collective bargaining (or negotiate) over wages and benefits" and separately whether they would be interested "in joining an organization that would represent employees who have filed grievances against their superiors or managers." The percentage of workers who answered positively to both questions is compared to those who answered affirmatively to neither, as are the responses for each representative voice question (see table 2.2, columns 2 though 4). Significant differences exist across the following variables:

- *Age:* The desire for collective representation is highest among the young and falls for older workers. Workers over the age of twenty-four are 10.2 to 15.5 percent less likely to want collective representation for both wages and grievances, and generally seem more opposed to collectively bargained wages than collective representation over grievances.

- *Tenure:* Worker preferences exhibit a U-shaped pattern for representation for grievances, with midtenure workers 8.5 percent less likely, and high-tenure workers 10.2 percent more likely, to want such representation. This is consistent with the life-cycle hypothesis, according to which skills, ability, earnings, and individual bargaining power all peak in the middle stage of one's career. When workers are beginning or ending their careers they may feel more vulnerable and so the desire for collective representation rises.

- *Income:* Higher-income workers are less likely to want collective representation, with that lack of desire peaking in the highest income category (over $100,000).

TABLE 2.2
Probability that workers prefer to individually deal directly with management to resolve workplace problems or prefer to deal collectively over a range of issues by selected characteristics, 1996

| | Preference for direct voice | | Preference for collective representation | | | | | |
| | To deal with workplace problems [1] Mean = 0.578 | | Over both wages/benefits and grievances [2] Mean = 0.360 | | Over wages/benefits only [3] Mean = 0.503 | | Over grievances only [4] Mean = 0.446 | |
	Mean	ΔProb	Mean	ΔProb	Mean	ΔProb	Mean	ΔProb
1. By gender								
Female	0.473	—	0.462	—	0.461	—	0.463	—
Male	0.527	-0.015	0.538	0.008	0.539	0.051	0.537	0.025
2. By age†								
18–24	0.118	—	0.104	—	0.104	—	0.104	—
25–34	0.247	0.084*	0.262	-0.139**	0.263	-0.202***	0.263	-0.111*
35–44	0.343	0.086*	0.333	-0.129**	0.335	-0.210***	0.336	-0.096
45–55	0.223	0.082*	0.226	-0.102	0.224	-0.168**	0.223	-0.075
55+	0.069	0.080*	0.075	-0.155**	0.074	-0.211**	0.074	-0.128
3. By education								
Less high school	0.118	—	0.106	—	0.106	—	0.107	—
High school only	0.229	-0.022	0.218	0.050	0.219	0.019	0.219	0.061
Some postsecondary	0.380	0.065	0.359	0.011	0.361	0.027	0.359	0.016
Postsecondary	0.273	-0.017	0.317	-0.033	0.314	-0.051	0.315	0.032
4. By tenure†								
Tenure low	0.277	—	0.245	—	0.246	—	0.246	—
Tenure mid	0.423	0.071	0.455	-0.061	0.454	-0.069	0.454	-0.085*
Tenure high	0.277	-0.015	0.281	0.086*	0.280	0.045	0.280	0.102**

	Mean	Prob	Mean	Prob	Mean	Prob	Mean	Prob
5. By income ($)†								
<10,000	0.083	—	0.066	—	0.065	—	0.066	—
10,000–29,999	0.361	−0.017	0.332	−0.056	0.334	0.039	0.333	−0.024
30,000–49,9999	0.369	−0.057	0.377	−0.068	0.379	−0.067	0.377	−0.043
50,000–99,999	0.159	0.011	0.192	−0.117	0.190	−0.109	0.191 2	0.086
100,000+	0.000	—	0.008	−0.238**	0.008	−0.367***	0.008	−0.205
6. By employment								
Part-time	0.228	—	0.191	—	0.192	—	0.193	—
Full-time	0.772	0.024	0.809	−0.010	0.808	0.001	0.807	−0.054
7. By union status†								
Member	0.590	—	0.537	—	0.540	—	0.539	—
Past member	0.124	0.111**	0.149	−0.116***	0.147	−0.191***	0.149	−0.081
Never Member	0.283	0.091**	0.307	−0.166***	0.306	−0.231***	0.306	−0.110**
8. By workplace size†								
<25 employees	0.095	—	0.109	—	0.110	—	0.109	—
25–99 employees	0.089	−0.196*	0.090	−0.005	0.089	0.046	0.089	0.039
100–499 employees	0.117	−0.210**	0.125	0.057	0.126	0.076	0.125	0.079
500+ employees	0.699	−0.133*	0.676	0.041	0.674	0.083	0.676	0.062
9. By ownership/sector								
Private firm	0.289	—	0.298	—	0.300	—	0.298	—
Public firm	0.254	−0.076	0.238	0.000	0.234	0.068	0.239	−0.008
Government	0.393	−0.046	0.384	−0.019	0.385	0.045	0.383	−0.015
Other	0.064	0.028	0.080	0.051	0.081	0.118*	0.080	0.091
10. Observations	685		917		917		918	
11. Pseudo R2	0.036		0.039		0.062		0.026	

Note: Numbers in Mean column refer to cell proportions, which may not add up to 1 due to rounding or missing response categories (not reported). Numbers in ? Prob column represent percentage point change in probability. Based on logit estimates, all available upon request.

*** denotes significant at the 1% level;

** denotes significant at the 5% level;

* denotes significant at the 10% level.

†Indicates that an explanatory variable with multiple regressors is jointly significant (i.e., the hypothesis that the coefficients of all its regressors are jointly zero is rejected).

- *Union status:* Not surprisingly, nonunion members are less disposed to prefer collective forms of representation than current members. However, it would appear that previous exposure to unions reduces the negative desire for collective representation; past members are 11.6 percent less likely to want collective representation for both wages and grievances than current members, while never members are 16.6 percent less likely.

The Demand for Union Voice: Frustrated Demand or Oversupply of Union Representation?

Under Canada's Wagner-derived system, workers desiring unionization must gain the support of a majority of their fellow employees before union membership is extended to all workers. This leads to frustrated or unmet demand on the part of nonunion members unable to move into a union job or to convince their fellow employees to unionize. Once the bargaining unit is certified, the union represents all employees in the unit, who must pay union dues. This leads to an oversupply of unionization for those who would prefer not to be represented by a union.

Drawing on the Angus Reid survey undertaken in mid-1996 and the Canadian Labour Survey (1996), we explore the extent of frustrated demand for, as well as oversupply of, union membership in Canada.[6] We employ a framework derived from Farber and Krueger (1993), Farber (2001), and Riddell (1993). We find that the realized demand for unionization (i.e., actual unionization rate or probability of being a union member), $Pr(U=1)$ for the economy as a whole was roughly 34 percent. Frustrated demand for unionization, $Pr(D=1, U=0)$ that is, the proportion of nonunion employees desiring union voice, accounted for roughly 19 percent of nonunion members. Oversupply of unionization, that is, the proportion of union workers desiring to be nonunionized $Pr(D=0, U=1)$, accounts for nearly 12 percent of union members.

Despite Canada's Rand formula, the numbers above demonstrate that frustrated demand for union membership is greater than union oversupply. We find that the total demand for unionization in Canada (both realized and frustrated demand), $Pr(D=1)$, is 42 percent. This figure includes all workers who would prefer unionization if it were available as well as existing union members who would prefer to remain so. Since essentially the same question was asked of both nonunion and union workers, it can be interpreted as the *potential unionization rate* in Canada in the absence of organizing and switching costs for union and nonunion workers, respectively.

We examine the determinants of the demand for union voice based on a set

---

[6] The Angus Reid survey asked nonmembers and members of unions: "All things considered, would you personally prefer to (belong to/remain a member of) a union?" The survey was conducted by telephone and yielded a representative sample of 1,495 working-age people in Canada.

of variables already used in previous estimates of the incidence of union voice and a few added variables drawn from recent theories of unions as experience goods (Bryson et al. 2005; Gomez and Gunderson 2004) (see table 2.3). Because unionization is highly experiential in nature, this means that the more you know about unions (either through contact via family members and friends who are members or through previous membership), the more you like them and are likely to want to join if given the chance (Freeman and Rogers 1999; Bryson et al. 2005). We test for these relations by including explanatory variables that control for past membership, family membership, and the attitudes of friends and relatives toward unions. Our expectation is that the more exposed a worker is to unions, the greater will be the demand for union services.

We find that the demand for unionization is highest among younger and lower-income workers, those in larger establishments, and those with current or previous exposure to unions. As well, having family members who are union members or peers who are supportive of unions is significantly and positively related to the desire for union membership, reinforcing the notion of unionization being highly experiential in nature. In addition, given that demand for unionization is highest among groups of workers least unionized (the young and those with lower income), then perhaps before workers can successfully gain employment in the unionized sector, or successfully organize, they require more time and experience in the labor market. As argued elsewhere (Bryson et al. 2005), the "transaction costs" of joining seem to decline as workers age and gain experience.

What Are Governments, Unions, and Employers Doing to Enhance Voice and Representation?

Government Actions on Voice and Representation

As indicated previously, governments in Canada do not prohibit employers from dealing directly with employees in the same way that employers are restricted in the United States. For that reason governments in Canada have allowed employers more latitude to develop nonunion forms of voice and representation.

The federal government in Canada emphasizes labor-management cooperative initiatives, largely through collective voice in the form of sector councils (Gunderson and Sharpe 1998). These are usually established at the industry level across the country, although they may cover specific occupations or even gender. Sector councils exist, for example, in steel, construction, biotechnology, and child care, as well as occupations such as boilermakers and commercial pilots. They deal with such issues as skill requirements, skill and human resource development, standards setting, and mobility. Approximately thirty councils

TABLE 2.3

The determinants of desire for unionization, based on the question: "All things considered, would you personally prefer to belong to a union?" (Mean probability = 0.47)

	Desire for unionization	
	Mean	ΔProb
1. By gender		
Female	0.449	—
Male	0.551	0.008
2. By age[†]		
18-24	0.099	—
25-34	0.264	-0.240***
35-44	0.331	-0.086
45-55	0.233	-0.137
55+	0.073	-0.067
3. By education[†]		
Less high school	0.102	—
High school only	0.218	-0.036
Some post-secondary	0.347	-0.126
Post-secondary	0.334	-0.069
4. By tenure		
Tenure low	0.237	—
Tenure mid	0.463	-0.008
Tenure high	0.297	0.007
5. By income[†]		
<10,000	0.064	—
10,000-29,999	0.305	-0.132
30,000-49,9999	0.383	-0.190*
50,000-99,999	0.197	-0.303***
100,000+	0.021	-0.367***
6. By employment		
Part-time	0.191	—
Full-time	0.809	-0.105
7. By union status[†]		
Non-member	0.537	—
Past member	0.157	-0.415***
Never member	0.305	-0.502***
8. By size of workplace[†]		
<25 employees	0.140	—
25-99 employees	0.091	0.107
100-499 employees	0.125	0.145*
500+ employees	0.644	0.109
9. By ownership/sector		
Private firm	0.282	—
Public firm	0.230	0.003
Government	0.360	0.033
Other	0.128	0.014
10. By union family member		
No union family member	0.556	—
Union family member	0.444	0.110***

TABLE 2.3
Continued

	Desire for unionization	
	Mean	ΔProb
11. By peer attitudes		
Not supportive	0.542	—
Family and friends are supportive of unions	0.458	0.358***
Observations		827
Pseudo R^2		0.301

Note: Numbers in mean column refer to cell proportions, which may not add up to 1 due to rounding or missing response categories (not reported). Numbers in Δ Prob column represent percentage point changes based on logit regression estimates (available upon request). Significance is denoted by *** at the 1% level ** at the 5% level and * at the 10% level. † Indicates that an explanatory variable with multiple regressors is jointly significant (i.e., the hypothesis that the coefficients of all its regressors are jointly zero is rejected).

currently exist, "covering" about 40 percent of the workforce, based on the assumption that all workers in a sector with a council are "represented" by the council. Where they are present, unions are involved in the formation and operation of the council. The importance of sector councils was reiterated in the federal government's recently announced Workplace Skills Strategy (WSS). Sector councils were specifically singled out as important components of that strategy.[7]

In the health and safety area, the federal government has emphasized voice and representation through the "internal responsibility system," whereby labor and management are jointly to improve health and safety at the workplace (in contrast to the U.S. model, which tends to emphasize specific regulations).[8] The internal responsibility system mandates employee voice and representation by giving employees: (1) the Right to Representation through health and safety committees in their workplaces, (2) The Right to Refuse unsafe work, and (3) the Right to Know or to be informed of workplace risks and hazards through information and labeling requirements.

A form of employee voice in the nonunion sector is also provided through *statutory* protection against wrongful dismissal, though this only exists in the federal government, Quebec, and in Nova Scotia.[9] *Unionized* employees, of course, have protection against unjust dismissal through the normal grievance procedure, and *individual* employees can also go through the courts, though only executives and higher-level personnel use the latter given the expense. To

[7] That identification was made when the minister of Human Resources and Skills Development announced that the government would be committing over $37 million for thirty-one projects under the Sector Council Program.

[8] The internal responsibility system in Canada is discussed in O'Grady (2000).

[9] In general the protection afforded to employees in the union sector appears to be stronger that the statutory protection available to nonunion employees. See Eden (1994) and McPhillips (2005).

provide protection for regular nonunion employees, a number of jurisdictions have given statutory protection so that redress, similar to that of a grievance procedure, can be sought through a board.

Employee voice can also be heard through complaints in the various dimensions of labor law including: labor standards (e.g., minimum wages, hours of work and overtime, advance notice); workers' compensation (e.g., appealing decisions); human rights and anti-discrimination; and pay equity. In general, however, the complaints often come from unions rather than individuals, given concerns over reprisals. Workers' compensation involves an interesting voice trade-off in that individual workers have given up their right to sue their employer in return for a more guaranteed form of "no fault" insurance in case of a workplace accident.

The most controversial issue involving employee voice in Canada is whether unions ought to be certified on the basis of card counting (usually 50 to 55 percent required) or voting (as is the case in the United States). Supporters of the latter argue that it is the normal democratic way of exercising voice in choosing representation without undue intimidation on the part of the union, while opponents argue that voting fosters undue employer influence and management opposition and intimidation in the period up to the vote. Certainly, the card-signing procedure has been singled out as an important institutional aspect that has fostered the higher degree of unionization in Canada compared to the United States, and the empirical evidence tends to bear this out.[10] Up until the 1980s only one jurisdiction required voting; currently six provinces covering about 75 percent of the workforce require a vote.

Union Actions on Voice and Representation

Unions in Canada have tried to strike a balance between a defensive strategy of protecting existing members, mainly from restructuring, and a more proactive strategy of recruiting new members through organizing campaigns.[11] The protection of existing members has focused on restrictions on layoffs and subcontracting as well as resistance to wage concessions and protection of pension benefits. Recruiting new members has focused on a wide range of strategies including new organizing in the growing service sector and social unionism involving coalition building, community activities, and political activism. As well, there is an emphasis on enhanced inclusiveness through providing voice and representation to a workforce that is increasingly diverse in terms of ethnicity, gender, immigrant status, and nonstandard employment status, espe-

[10] See Riddell (2004) for evidence as well as a discussion of the increased prominence of the vote regime.

[11] Union strategies in this area are discussed in Kumar and Murray (2003) and Yates (2003) and references cited therein.

cially in the service sector. Trying to have organizer characteristics match the characteristics of the groups that are being organized has often been a strategy employed. Perhaps somewhat surprisingly, Canadian unions have not generally protested the legal regime that accommodates nonunion forms of representation. Whether this reflects their belief that they may evolve into more formal unions, or that they protect unions by providing similar situations in the nonunion sector, is an open question.

There has generally been a shift away from traditional, narrow business unionism with its emphasis on job control and the specification of detailed work rules and narrowly defined job classifications as well as pattern bargaining. There has been more emphasis on social unionism and issues such as child care, parental leaves, and protection against harassment. Although increased emphasis has been placed on new organizing, there is, nevertheless, a perception that the best way to appeal to new members is to protect and represent existing members. In some cases, unions have engaged in "community unionism" to enhance their image by providing services to the broader community, but these have generally been cut back because of expense and the pressure to provide more immediate results.

Organizing activities in Canada generally take place in a decentralized and uncoordinated fashion, and sometimes involve interunion disputes and raids. The central bodies play a very limited role, tending to focus on education, research, and some involvement in training. They lobby for political changes that are favorable to unions and their members as well as more general policies that enhance their social unionism image, but tripartite corporatist arrangements involving social partnerships on national issues have not developed.

Unions differ substantially in their strategies. The Canadian Auto Workers Union (CAW) has espoused a more adversarial, noncooperative social unionism approach, perhaps because of being protected by the sustained growth in the auto sector. Other unions have been more cooperative, as evidenced by the growth of labor-management committees in recent collective agreements (Payette 2000). Many of the traditional industrial unions have survived by expanding into the growing service sector, trying to become more like general unions, providing services across a diversified range of industries.

In essence, Canadian unions have changed, but there has not been a fundamental transformation in their strategies for voice and representation. Union bargaining power has declined and unions have shifted somewhat from their monopoly face to their voice face, as evidenced by the decline in the union wage premium in recent years (Gunderson and Hyatt 2005). Has their incremental change strategy been successful? Unionization in Canada has declined by about seven percentage points since the mid-1980s (Riddell and Riddell 2004). Nevertheless, unions appear "alive and well" at about 30 percent of the potentially "organizable workforce" (more than twice the U.S. level), and they have staved

off the precipitous decline in union membership that has occurred in most in-
dustrialized countries.

Employer Actions on Voice and Representation

Employers in Canada have increasingly tapped into employee voice in a direct
fashion through various mechanisms: employee involvement schemes, work
teams, quality circles, suggestion schemes, nonunion grievance systems, and
problem-solving groups (Verma and Taras 2005). This is part and parcel of the
trend toward "progressive" human resource management, with the rationale
being to foster a high-commitment workforce (largely for purposes of quality
and flexibility) as well as to foster the knowledge economy by tapping into
those closest to the production decisions. Such employee voice, however, is sel-
dom accompanied by any power shift, since ultimate decisions remain firmly
in the hands of management.

Progressive human resource management practices are obviously potential
alternatives to the stronger form of voice and representation through unions.
Nevertheless, Canadian managers tend not to resist unions as strongly as U.S.
managers (Thompson and Ponak 2005), although resistance is increasing, in
part because of the pressure from international competition and especially the
less-unionized United States. It is also the case that Canadian employers tend
not to pressure for radical change (e.g., right-to-work laws) as opposed to marginal changes (e.g., the shift from card to vote regimes or allowing replacement
workers in certain situations).

Implications for the Future

In this chapter we have examined the state of worker voice in Canada during
the mid- to late 1990s. We find that roughly 30 percent of all workers (in the
employed non–self-employed population) had no formal voice, while 55 percent had access to some form of voice, defined as nonunion representation
and/or bargaining, or union bargaining between employees and management.
By and large, despite a legal environment that permits nonunion voice vehicles, the majority of all voice in Canada is union only (i.e., collectively bargained voice), with 42 percent of all workers (and 76 percent of those with
voice) having the union-only form of voice. Roughly 14 percent of all workers
(24 percent of the voice population) had some form of nonunion voice at work.

In terms of employee satisfaction and positive attributes associated with a
workplace or job, the presence of voice does seem to cohere quite strongly with
positive attributes such as the presence of a grievance procedure or high-commitment workplace practices. We found little evidence, however, for substitu-

tion of voice vehicles, as the different forms of voice generally varied in the same fashion across any given worker characteristic. The one exception occurred in the case of young workers, who seem to be significantly less likely to have union voice but significantly more likely to have access to nonunion voice.

When Canadian workers were asked generally about their preferred type of voice (direct versus collective or union versus nonunion), the majority seemed to prefer direct individual voice (57.8 percent) when it came to dealing with individual problems at the workplace. However, workers in larger establishments had opposite preferences. As establishment size increased, workers were much more likely to want collective voice, presumably in keeping with expectations about the value of collective voice when distance from management increases. The stage in the life cycle of a worker also seems to play a role in explaining preferences for collective versus direct one-on-one forms of voice. Generally speaking, the youngest and oldest workers and those with the least and most tenure are more likely to desire collective representation, as compared to middle-aged or middle-tenure workers.

Finally, in examining the representation gap as it pertains to the desire for union voice, we found that Canada, like the United States, has a substantial proportion of workers who desire union representation but who are not getting it. If all worker desires for (and against) union voice were met, the proportion of workers with union membership would be close to two-fifths of the workforce (42 percent), substantially higher than the 34 percent unionized at the time of the Lipset-Meltz survey. Frustrated desire for unions is highest among the youngest and most economically disadvantaged. Another significant explanatory factor is previous exposure to union voice. Workers who are current or past members are more likely to desire union voice when compared to those who were never members. Social capital is also an important determinant, as workers with family who are union members or who have peers with positive attitudes toward unions are more likely to desire unionization.

In summary, in terms of the demography of voice, it (and especially union voice) is most prominent among workers who are older, have long tenure, and who are working in large establishments and in the public sector. Younger workers, however, are more likely to have access to nonunion voice. The desire for voice is highest for workers who are younger, lower income, in larger establishments, and who have current or previous exposure to unions, or whose family members are unionized or whose peers are supportive of unions. Frustrated or unmet demand for voice is highest among the young and those with lower income because they have the highest demand for, but lowest supply of, voice and especially union voice.

The three major actors in Canada's employment relations system are all taking actions to affect voice and representation of workers. Governments in Canada have provided a legal environment that is conducive to nonunion forms of voice; encouraged collective voice through sector councils; fostered the internal responsibility system in health and safety, especially by mandated voice through the Right to Representation in joint health and safety committees and the Right to Refuse unsafe work; provided some statutory protection against wrongful dismissal procedures in some jurisdictions; provided legal protections in areas such as labor standards, workers' compensation, human rights, antidiscrimination, and pay and employment equity initiatives; and shifted from certification through card check to votes.

Unions have moved somewhat away from their monopoly face toward their voice face, reduced their emphasis on job control, and focused more on new organizing and social unionism. However, this shift has been incremental.

Employers have increasingly tapped into employee voice in a direct fashion through means such as employee involvement, work teams, quality circles, nonunion grievance procedures, and problem-solving groups, but without giving up ultimate decision-making power. Some of these changes have been made to provide an alternative to unionization; although Canadian employers do not resist unions as much as do their U.S. counterparts, there is some trend in that direction.

As we have noted, Canada is one of the few countries in the Anglo-American world where decentralized bargaining prevails and unionization has not plummeted. The divergence between Canada and the United States is particularly remarkable. In the mid-1950s, both were slightly more than 30 percent unionized. In the United States, unionization has declined to about one-third that level. In Canada, it has fluctuated somewhat, but currently is close to its earlier level and twice the U.S. rate. Numerous reasons have been offered to explain the divergence: less restructuring away from highly unionized sectors in Canada and especially the public sector; less effective management opposition in Canada; more of a collectivist vs. individualist attitude in Canada; more innovative union activity in Canada, especially with respect to organizing, political pressure, and pursuing a social agenda; and—most importantly—a legal regime in Canada that is more "union friendly" in areas such as certification and decertification procedures, bankruptcy and succession rights, first-contract imposition by boards, restrictions on employer campaigning, and union-security provisions, such as the Rand formula and no right-to-work legislation (Lipset and Meltz 2004; Murray 2005; Riddell 1993; Taras 2001).

Can Canada maintain its unionization level? Potentially yes, given that most of the factors that account for the divergence with the United States are not likely to change much in the future and these forces have already played themselves out. A greater competitive threat from deunionization in the United States is not likely to be in the cards, given that private sector unionization in the United States is already below 10 percent. As well, unions in Canada have increasingly emphasized their voice face rather than monopoly face, and this should engender less management opposition. The legislative initiative that has had the greatest impact in dissipating unionization in Canada, the shift from a card to a vote regime, has already largely occurred, with 75 percent of the workforce under a vote regime. Furthermore, there does not appear to be any employer or political groundswell for radical change (e.g., right-to-work legislation) compared to marginal changes (shift from cards to votes or allowing replacement workers during strikes in some situations).

Chapter 3

What Voice Do British Workers Want?

ALEX BRYSON AND RICHARD B. FREEMAN

Throughout most of the postwar period trade unions were the predominant institution delivering worker voice in Britain. Labor relations were voluntaristic, but public policy gave tacit support to unionization. Union density was high, reaching 65 percent of workers in establishments with more than twenty-five employees in 1980, according to the Workplace Industrial Relations Survey. Lay representatives, rather than paid union officials, delivered most union services at workplaces where firms recognized unions.[1] In the 1960s and 1970s collective bargaining agreements were often struck above the workplace level at the level of organizations, sector, or nation. At the same time there was considerable labor unrest at workplaces, where shop stewards and militant workers had considerable independence in calling wildcat strikes (Donovan 1968). This system began to change with the unraveling of the social contract between the Labour government and the unions in the "winter of discontent" in 1979, and disappeared during the Margaret Thatcher and John Major years that followed.

Under Prime Ministers Thatcher and Major the Conservatives "set about dismantling the props to joint regulation and restricting the power of trade

---

[1] In Britain, when an employer agrees to negotiate with a union over pay, the union is said to be "recognized." If the firm recognizes the union for pay bargaining, it will generally recognize the union for negotiations over nonpay terms and conditions and in procedural matters such as grievance handling.

unions" (Millward, Bryson, and Forth 2000, 230). Legislation limited the conditions under which unions could legally engage in industrial action, and made unions and their officials financially liable for unlawful actions. The government fought against striking workers in the miners' strike of the mid-1980s, and limited collective bargaining through the introduction of Pay Review Bodies in the public sector. The change in public policy undermined the perception that unions were the socially desired form of worker representation in dealing with employers.

In the early 1990s the government outlawed the closed shop, which required workers to join a trade union as a condition of employment. This made it difficult to maintain union density in unionized workplaces because nonmembers could free ride on union-negotiated improvements to pay and conditions, while the unions could not "privatize" the public goods they produced in the workplace to deliver them to members only. As a result, the proportion of nonmembers grew so that at the turn of the twenty-first century, around 40 percent of workers in unionized establishments were free riders.[2]

From the mid-1980s to the early 2000s the proportion of employers who used collective bargaining to determine pay fell, and collective bargaining was decentralized to workplace level (Millward, Bryson, and Forth 2000, chapter 6; Kersley et al. 2005). Between 1984 and 1998, the proportion of workplaces with twenty-five or more employees with recognized unions dropped from 67 percent to 42 percent. Less than one-third of this decline was due to changes in the distribution of workplaces among employers (Bryson et al. 2004).[3] The decline in unionization did not, however, increase the proportion of workplaces with no worker voice. Instead, there was a growth of nonunion voice institutions, creating competition in the market for representation and participation. Management in new establishments chose direct communication as their preferred voice regime (Bryson et al. 2004). The proportion of the workforce in unions plummeted from around half in the early 1980s to under one-third by 2003, by which time one-half of the British workforce had never been in a union (Bryson and Gomez 2005).[4] Direct communication between workers and management became the predominant institution for delivering worker voice (Millward, Bryson, and Forth 2000; Kersley et al. 2005, 2006).

[2] In the 2001 BWRPS, 36 percent of workers who said there was a union they could join at their workplace reported that they were not members. In the 1998 WERS, 44 percent of workers in unionized settings were not members.

[3] Between 1998 and 2004 union recognition stabilized among workplaces with twenty-five or more employees. However, among smaller workplaces with 10–24 employees it fell from 28 to 18 percent (Kersley et al. 2005).

[4] Union density figures vary somewhat across surveys. The British Social Attitudes Survey (BSAS) indicates a fall from 49 percent in 1983 to 31 percent in 2001, with the trend closely resembling the Labour Force Survey data since it became available in 1989 (Bryson and Gomez 2002; Palmer, Grainger, and Fitzner 2004).

The victory of the Labour Party in 1997 shifted public policy in ways more conducive to unionization. The 1999 Employment Relations Act (ERA) made it easier for workers to organize unions, albeit through more formal procedures than traditional British voluntarism. The gradual acceptance of the EU directive on works councils, which began in 2000, guarantees a new form of collective voice at workplaces, which presents both an opportunity and challenge to unions. As a result, the decline in union membership and density began to stabilize in the mid-2000s, and density rose slightly from 2004 to 2005.

The Situation in the Early 2000s

In 2005 union density was 29.0 percent. Membership rates differed by age, education, occupation, working hours, sector, and workplace size (Grainger 2006). However, the growth of unionization among professionals in the public sector and falling unionization among manual workers in the private sector eliminated historical differences in manual/nonmanual unionization rates (Bryson and Gomez 2002, 51–56). Similarly, the concentration of women in the more heavily unionized public sector eliminated the historical difference in male/female unionization rates.

Because there is no British legislation comparable to the American NLRA Section 8(2) that prohibits company unions and practices that might be construed as amounting to company unionism, workers in the United Kingdom have a more heterogeneous set of options for representation than do U.S. workers. The proportion of workplaces with ten or more employees with specified forms of voice for workers in 1998 and 2004 can be seen in table 3.1. The data show that the percentage of workplaces covered by unions fell from 33 percent to 27 percent between 1998 and 2004. Among workplaces that recognized a trade union, moreover, the proportion of unionized work sites with a union representative at their immediate workplace fell by ten percentage points. In the late 1990s, around 15 percent of employees worked in workplaces where there were nonunion employee representatives (Bryson 2004). The workforce elected roughly half of these representatives while the rest were volunteers or management appointees. Most nonunion representatives were attached to joint consultative committees, the traditional method used by employers to consult with employee representatives. These committees, operating at the workplace or organization level, provide a formal setting in which the employer can consult staff representatives, though they rarely engage in negotiation over terms and conditions (Cully et al. 1999, 101–2).

There is a mixed pattern of change in the prevalence of employer-sponsored voice institutions from 1998 to 2004. The proportion of workplaces with problem-solving groups involving nonmanagerial employees increased, but the

TABLE 3.1
Percentage of workplaces with specified labor—management voice practices, 1998–2004

	1998	2004
Representative voice		
Workplaces that recognize unions	33%	27%
Unionized workplace with union representative		
at own workplace	55	45
Problem solving groups with nonmanagers	16	21
Joint consultative committees	20	14
Consultative forum above workplace level	27	25
Communication		
Meetings with entire workforce/team briefings	85%	91%
Regular newsletters	40	45
E-mail	—	38
Intranet	—	34
Employee surveys	—	42
Information Disclosure		
Investment plans	50%	41%
Financial position of workplace	62	55
Financial position of organization	66	51
Staffing plans	61	64

Source: Kersley et al. 2005.

proportion of workplaces having joint consultative committees and higher-level consultative forums declined, possibly because employers anticipated that mandated works councils would supplant these forms of nonunion voice.

Where the prevalence of nonunion voice continued to expand was in management-sponsored forms of two-way communication between management and employees without the mediation of a representative, that is, worker participation rather than representation. Managements increasingly held regular meetings with the whole workforce ("town hall meetings" in the U.S. vernacular) and formed briefing groups or problem-solving groups, where workers could voice their opinions and concerns to management. In addition, firms increased their ways of communicating (one-way) to workers, with many using e-mail and Intranet to send messages to employees.

But there was a sizeable drop in the proportion of workplaces disclosing information on many key issues, such as investment plans, and the financial position of the workplace and organization. Again, in some cases, this may reflect an expected transition to works councils covered by the EU Social Charter, which mandates some disclosures of information.

The growth of nonunion channels of voice for workers has generated great debate within the union movement. Union "modernizers" maintain that union success depends on the ability of unions to foster collaborative relations with employers by bringing "added value" to the firm. Under former general secretary John Monks, the Trade Unions Congress favored partnership agreements between employers and unions, without great concern that this strategy might undermine the independence of trade unions. The government's certification officer establishes whether a union is truly independent of the employer, as defined by statute.[5]

Other trade unionists are dubious about the benefits of "partnership" for unions and their members. The election of more radical union general secretaries in some of Britain's largest unions in the 2000s gave momentum to those disillusioned about the gains made through partnership or collaboration with the Labour government. The new leaders, called "the awkward squad" by some, favor a more militant unionism that questions the gains to be made through collaboration with employers (Charlwood 2004).[6] Some academic researchers have found the benefits of partnership to be minimal (Kelly 2004). From the perspective of our analysis, however, the critical issue is less how union leaders or researchers assess the competing institutions of voice, and the virtues or vices of union-management cooperation, than how workers view these institutions and relations.

Data and Method

To assess the preferences of British workers among union services, firm-based institutions, and nonunion works councils, we analyzed data from the 2001 British Worker Representation and Participation Survey (BWRPS) and the 1998 Workplace Employment Relations Survey (WERS). The BWRPS asked some 1,300 randomly chosen British workers about their situation at work and their attitudes toward unions and other labor institutions (Diamond and Freeman 2001). It was conducted as part of the monthly British Market Research Bureau Omnibus Survey. Interviews were conducted using face-to-face computer-assisted personal interviewing (CAPI) techniques. In total, some 3,614 interviews were conducted as part of the Omnibus survey. Of these, 1,355 people were eligible to take part in the BWRPS. The weighting schema

[5] Section 5 of the Trade Union and Labor Relations (Consolidation) Act of 1992 defines independence. If the union is deemed independent it receives a certificate of independence in accordance with Section 6 of the act. Some employer-specific bodies known as staff associations do attain independent status, whereupon there is little to distinguish them from trade unions.

[6] Some on the political left favor greater union political engagement to produce a more union-oriented agenda for future Labour governments. The New Labour case for unionism (associated with the Labour Party leadership) has been based on its value-added economic benefits. While the Left characterizes voice as a human right, enshrined in international conventions, it has yet to be recognized as such by employers (Coats 2004) and union advocates must make the case that union voice is the best type to guarantee equity.

used in this analysis ensures that demographic profiles match those for all employees in Great Britain aged fifteen or over.

The WERS is a nationally representative survey of workplaces with ten or more employees covering all sectors of the economy except agriculture. With weighting to account for complex survey design, results can be generalized with confidence to the population of workplaces in Britain employing ten or more employees. It asked managers, employees, and union representatives about labor relations policies and practices (and other issues). Our analyses use two elements of the survey. The first is the management interview, conducted face-to-face with the most senior workplace manager responsible for employee relations. Interviews were conducted in 2,191 workplaces with a response rate of 80 percent. The second element is the survey of employees within workplaces where a management interview was obtained. Self-completion questionnaires were distributed to a simple random sample of twenty-five employees (or all employees in workplaces with 10–24 employees) in the 1,880 cases where management permitted it.[7] Of the 44,283 questionnaires distributed, 28,237 (64 percent) usable ones were returned.[8]

Both surveys ask workers about the problems they face at their workplace and the perceived effectiveness of unions or management in dealing with these problems. We combine the responses of individuals to similar questions into single measures designed to reflect the underlying or latent factor associated with the questions. For instance, we summarize the responses of workers to questions about workplace problems, difficulties with management, and gaps between their desired and actual influence on decisions into a single measure of "needs" for representation or participation comparable to thermometer scales of temperature, with higher values reflecting greater workplace problems or needs.

We focus on summary measures rather than on single variables for three reasons. First, because the summary measures reduce the danger that the wording or placement of particular questions will create measurement error or bias in responses. Conceptually, there is a near infinite list of questions on a particular issue, from which surveys select a handful. Averaging across the questions in a particular survey provides a more reliable and hopefully valid measure of the real situation or attitudes than any single question. Second, we focus on summary measures because they facilitate comparisons of results across surveys. The BWRPS and WERS ask different questions about workplace problems or needs. Summary variables subsume the differences into a single mea-

---

[7] The probability of worker selection is the product of the probability of the workplace being selected and the probability of an employee being selected from within that workplace.

[8] The weighting scheme compensates for sample nonresponse bias detected in the employee survey (Airey et al. 1999, 91–92). For details of the first findings from the 2004 survey, see Kersley et al. (2005).

sure, which provides a natural way to compare responses. Third, we focus on summary measures because they make it easier to discern patterns associated with workplace relations and worker attitudes than seriatim analysis of individual questions.[9]

Quantifying Employee Needs

The BWRPS asked employees about the workplace factors likely to generate employee needs for representation or participation in four ways. It asked about: (1) the influence workers had and wanted in different workplace decisions; (2) the grades workers give to management in dealing with workplace issues; (3) the presence of particular problems at the workplaces; and (4) general workplace climate. We coded responses to questions in each of these areas into 0/1 variables, where 0 means no problem/need and 1 means a problem/ need.

In the influence questions, we said there was a problem when workers wanted "a lot" of influence in an area but did not have it. British workers showed substantial needs/problems in determining pay raises and deciding perks and bonuses—traditional trade union domains (Diamond and Freeman 2001).

On the grade questions, the survey asked workers to grade management with a school grade scale from A to F. We coded D/F grades as a 1 for problem or need. Few British workers give management D/F on understanding and knowledge of the business, but many gave such grades in granting pay increases, sharing authority, and making work interesting.

On the questions that asked workers to identify unfair practices, the most common unfair practice was preferential treatment by management or senior staff. The second most common was payment of unfair wages. This was followed by unfair dismissal or discipline and bullying. Discrimination was the least cited problem. Taking all of these questions, 39 percent of workers cited at least one unfair practice area as being a problem at their current workplace.

The questions about general workplace climate included trust in management, security of employment, pleasantness of jobs, and employee-management relations. Again, we counted a problem or need only when workers reported that an area was particularly bad.

Altogether, we used twenty-six BWRPS items to measure problems at workplaces. Because the BWRPS had a split sample design, however, it asked some items of only half of respondents, so that we have observations for each individual on only twenty-three items. We constructed a Workplace Needs (WN)

---

[9] For more information on the statistical tests underpinning these summary measures, see Bryson and Freeman (2006).

measure by counting the numbers of times workers reported a problem/need. The WN variable can vary from zero (no problems reported) through 23 (worker reports problems for every item).

Following a similar strategy, we examined the WERS questions that related to problems or needs at the workplace. We took responses on thirteen questions, and coded them 1 if workers reported a problem or were dissatisfied with their situation and 0 otherwise. We then summed the responses to form a single scale of workplace needs. The WERS scale takes the value 0 when workers report no problems and 13 when they report the maximum number of problems. The exact items used in both of our indices can be seen in appendix A.

Our analysis yielded five findings about the needs/problems workers have at their workplace and the factors that influence them.

Finding 1: Workplace needs are not normally distributed

The distribution of the Workplace Needs variables from both data sets can be seen in figure 3.1. Both distributions show a concentration of observations at the lower end of the scale. The modal score for the BWRPS index is zero, given by 23 percent of workers. Fifty-four percent of workers report problems on fewer than three of the items, while just 10 percent of workers accounted for 52 percent of all the reported problems. The WERS index shows comparable nonnormal bunching of responses at zero and a relatively thick tail of responses at higher values.

If the distribution of problems was generated by the random arrival of problems with a given probability for all workers we would expect our thirteen or twenty-three items to generate a bell-shaped curve. Responses would be bunched around the mean value and tail off at lower and higher values. The distributions seen in figure 3.1 follow a different pattern, with most workers having few or no problems and some workers having many problems. The reason the distribution takes on the nonnormal shape is simple: the needs of workers on different items are not independent. Knowing that a worker reports needs on a particular item gives information about their likelihood of reporting needs on other items.

There are three possible reasons for the nonindependence of the reports of needs. One possibility is that it reflects workers' personal characteristics—their age, gender, years of schooling, for which we have measures, or their unobserved psychological attributes, for which we have no measures. In this case, a given worker may see more problems or get into more problems than another worker in the same objective situation. The individual nature of reported needs is unlikely to translate into a collective response.

The second possibility is that the nonindependence reflects attributes of the workers' industry or occupation or sector of work, which most workers in that

A. BWRPS (based on scale from 1 to 23)

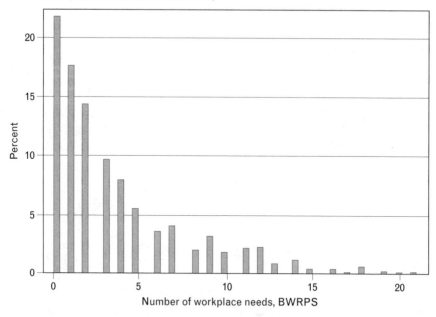

B. WERS (based on scale from 1 to 13)

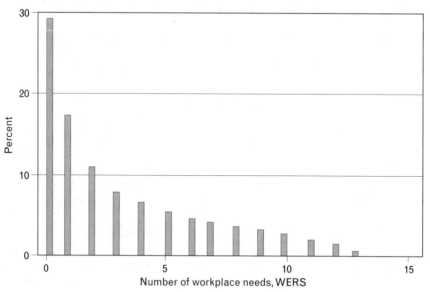

Figure 3.1: The distribution of needs for representation and participation

area would report. If this were the case, the data would reveal a concentration of needs in particular parts of the labor market.

The third possibility is that the nonindependence of needs reflects labor practices at particular workplaces. A workplace with considerable labor-management conflict might, for example, generate lots of problems, while one with good labor relations might generate few problems. In this case, when a worker reports many needs, he or she is reporting what others would also report, which is likely to translate into a general desire for representation at a workplace.

To examine the impact of demographic factors, and of job and industry, on the needs reported in the BWRPS and WERS, we estimated linear regression equations relating our WN measure to measures of types of work and workplace, and to age, gender, and other personal attributes. To measure the extent to which workplaces per se generate needs/problems, we made use of a unique aspect of the WERS design—that it obtained worker reports on workplace conditions from multiple worker respondents at the same workplace. In these data the effect of a workplace on needs/problems will show up in many workers at the same workplace reporting many or few needs.

Finding 2: Needs/problems are more related to industry or occupation of work than to the demographic characteristics of workers

The easiest way to summarize the evidence behind finding 2 is to compare the variation in the number of needs among industries/occupations with the variation across workers with different demographic characteristics. If the number of needs varies more by industry or occupation than by demography, needs would be more strongly associated with attributes of workplaces than with attributes of individuals. This was the case in both the BWRPS and WERS. For instance, in the BWRPS the industry with the highest number of needs was manufacturing, where workers reported 5.7 needs, while the industry with the lowest number of needs was hotel and catering, with 2.3 needs (figure 3.2). Similarly, among occupations, operatives had an average of 6.0 needs, whereas managers reported just 2.3 needs. By contrast, there was a much smaller difference in the mean number of needs by gender (4.1 needs for men versus 3.1 needs for women); or by age (3.5 needs for workers 25–34 versus 2.9 needs for workers 55–64).[10]

Finding 3: Workplaces generate different needs for employee representation or participation

To see whether the needs/problems that workers report are workplace related we created a data file from the WERS that gave the number of needs reported

---

[10] Multivariate statistics, such as F-tests of the contribution of these different sorts of factors, support this evidence. See Bryson and Freeman (2006).

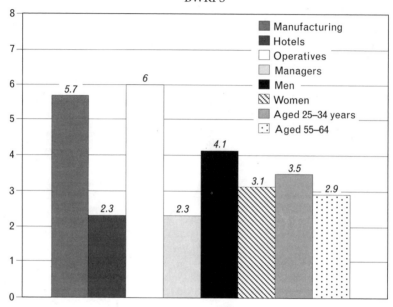

Mean needs
BWRPS

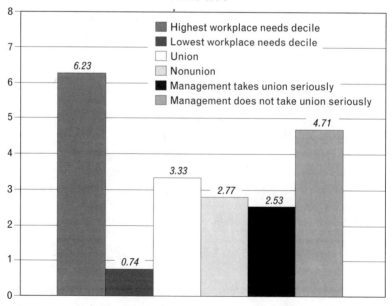

Mean needs
WERS 1998

Figure 3.2: Worker reports of needs/problems by industry, occupation, demographic characteristics, and workplaces

by 25,451 employees at 1,759 workplaces for which we had valid data—giving us an average of 14.5 worker reports on needs per workplace. Using several statistical tests, we found that the workers at a given workplace gave sufficiently similar reports of numbers of needs to conclude that workplaces themselves vary in their creation of needs. To demonstrate this without complicated statistics, we tabulated the average number of needs for each of 1,759 workplaces and ranked the workplaces by average needs. This tabulation shows that workplaces in the upper 10 percent of the distribution of needs averaged 6.23 needs on the WERS scale from 0 to 13; whereas workplaces in the lower ten percent of the distribution of needs averaged 0.74 needs (figure 3.2).[11] Such wide variation by workplace makes a prima facie case that the differing labor situations at workplaces are a key factor in worker reports of problems or needs.

Unions and Human Resource Policies

To what extent can we identify the impact of unions and human resource policies on workplace needs?

A priori, it is unclear whether unionism will increase or decrease perceived needs/problems. As the traditional worker organization for dealing with workplace problems, unions could make workers more aware of problems and thus more likely to report problems even if there are no more problems at their workplace than elsewhere (Freeman 1978; Freeman and Medoff 1984). Unions might also be associated with more problems if workplaces with many problems induce workers to unionize and the union fails to resolve the problems, leading problems and unionism to be positively associated for a very different reason. On the other hand, if unions help solve workplace problems workers at sites with recognized unions may report relatively few problems.

Similar considerations apply to the potential association between management human resource practices and numbers of reported problems. Absent a human resource office or an open door policy, workers may ignore some problems because there is no way to resolve them. In the presence of mechanisms to discuss problems and to deal with them, workers may notice more problems. However, if the institutions solve those problems, they may report fewer problems.

To determine how union status and human resource practices affect the number of problems, we regressed the number of problems on measures of unionism and human resource practices, along with other potential determinants of problems. Using the WERS, we also compared the average number of

---

[11] Alternatively, average needs at the tenth percentile were 1.25, whereas average needs at the ninetieth percentile were 5.09.

needs at workplaces by union status and human resource practices. Given the crosscurrents of possible effects, it is perhaps not surprising that we found a complex pattern of relations.

Finding 4: Unionized workers report more problems except when they say they have a strong union that has a good working relation with management

Because there are nonunion as well as union members at sites where management recognizes unions and at sites where management does not recognize unions, we compare numbers of problems by the union status of workplaces and by the membership of workers in unions as well.

In the BWRPS, workers at unionized workplaces reported 4.20 problems, while workers at nonunion workplaces reported 3.08 problems. Adding diverse regression controls barely changed the difference between the two types of workplaces. Moreover, at both union and nonunion work sites, union members reported more problems/needs than nonunion members. At unionized workplaces, members reported 4.69 problems, while nonmembers reported 3.26 problems. At nonunionized workplaces, members reported 5.04 problems, while nonmembers reported 2.95 problems. Similarly, in the WERS, whether we look at unionization of the workplace or union membership, unionism is associated with more reported workplace problems. The mean number of problems reported by workers in unionized workplaces in the WERS was 3.33, whereas the mean number for those in nonunionized workplaces was 2.77 (figure 3.2) Across all sites, union members reported 3.68 workplace problems compared to 2.72 reported by workers at nonunion sites.[12]

These contrasts do not, however, tell us whether unionism raises the reported numbers of problems or whether unions organize workplaces or workers with more needs, nor whether, faced with a given set of problems, unions help resolve them, per the "value added" notion of union contribution to the firm. To examine this issue, we compared the problems at unionized workplaces with different reported union-management relations and by different levels of union power. In BWRPS, workers who said that unions and management worked in partnership reported 3.34 problems, whereas workers in unionized workplaces where they did not think management and unions worked in partnership reported 5.18 problems. In WERS, workers who said that "management takes the union seriously" reported 2.53 problems, whereas

---

[12] Given that the needs variable averaged 3.57 in the BWRPS and 3.10 in the WERS, the differences between the number of problems in union and nonunion workplaces in the two surveys was larger in the BWRPS. In that survey, workers in nonunion workplaces score 86 percent of the overall mean on problems, whereas those in union workplaces score 118 percent of the mean, a difference of 32 points. In WERS, workers in nonunion workplaces score 89 percent of the mean while workers in union workplaces score 107 percent of the mean for all WERS workers, a difference of 18 points.

those who said that management does not take the union seriously reported 4.71 problems (figure 3.2). In addition, workers who report that the union is effective at their workplace report fewer problems than workers who say that the union is not effective; and workers who say the union has just enough or too much power report fewer problems than do workers who say the union has too little power. The implication is that when employers treat unions seriously or there is a balance of power at the workplace so that unions are effective, unionization reduces problems. In this situation, cooperation also reduces perceived problems.

Finding 5: Nonunion channels of voice reduce workplace problems/needs

The two data sets contain information on different human resource practices, but they show consistent results. The BWRPS asked workers about an open door policy, joint consultative committees, a grievance system, and a human resource department. Regression analysis of the number of needs/problems on the presence of these practices (and other determinants of needs/problems) shows that joint consultative committees and open door policies reduced the number of needs, while the other two had little or no effect. The WERS asked about the presence of joint consultative committees, grievance procedures, the presence of a human resource specialist, quality circles, regular meetings with management, and monthly team briefings. Regression analysis shows that regular meetings with management and the presence of quality circles reduce the number of workplace needs, while the other institutions have little or no effect. Indeed, in some calculations, some of these practices had modest positive effects on the number of needs/problems. While the two surveys differ in their estimates of the impact of joint consultative committees on needs, the overall pattern of results supports the generalization that nonunion channels of voice reduce problems, albeit with uncertainty about the specific forms that accomplish this.

Summary of Findings

The problems/need for representation and participation reported by workers vary across workplaces and by types of jobs. Unionism raises the number of reported problems, while firm-based nonunion channels of voice reduce reported problems; but unions that work effectively with management and those that have sufficient strength to be taken seriously by management reduce the number of problems at union workplaces.

Workers' Choice of Institutions for Voice

The United Kingdom has a diverse set of institutions through which workers can seek to resolve workplace problems. Our analysis posits that the way workers want to deal with the problems depends on the type of problem they face, the number of problems/needs, and the efficacy with which they believe the different institutions can resolve them. The evidence yields six more findings that illuminate these relationships.

Finding 6: Worker preferences for collective or individual voice depend on the problem and on the worker's union status

Preferences between collective voice and individual voice in dealing with workplace problems are potentially critical to the choice of workplace institutions. Some workers have a collectivist bent, preferring to deal with problems with fellow employees. Other workers prefer to deal with workplace issues by themselves. At the same time, there are distinctions between problems that affect an entire workplace and thus may be more readily resolved by collective action and problems that can be resolved individually by one-on-one meetings with management.

To see how workers differ in their collectivist or individual orientation, the BWRPS used a split sample design. It asked half the sample whether they agreed with the statement: "In the long run, the only person one can count on at work is yourself"; and asked the other half of the sample, "Working with others is usually more trouble than it is worth." Persons who agree with the statements have an individualist orientation, while those who disagree have a collectivist orientation. Almost half of respondents count as individualist on the first question, whereas only 19 percent count as individualist on the second question. One interpretation of this huge difference is that it reflects the fact that many people who count on themselves in the long run appreciate that it may be fruitful to work with others in the short run. There was virtually no difference between union and nonunion workers in their responses to these questions.[13]

To see whether workers view specific problems as being more amenable to individual voice or collective voice, the BWRPS used another split sample question. It asked half of the sample whether they preferred to deal with problems through a group of colleagues or fellow workers or on their own and asked the other half whether they preferred to deal with problems with a trade union/staff association representative or on their own. The responses show differences

---

[13] On whether working with others was usually more trouble that it is worth, 21 percent of union members agreed and 18 percent of nonunion members agreed. On whether in the long run the only person one can count on at work is oneself, 45 percent of members agreed compared to 48 percent of nonmembers.

by issue and also by union status. In both designs, workers preferred solving problems relating to promotion and training and skill development on their own and preferred to deal with problems of discrimination through a trade union. Union members favored collective solutions to negotiating salary and working hours and conditions, while nonmembers preferred negotiating on their own. Moreover, regardless of the question, union members preferred a more collectivist solution. When nonmembers desired collective action, moreover, they favored using colleagues or a group of fellow workers rather than a trade union or staff representative, while union members sometimes preferred the union and sometimes preferred colleagues or a group of fellow workers.

The finding that there is little difference in collectivist orientation between union and nonunion members and large differences in their desire for union solutions to specific problems suggests that the experience of unionism affects preferences for institutional solutions.

Finding 7: Nonunion members at unionized sites and workers at nonunion sites desire some union services

In Great Britain approximately 40 percent of workers at a workplace with a recognized union do not join the union. Do these "free riders" reject the union option utterly or do they have some desire for union representation? The BWRPS asked respondents about their desire for union services in six areas (table 3.2). Three-quarters of *nonmembers* at union workplaces expressed desire for union services on at least one item, and over half wanted union representation on at least three items. Ten percent of the nonmembers said that they would be very likely to join a union if asked, and 26 percent said that they would be quite likely to join a union if asked. So why don't they join? One reason is that the union does not ask them: 56 percent of nonmembers eligible to join a union at their workplace say they were never asked to join; many of these workers were young or recent hires to the establishment. Since these workers could have asked members how to join if they "really wanted to," the BWRPS went further to ask nonmembers to assess the factors that contributed to their remaining nonunion.

Sixty-nine percent of nonmembers cited as either "quite important" or "very important" at least one of the four reasons that the survey offered to explain their behavior.[14] Thirty-eight percent said that a quite/very important reason they did not join was because they perceived that the "union doesn't achieve anything." Nearly the same proportion (35 percent) of nonmembers said that a quite/very important reason was that they got the benefits and did not need

---

[14] Only 10 percent of nonmembers say all four reasons were "not at all important" so that, for a small minority, the question is not getting at their reasons for not joining.

TABLE 3.2
Desire for union representation and union membership, BWRPS

	Unionized workplace		Non-union workplace	
	Union member	Nonmember	Union member	Nonmember
Number of issues where union representation desired:				
0	4	24	10	38
1–2	10	20	30	25
3–5	66	40	55	28
All 6	20	16	5	9
Likelihood of joining union if asked:				
Very likely	—	10	—	16
Quite likely	—	26	—	30
Workplace will work better with trade unions				
Agree	67	34	54	20
Neutral	29	56	38	68
Disagree	3	11	9	13
Workplace will work better with collective voice arrangement				
Works council only	5	20	27	34
Works council and union	80	51	45	21
Union only	12	9	11	4
Neither	4	21	17	41

Notes:

1. Figures in the upper panel show the percentage of workers preferring a "trade union or staff association representative" to deal with the cited problems at the workplace, rather than deal with the problem "by themselves." The six items relate to sexual/racial discrimination, negotiating salary, negotiating working hours and conditions, promotion, bullying, and training and skill development.

2. To obtain the likelihood of joining, nonmembers in unionized workplaces were asked: "If someone from the union at your workplace asked you to join, how likely is it that you would do so?" Nonmembers in nonunionized workplaces were asked: "If a group of workers at your workplace formed a union and asked you to join, how likely is it that you would join that union?"

to pay for membership—classic free riders. Nonmembers also identified pecuniary and nonpecuniary costs of membership. Thirty percent said that they were deterred from joining by a membership fee that they regarded as too high, while 28 percent said they had not joined because "people doing my job don't join trade unions."

What about workers in workplaces without a union? The BWRPS asked them about their desire for union representation on six separate items. Six in ten said that they wanted a union to represent them on at least one item, and one in ten wanted union representation on all six items (see column 4 of table 3.2). Sixteen percent of nonmembers in nonunionized workplaces said they would be very likely to join a union if one existed at their workplace, and another 30 percent said they would be quite likely to join.[15] These figures are

[15] These data are consistent with data from the 1998 British Social Attitudes Survey, which found 39 percent said they would be "very" or "quite" likely to join a union if asked (Bryson and Gomez 2003a). BSAS 1998 asks employees in nonunionized workplaces: "If there were a trade union at your workplace, how likely or unlikely do you think you would be to join?" with precoded answers ranging from "very likely" to "not at all likely."

larger than the comparable figures for nonmembers at union work sites. One reason is that in union workplaces, nonmembers are a selected group with less desire for unions. Another reason relates to the way the survey asked workers in nonunion sites about joining a union. It posed a scenario in which a group of workers at their workplace had formed a union and asked the individual to join,[16] which makes the cost of organizing the institution lower than it would be in reality. Taking this criticism a step further, our next result suggests that we should view the responses to the question about "likely to join" as possibly exaggerated.

Finding 8: Workers doubt unions' ability to change workplace outcomes

A potentially important element in workers' choice of unions as their preferred labor market institution is whether they believe a union can deliver the services they want. The BWRPS asked workers in unionized settings whether they thought their workplace would be better or worse without the union, whereas it asked workers in nonunion settings whether they thought their workplace would be better or worse with a union. If unionized and nonunionized workplaces operate equally effectively with respect to workers, and if workers favor whatever status quo works effectively, the proportion of workers in a union setting saying their workplace would be better absent the union would be about the same as the proportion of workers in a nonunion setting saying their workplace would be better with a union. The evidence in table 3.2 contradicts this "null hypothesis." At unionized workplaces the majority of workers believe that the workplace would be worse if there was no union, while few believe that the workplace would be better. By contrast, at nonunionized workplaces, most workers think that the union would make no difference, though more think the workplace would be better with a union than think it would be worse. The implication is that while workers in unionized workplaces believe that unions are doing a good job, workers at nonunion sites are not convinced unions would make enough of a difference to attract them.[17] If we define British workers truly likely to join unions as those who report they are very likely to join and who believe a union would make the workplace better, 10 percent of nonunion employees in nonunion workplaces would be classified as wanting unionization. This finding, coupled with declining union density in workplaces with unions available, raises questions about just how big any union representation gap is in Britain (Bryson and Freeman 2006).

[16] See footnote 2 to table 3.2.

[17] The desire for union representation is strong among union members. Only one in twenty members do not want union representation on any items, while nine in ten want union representation on at least three of the six listed (column 1 of table 3.2).

Finding 9: Workers see works councils and unions as complements

New EU-inspired legislation requires employers to inform and consult their workers regularly about workplace policies and issues through works councils. Prior to the legislation, most workers said they favored such requirements (Diamond and Freeman 2001, exhibit 20). If workers see these new institutions as substitutes for unions, the union share of the market for voice in the United Kingdom could fall over time. If workers see these new institutions as working better with unions, they could spur a renascence of unionism in the United Kingdom.

Most workers see works councils as complementary to unions (table 3.2), which is how councils and unions have operated in much of continental Europe. Three-quarters of workers believe their workplace would work better with some form of collective representative worker voice. Two-thirds think the workplace would be better with a works council. And in two-thirds of these cases (nearly half of all workers) workers want a combination of works council and union. Union members strongly prefer the combination of a works council and union to other options. Nonmembers working in workplaces with a union also prefer the combination of a works council and a union to other options.[18] However, nonmembers have a less favorable view of collective representation, and where they do favor collective representation, they prefer works councils over unions.

In addition, over a third of nonmembers said that they wanted neither institution at their workplace, and 30 percent said that they wanted a works council only—which suggests that over half of nonunion workers would not want unions if works councils were widely available. On the other hand, while just 5 percent of nonmembers see a union by itself as the best way of dealing with an employer, 29 percent of nonmembers made a combination of works councils and trade unions their first choice. This suggests the advent of works councils creates an opportunity for unions to expand their influence in the workforce.

Finding 10: Workers with lots of problems want unions

The link between worker needs and their preference for institutions lies at the heart of our model of what workers want in the form of voice. The notion is that workers identify workplace problems, which they attribute to management, and seek solutions in some form of independent voice, of which unionism is the strongest form, if they believe that the union can solve the problems.

The evidence shows that the number of problems/needs is associated with the desire for unionism. One way to see this is to estimate how the number of

---

[18] This supports the contention that unionization is an "experience good"—something that workers are more likely to value having experienced it (Bryson and Gomez 2003b).

problems affects workers' preference for having a works council and a union, which is arguably the strongest form of representation for workers, relative to having only a union, which is arguably the second strongest form, relative to having only a works council, relative to having no worker institution. In the BWRPS the greater the number of needs, the greater the desire for the stronger forms of representation: the mean number of needs is 4.71 for those wanting a combination of works council and union, compared with 3.68 for those wanting a union only, 3.01 for those wanting a works council only, and 2.11 for those with no desire for collective representation. This relationship holds when controlling for other factors (Bryson and Freeman 2006). Separate analyses of workers in the unionized and nonunionized sectors show that, in the union sector, those with more needs prefer union involvement but are indifferent as to whether the union operates in conjunction with a works council; and that the more effective a union is in delivering services, the more workers favor the union-only option.[19] Overall, however, union members prefer the union option over the union plus works councils option. Among nonunion workers, more needs implies a desire for works councils and a union.

The number of problems workers have also affects their desire for a switch in the union status of their workplace. Multivariate analyses of BWRPS reveal that in unionized workplaces workers with greater needs are more likely to say that the workplace would be worse off if it lost union representation than are workers with fewer needs. Similarly, in nonunion workplaces, those workers with the greatest needs are the most likely to say the workplace would be better with a union.[20]

Further analyses of the BWRPS show that needs increase worker desire for unions to negotiate for them and to protect them but do not affect workers' desire for the union to help on issues of career promotion.[21] At the same time, the presence of a union on site that the worker can join increases the worker's desire for union representation in all three areas. Finally, analysis of WERS data shows that greater needs raise worker desires for unions in the areas of representation in pay, making complaints, and in disciplinary matters. Moreover, the effect of problems on desire for union representation is larger for workers in nonunion workplaces than for those in union workplaces.

---

[19] Union effectiveness in delivering terms and conditions is measured using a scale based on employee ratings of their ability to win fair pay, promote equal opportunities, work with management, make work interesting, and protect workers (Bryson and Freeman 2006).

[20] Studies that link job dissatisfaction to desire for unionization are consistent with these results (e.g., Leigh 1986).

[21] The survey asked split sample questions. Half of the survey was asked about negotiating salary and half about negotiating hours and conditions, which we combine into a want for union negotiating; half was asked about bullying and half about sexual or racial discrimination at the workplace, which we combine into a want for union protection; and half was asked about promotion or training and half about skill development, which we combine into want for union representation on career development.

Finding 11: Union effectiveness and managerial policies influence the desire for unions, independent of needs

Workers are more likely to choose unions when they believe unions "make a difference to what it is like to work here" and where unions "take notice of members' problems and complaints." The managerial policies that significantly affect the desire for union representation are grievance procedures, joint consultative committees, and the presence of a human resource specialist, all of which are *positively* related to the probability that a worker will want union protection. There are two ways to interpret this. One possibility is that management introduces these policies because workers are prounion but that the policies do not noticeably reduce that tendency. Another is that the policies work sufficiently poorly that workers see unions as a way to make them work better.

There is likely, moreover, to be a significant feedback relation between union effectiveness and managerial policies. When a union has real workplace power, management is likely to treat it as a partner (Boxall and Haynes 1997), which in turn will increase union effectiveness and the desire of workers for unions.

Finding 12: Workers in the United Kingdom want cooperation, not confrontation

Workers and management can interact conflictually or cooperatively. Unions can follow the "modernizers" agenda and seek cooperative relations with management, including partnership arrangements with firms, without accepting the management agenda, or they can raise red flags in confrontation in the Arthur Scargill tradition of union militancy. Management can also choose cooperation or confrontation. It can take union concerns on a variety of issues seriously, or try to minimize the areas where it deals with unions.

The vast majority of workers prefer a worker-based organization that "work(s) with management to improve the workplace and working conditions" to an organization that declares its main function as "defend(ing) workers against unfair treatment by management." Seventy-one percent of members and 73 percent of nonmembers in BWRPS preferred the organization that worked with management to the organization that made defending workers its main function. Union members prefer this even though most regard defending workers against unfair treatment to be one of the principal goals of their union. One reason for the desire for cooperative relations is that the number of workplace problems falls when management and their union work cooperatively.[22] Another reason for the desire for cooperative relations is the stress

---

[22] Freeman and Rogers (1999) examined the meaning of cooperative relations by asking U.S. workers whether it involved management giving on some issues, sharing power and authority, or simply

and strain that can come to workplaces when management and unions are at loggerheads. A third reason is that when unions and management are at loggerheads a poor climate of employment relations ensues, which can affect unions' ability to deliver for workers (Freeman and Medoff 1984).

Workers' desire for unions and management to work cooperatively requires decisions by both parties. The union may choose a cooperative or "partnership" stance but find that management treats this as a sign of weakness and exploits or rejects it. Only a union with sufficient bargaining power will be treated as a viable partner by management and will reduce problems/needs at the workplace. Similarly, management may choose a cooperative stance but find that the union treats this as a sign of weakness and uses it for its advantage.

What Is Being Done?

Unions, employers, and government have responded to the emerging market for voice in several ways.

Trade union representatives have increasingly sought to recruit new members at their workplace. The 2004 WERS survey shows that 77 percent of union representatives attempted to recruit new members in the preceding year. Among those who specified the nature of the recruitment, 85 percent sought to recruit nonmembers at workplaces where unions negotiated pay and working conditions, thus addressing the critical free rider or "infill" problem, and virtually all of them (94 percent) said they had some success. A smaller proportion (39 percent) had attempted to sign up members in workplaces that had no collective bargaining (Kersley et al. 2005). The TUC developed some innovative websites to exploit the reach and low cost of the Internet to improve union services to workers. The site http://www.worksmart.org.uk provides information to primarily nonunion workers about their rights at work and ways to deal with workplace problems. The TUC also offers union health and safety representatives a weekly e-mail with the latest information on issues relating to occupational health and safety; and it has created a special representatives-only website that offers bulletin boards for union reps to discuss ways to deal with problems, http://www.unionreps.org.uk (Freeman 2005a). Analysis of the union reps website shows that it connects representatives from many unions and areas so that the collective wisdom of reps can be brought to bear on helping representatives deal with workplace problems at virtually zero cost (Freeman and Rehavi 2006). In addition, using government legislation that provides financial support for educational activities, unions have trained learning rep-

---

meeting pleasantly while keeping control. Workers interpreted cooperation as sharing at least some decisions rather than as a sham.

resentatives at many work sites, to help workers find the appropriate ways to enhance their skills. Still, as can be seen in table 3.1, WERS finds that the proportion of workplaces covered by unionism fell from 33 percent to 27 percent between 1998 and 2004, and the proportion of unionized work sites with a union rep at the immediate workplace fell by ten percentage points.

Surprisingly, perhaps, the spread of nonunion voice channels has slowed in the United Kingdom. There is an increase in the proportion of workplaces with problem-solving groups involving nonmanagerial employees but a decline in the proportion of workplaces having joint consultative committees and higher-level consultative forums (see table 3.1), possibly because employers anticipate that these forms of nonunion voice will be supplanted by mandated works councils. As suggested earlier, this may reflect an expected transition to works councils covered by the EU Social Charter, which mandates some disclosures of information.

Indeed, the biggest change in the way the United Kingdom provides voice to workers is through the Labour government's January 2000 reversal of the United Kingdom's "opt out" from the 1994 European Works Councils Directive that established works councils in large firms. In June 2001 the government acceded to the EU labor law that requires firms with more than twenty staff in a single workplace or fifty staff in scattered sites to consult employees on major decisions. While U.K. legislation gave companies from three to seven years to adjust to the new legislation, the United Kingdom is joining the other EU countries in establishing a works councils–based industrial relations system. With the United Kingdom accepting works councils, British workers will have the widest choice of institutions of voice in the Anglo-American world. They will be able to combine nonunion mandated works councils with unionization if they desire, stick to unions with no complementary institutions, or select works councils or firm-sponsored nonunion forms of voice. Firms will be able to influence workers' choice through their human resource policies, though some formal policies may increase workers' desires for unions. The good news for unions is that many workers view unions as a desirable form of voice and that works councils and employer personnel practices do not have a pronounced impact in reducing worker desire for unionization. The bad news for unions is that worker doubts about union effectiveness, lack of union recruitment activity, free-riding behavior, and the perceived direct and indirect costs of unionizing have led many to believe that unions will not make their working life better.

Our analysis shows that workers with greater workplace needs are more desirous of unions but that their preferences are fine grained. Workers want unions to negotiate wages and working conditions and for protection against arbitrary employer actions but do not see unions as helping them progress in their careers, though it is possible that union learning reps could change this perception. Many workers see no major workplace problems that would impel them to form or join unions. Effective union representation of workers is also dependent on management-union cooperation, which workers prefer to confrontation. However, unions cannot impose this on management, and cooperation works only when unions are operating from a position of some strength.

The way unions and firms respond to the advent of mandated works councils to meet workers' desires will play a major role in determining the institutions of voice at British workplaces. Given the variety of workplace experiences and worker attitudes, we do not expect a single form will dominate the market for voice, as unions once did in the 1970s. If workers obtain what they want, we can expect to see some combination of unionism and works councils in most U.K. workplaces. For this to occur, unions will have to deliver positive value on two fronts: providing tangible benefits to members, while adding value to employers who can influence the costs/benefits of membership and the climate of employment relations. The union–works council combination is the institutional framework that offers the greatest potential for accomplishing these dual gains, but it is also a combination that makes greater demands on both unions and firms.

Appendix A

The BWRPS Index

We developed this index by counting one point every time a respondent thought that "having a lot of influence" was "very important," but did not have "a lot of influence" in relation to "deciding how to do your job and organize work," "setting working hours including breaks, overtime and time off," "deciding how much of a pay rise the people in your work group or department should get," "the pace at which you work," "deciding how to work with new equipment or software," "deciding what kinds of perks and bonuses are offered to employees." A point was added every time the respondent gave management a D, E, or F grade in relation to "promoting equal opportunities for women and ethnic minorities," "understanding and knowledge of the business," "keeping everyone up to date with proposed changes," "concern for employees," "willingness to share power and authority with employees in the workplace," "making work interesting and enjoyable," "giving fair pay increases and bonuses." A point was also added each time respondents reported one of the following problems at work: "workers being paid unfair wages," "workers being disciplined or dismissed unfairly by management," "preferential treatment by management or senior staff," "bullying by management or fellow workers," "sexual or racial discrimination." Finally a point was added every time the respondent thought managers were not "understanding about employees having to meet family responsibilities," disagreed with the statement "people here are encouraged to develop their skills," disagreed with the statement "my job is secure in this workplace," disagreed that "my job is interesting and enjoyable," rated management-employee relations as "poor," and was not satisfied with their "influence in company decisions that affect your job or work life."

The WERS Index

We developed this index by counting one point for each of the following: disagree that "I feel my job is secure in this workplace" (qa8c=4|5); dissatisfied with "the amount of influence you have over your job" (qa10a=4|5); "the amount of pay you receive" (qa10b=4|5); "the sense of achievement you get from your work" (qa10c=4|5); "the respect you get from supervisors/line managers" (qa10d=4|5); disagree that "managers here are understanding about employees having to meet family responsibilities" (qb5b=4|5); disagree that "people working here are encouraged to develop their skills" (qb5c=4|5). In addition, A point was added every time the respondent gave management a D or F grade in relation to "keeping everyone up to date about proposed changes" (qb8a =4/5); "providing everyone with the chance to comment on proposed changes" (qb8b=4|5); "responding to suggestions from employees" (qb8c= 4|5); "dealing with work problems you or others may have" (qb8d=4|5); "treating employees fairly" (qb8e=4|5); and if they viewed relations between management and employees as poor or very poor (qb9=4|5).

Chapter 4

Employee Voice in the Irish Workplace
Status and Prospect

JOHN GEARY

The "Irish model" of industrial relations has attracted attention interna-
tionally for its attempts to refashion its erstwhile decentralized system of wage
bargaining in favor of a more centrally coordinated approach. The participation of unions in a succession of "social partnership" agreements, beginning in
1987, has set Ireland apart from Britain, the source of many of its labor market institutions. Although it has been common to categorize Ireland along with
Britain—and by extension other Anglo-American countries—as sharing one
relatively homogeneous industrial relations system, any such easy labeling of
the Irish case is now devoid of credible meaning. Among Anglo-American
countries, the voice permitted Irish unions in macroeconomic management
and social policymaking is singular. The question of whether unions and workers have enjoyed a commensurate level of influence or "voice" within Irish
workplaces is another matter.

In this chapter I catalogue the provisions for employee voice in the Irish
workplace, based on the findings from two recently conducted surveys. The
chapter provides an overview of Irish industrial relations, considering the
wider political context before discussing the challenges confronting trade

    I would like to thank Peter Boxall, Paddy Gunnigle, Peter Haynes, and Bill Roche for their comments
on a previous draft of this chapter. The help and advice provided by Teresa Brannick is particularly appreciated. I am also grateful to Nicola Tickner and her colleagues at the Central Statistics Office for providing me with data from the QNHS.

unions. It then outlines the methodology employed in the two surveys, analyses the findings, and discusses the postures and initiatives pursued by the social partners—unions, employers, and government—with respect to employee voice. I conclude the chapter by summarizing the main findings and outlining the prospects for employee voice in the future.

The Industrial Relations Context

As in the other countries examined in this book, employee voice in Ireland was conventionally understood as being synonymous with union voice. Certainly, along with the United Kingdom, Ireland differs from other European countries in not possessing a general, permanent, and statutory system of employee information and consultation.

Employees in Ireland enjoy a constitutional right to join a union of their choosing. They may request their employer to recognize that union for the purposes of negotiating terms and conditions of employment. The employer, however, is free to concede or refuse union recognition. It is a "voluntary" concession on the part of employers. Nonetheless, most Irish employers have traditionally felt constrained to recognize a union where the majority of their employees request recognition. In this context, too, the Labour Court and the Labour Relations Commission have often prevailed on otherwise reluctant employers to recognize trade unions where workers have been able to make a demonstrable case that this is what the majority of workers want.

In contrast to almost all other European countries, Irish political parties' views on the rights and status of unions have not diverged significantly. Any differences that may have been apparent in past decades have certainly diminished in recent years as the two largest parties, Fianna Fàil and Fine Gael, came to adopt a shared position on the importance of social partnership agreements and unions' role therein. In not maintaining a major party of the left, Ireland is distinguished from its European neighbors and only really finds its equivalence in the United States, where the Left is also effectively nonexistent. In this context, levels of trade union membership have remained unaffected by the political complexion of governments (Roche and Larragy 1990), and, in spite of the absence of a major party of the left, Irish unions have prospered comparatively well in comparison to their European counterparts (see Ebbinghaus 2002).

Union density peaked in the early 1980s at around 62 percent. Shortly thereafter, as in many other European countries, union density went into a slow, steady decline and is currently estimated to be 35 percent.[1] There is no doubt-

---

[1] Note that the 1980 figure is derived from the DUES (Development of Unions in European Societies) Project (see Roche and Ashmore 2002). Its data set is constructed on the basis of annual returns from unions. Data for 2004 is obtained from the Quarterly National Household Survey (QNHS, quar-

ing that the decline in density over the last twenty years is the most severe and critical ever experienced by the Irish union movement. Despite a modest increase in 2002, the decline has been consistent and steep.

The data reported in table 4.1 provide a detailed breakdown of recent trends in union density. Taking economic sector first, only the agriculture, forestry, and fishing sector, albeit from a very low level of unionization, recorded an increase in union density between 2000 and 2004. In all other sectors density declined, in some instances, as in "other production industries" and construction, by more than seven percentage points. The former comprises a very disparate group of industrial sectors; as well as traditional manufacturing industries in which Irish-owned companies predominate, and which are highly unionized, it also includes new high-tech firms in the computer and software industries, many of U.S. origin, which rarely concede union recognition. The decline in union density in the "other production industries" sector reflects the recent employment growth and concentration of employment in these new industries. Although the Quarterly National Household Survey (QNHS) data do not classify union membership by public and private sectors, it is clear from the available data that the decline in union density has been particularly marked in industries in which the private sector predominates.

Turning to the decline in union density among different occupational groups, two groups—craft workers and plant and machine operators—have witnessed a significant decrease between 2000 and 2004. The context and reasons for this decline vary significantly, however. With respect to the latter, employment levels decreased by 16 percent, and the fall in density is attributable in large part to the decline of traditional low-skilled industries and employment in Ireland. In contrast, craft employment expanded by 10 percent, and notwithstanding an increase in membership, union density declined by over 7 percent. With the exception of associate professional and technical employees, whose union density increased marginally, all remaining occupational groups witnessed a decline in union density against a background of significant employment expansion.

Interestingly, unionization increased by a small proportion among employees in part-time employment, where it is concentrated among part-time female employees. This increase needs to be put in the context of exceptional employment growth in this segment of the labor market: part-time employment grew by 16.5 percent between 2000 and 2004. In comparison, full-time employment grew by 8.5 percent, but union density in this segment fell by over four and half percentage points.

---

ter three). This is a quarterly labor force survey that is based on a weighted sample of thirty-nine thousand households and was obtained from the Central Statistics Office (CSO). Unfortunately, there is no CSO data on union membership going back to 1980. The sharpness of the decline in union density here portrayed is probably overstated by the use of these different data sets.

TABLE 4.1
Trade union density, 2000–2004[a]

Employment characteristics	2000	2004	Change
Sector			
Agriculture, forestry, and fishing	11.19 %	14.17%	2.98%*
Other production industries	45.38	37.61	−7.77
Construction	34.40	26.86	−7.54
Wholesale retail	22.45	18.25	−4.20
Hotels and restaurants	14.87	12.15	−2.72
Transport, storage, and communication	52.15	48.96	−3.19
Financial and other business services	27.16	22.74	−4.42
Public administration and defense	80.80	78.07	−2.73
Education	66.44	61.08	−5.36
Health	57.59	52.12	−5.47
Other	19.81	18.09	−1.72
Occupation			
Managers and administrators	31.56 %	28.84%	−2.72%
Professional	53.26	46.24	−7.02
Associate professional and technical	52.51	52.52	0.01*
Clerical and secretarial	39.40	36.10	−3.30
Craft and related	41.01	33.33	−7.68
Personal and protective service	32.03	30.40	−1.63
Sales	21.47	17.31	−4.16
Plant and machine operatives	49.52	41.15	−8.37
Other	30.79	28.15	−2.64
Employment Status			
Full-time (total)	43.23 %	38.09 %	−7.78%
Part-time (total)	19.28	19.93	0.65*
Part-time (male)	10.15	7.93	−2.22
Part-time (female)	21.93	22.67	0.74*
Age			
< 24	20.74%	17.70 %	−3.04%
25–39	41.13	34.55	−6.58
40–54	45.00	44.64	−0.36
55+	38.35	38.45	0.10*
Total	39.12%	34.77%	−4.35%

Source: The data is derived from the Quarterly National Household Survey (QNHS, 2000 and 2004, quarter three).
Note: * highlights an increase in union density between 2000 and 2004.
[a]The data are derived from the number of employees who answered "yes" to a question on membership of a trade union or staff association. Those respondents who did not state whether they were in a union are excluded from the present analysis.

Perhaps not surprisingly, unionization is lowest among new entrants to the labor market: 17.7 percent of employees under twenty-four years of age are in unions, whereas 44.6 percent of those between forty and fifty-four years of age are union members. Union density declined in all but one of the four age cohorts in recent years. The decline is most steep among those employees between twenty-five and thirty-nine years of age.

The reasons for the decline in union density in Ireland are similar to those observed in the other countries reviewed in this book; in particular, a shift in the structure of employment away from sectors where unions have been strong traditionally to expanding sectors, such as services and high-technology industries, and the growth of part-time and temporary employment. But structural changes in themselves only account for part of the change (Roche 2001). Other factors are perhaps unique to Ireland and reflect Ireland's industrial development strategy and associated dependence on foreign investment. Up until the mid-1980s, development agencies and Irish public policy, more generally, were positively disposed toward union recognition to the extent that incoming multinational companies were often encouraged to recognize unions. This position was reversed, however, in the face of intensified international competition to attract inward investment and an increased assertiveness on the part of employers, particularly those of U.S. origin, to remain nonunion. As a consequence, since the mid-1980s union nonrecognition has become strikingly evident among U.S.-owned companies (Geary and Roche 2001). In turn, unions have had to concede that a dogged pursuit of union recognition in these sectors would not only be likely to yield modest returns but would be ill-advised politically if such campaigns resulted in capital flight or jeopardized future inward investment.

Recent research also confirms a general hardening of employer opposition to union organization in the private sector. Union officials report that many employers use coercive measures to forestall recognition, including victimizing activists (48 percent), sacking union activists (22 percent), and threatening closure or relocation (38 percent) (D'Art and Turner 2005). Only 5 percent of employers were reported as having encouraged employees to join a union, and 27 percent allowed union organizers access to the workplace. In the face of such resistance, the proportion of cases where unions were successful in securing recognition declined from two-thirds in 1999 to 40 percent in 2002. D'Art and Turner (2005, 129) highlight the conclusion that the stratagems used by Irish employers to suppress union organization in recent years have become "sophisticated and intense." There is also evidence that Irish employers in the 1990s were more likely to introduce change unilaterally than to engage unions through partnership arrangements or at arms-length through collective bargaining (Roche and Geary 2000).

Over the last twenty-five years or so, then, trade unions in Ireland have faced a difficult and, at times, hostile environment at the workplace level. While national social partnership agreements have provided unions with "a place in the sun" and enhanced their influence over government macroeconomic strategy and social policy decision making, the decline in union density continues, particularly in the private sector, as unions confront significant obstacles to organization in new, expanding sectors of the economy as well as "old" expanding sectors such as construction. Increasingly, the greatest concentration of union members is in the public sector and in traditional manufacturing industries, construction, banking, and insurance. In accounting for the erosion of unions' membership base, structural shifts in employment are an important factor, but so are the shifting postures of employers toward union recognition, particularly those of U.S. origin. Employers, too, are placing a greater emphasis on direct employee involvement, even in unionized companies, as well as exhibiting a confidence and assertiveness in introducing changes on the basis of managerial prerogative.[2] With this duality in union fortunes—accorded a central role in macroeconomic management and social policy development, but increasingly marginalized and by-passed at the workplace level—observers have come to talk of a system of industrial relations in Ireland that is represented by a "truncated partnership." Trade unionism, once the dominant employee voice mechanism, faces significant challenges in the Irish workplace.

Data Sources

The analysis in this chapter draws from two data sources—the National Centre for Partnership and Performance/Economic and Social Research Institute/University College Dublin (NCPP/ESRI/UCD) Survey of Employees' Attitudes and Expectations of the Workplace (2003) and the UCD Employee Voice Survey (2005). Both are nationally representative surveys. Together, they provide the most comprehensive picture to date with respect to the structures and provisions for employee voice in Irish workplaces. The former survey obtained a total of 5,198 responses, a response rate of 46.5 percent. The latter is based on 1,420 responses and achieved a response rate of 56 percent. Both surveys were administered by telephone, the former as a stand-alone study in the summer of 2003 and the latter as part of a larger omnibus survey in the spring of 2005. In both studies, the resulting data were reweighted to adjust for any discrepancies in the distribution of key analytical variables, such as gender, age, level of educational attainment, social class, size of establishment, and sector between the sample and population distributions.

---

[2] Substantial numbers of firms have introduced direct participation arrangements—up to two-thirds of employers in the private sector. Where such mechanisms are in use, however, clear differences of view exist as to the extent to which employees are permitted to influence management decision making. Employers' claims that they inform and consult with employees and value such arrangements are in significant part challenged by employees. This gap in perceptions is evident in both survey and case study research (see Geary and Roche 2005).

TABLE 4.2
Trade union reach and density

	Trade union/staff association in workplace (union presence)	Member of trade union/staff association (union density)
Yes	52.5 %	37.7%
Public sector	90.7	68.8
Private sector[a]	43.6	30.4
Manufacturing	59.2	40.0
Construction	43.1	33.7
Wholesale retail	38.9	28.8
Hotel restaurants	23.8	13.0
Transport and communication	63.3	50.3
Finance and other business services	41.1	27.6
Public administration and defense	90.5	72.1
Education	73.8	47.8
Health	67.6	52.8
Other services	24.8	16.5
Size of workplace		
1–4	17.9	14.0
5–19	35.8	26.3
20–99	58.4	40.9
100+	75.0	54.7

Source: NCPP/ESRI/UCD (2003) data set.
[a]Includes employees working in commercial semistate companies. If they are excluded, union density in the private sector is 28.2 percent.

Union Voice: Reach and Members

Union Presence and Density

Table 4.2 details the extent of union reach and density in Ireland. Just over half of those interviewed indicated that management recognized a union in their workplace, and almost 38 percent of all employees are union members, a figure that is not too dissimilar to that found in recent Quarterly National Household Surveys. Not surprisingly, the NCPP/ESRI/UCD data also reveal sharp differences in union presence and membership across sectors. The vast bulk of employees (91 percent) in the public sector said a union is recognized in their workplace, in comparison to 44 percent of employees in the private sector. While over two-thirds of public-sector employees are union members, less than a third of their private-sector counterparts are members. The highest concentrations of union membership are in public administration and defense, followed closely by education, health, and transport and communication, where the state is also a major employer. The hotel and restaurant sector has the lowest levels of unionization. Four of every ten employees in manufacturing are unionized. A third of employees in construction are unionized, and a little over a quarter are unionized in finance and other business services. Finally, union density increases with workplace size: only 14 percent of workers in very small workplaces are union members, while more than half of those employed in large workplaces (100-plus employees) are unionized.

Who Are the Union Members?

When union members are profiled on the basis of individual-level characteristics, it is notable that there is virtually no "gender gap": almost four out of every ten males and females are unionized. There is a curvilinear relationship between age and union membership: unionization is lowest among young workers, below average in the oldest age cohort (55 years and over), and highest among employees in the intervening age groups. Employees with no educational qualification are less likely to be union members, but otherwise there is little variation by level of educational attainment. As might be expected, union density increases with job tenure, and, as seen with the QNHS data, those in part-time employment are less likely than those in full-time employment to be members. Permanent employees are nearly twice as likely to be unionized as temporary or casual employees.

There are some pronounced variations in union density across occupations in the public and private sectors. Managerial and professional employees in the public sector are four times more likely to be in unions than their counterparts in the private sector. Indeed, union density is at its highest for all occupational groups among these latter two categories in the public sector. In contrast, craft workers and plant or machine operators are the most highly unionized occupations in the private sector. Employees classified as occupying "elementary" jobs have comparatively low levels of unionization.

Union Voice and Employees' Views

Between 1980 and 2004, the Irish trade union movement suffered a near precipitous decline in its membership base—as measured by union density. The fundamental question arises as to whether continuing union density decline in Ireland is due to employer opposition to union organization and/or to an already weak or weakening commitment to, and belief in, unions among members.

Union Members in Unionized Workplaces

Union members in unionized workplaces were asked why they *continued* to be union members. For a significant number, union membership is experienced as a constraint; that is, it is perceived either as a condition of employment (69 percent) or as a consequence of informal pressure from work colleagues (68 percent). However, the predominant reasons related to the perceived advantages that union membership bestowed, principally the protection unions offered members (93 percent) and unions' ability to secure better wages and conditions of employment (89 percent). The role unions play "in creating a more just society" also figured prominently (83 percent). The differences across occupational groups as to the reasons for continued union membership are relatively small.

One reading of these findings is that union members in Ireland exhibit an instrumental orientation to their union—they continue to be members because unions are perceived as capable of voicing and defending their immediate workplace interests. Another reading is that union membership remains, if only in part, an involuntary act, and that many employees feel compelled to remain union members. To the extent that the latter is the case, the argument might be advanced that union organization is built on fragile foundations and is vulnerable in the long term. To examine employees' orientation to unions further, a series of additional questions were asked with respect to the importance members attach to union membership, the perceived effectiveness of unions, as well as members' commitment to unions.

First, union members in unionized workplaces were asked whether union membership had become more or less important over the last five years. In response, only a small minority (9 percent) indicated that membership had become less important, compared with 37 percent who said it had become more important. The remainder (54 percent) said there had been little or no change. Respondents were also asked: "How likely do you think it is that you would quit being a union member in the next year or so?" Only 1 percent said that it was "very likely" and 5 percent that it was "quite likely," while over a quarter (26 percent) and over two-thirds (68 percent) said it was "not very likely" and "not at all likely," respectively. Another question examined members' views of the effectiveness of unions in representing employees' interests. The predominant view was that unions had been effective: three-quarters (74 percent) said that unions were either very or quite effective, 17 percent reported that were not very effective, and only 5 percent saw unions as being ineffective. Employees' experience of union representation seems to have led them to value union membership as being to their advantage.

It is also possible to examine attitudes toward unions in more detail by exploring members' commitment to unions. Union commitment is measured using a five-item scale (alpha = 0.72) adopted from Gordon et al. (1980). From the pattern of responses, it is possible to identify four descriptive categories: those respondents who are "highly committed" to unions and whose composite score is consistent with an average overall pattern of response within the "agree" to "strongly agree" range; those members who exhibit little or no commitment, with composite scores falling on average within the "disagree" to "strongly disagree" range; and, between these two intervals, those members whose commitment to unions tilts either toward a "moderately positive to a neutral" position, or toward a "neutral to moderately negative" position. The analysis shows that while a substantial proportion of union members are highly committed to unions (26 percent), the greater proportion of the sample is concentrated in and around the neutral position, but, within that latter cohort, the majority is positively *inclined* toward trade unions. It also emerges that those who are unequivocally not committed to unions (4 percent) are a very small proportion of union members.

The results reported here suggest that, on the whole, Irish trade union members are positively disposed toward union membership, value being members, and are generally committed to trade unionism. To this extent, it would seem that union organization is built on relatively robust foundations, and that there is little evidence to suggest a weakening in members' orientation toward unions.

What Accounts for This Pattern of Results?

To examine the effects of various possible influences on commitment to unions, a series of measures were devised to see whether they were associated with high levels of union commitment. To this end, respondents were asked whether "partnership" committees were present in their workplace and whether they personally participated in them. A variable measuring the effectiveness of workplace partnership was also devised. A number of questions were asked about direct participation: where such practices existed, whether respondents participated, and how much influence employees had over the organization and planning of work.

From a series of regression analyses, it is possible to derive some indication of the relative importance of the various influences that affect union members' commitment to trade unions. Many of the variables identified in the literature as being potentially related to union commitment, such as sector, workplace size, employment status, age, length of service, and staff category, were found not to be important influences in the Irish case, although there was a significant relationship with gender with female union members being more committed to unions. The single greatest influence is respondents' perception of union effectiveness in representing members' interests: the more effective members believe unions to be, the more committed they are to trade unions. Not surprisingly, there is also a relationship between the occupancy of representative positions (shop stewards) and levels of union commitment. With regard to the existence of partnership arrangements between management and unions, the mere presence of partnership committees in a workplace and participation therein is not sufficient to engender greater union commitment. It is only when such partnership committees are perceived to deliver beneficial outcomes for employees that they can be said to engender greater commitment to unions. The results with respect to direct participation and levels of work group discretion, on the other hand, were nonsignificant, and thus explain little of the variance in union commitment. Nevertheless, these results would seem to show that unions have neither benefited from, nor been disadvantaged by, their members engaging in various forms of direct participation.

In summary, union members in Ireland appear in large measure positively disposed toward their unions. Commitment levels are in large part accounted for by personal attitudes toward unions, in particular the perceived effectiveness of unions in representing workers' interests and the success of partnership arrangements. These influences remain robust when other factors are controlled for, including the structural contexts in which respondents are employed, members' age, and the climate of management-employee relations. The focus now turns to employees' views of union voice and, in particular, the roles members would wish unions to perform, in terms of bargaining priorities and representative postures vis-à-vis management.

Whither a "Priority Deficit"?

Respondents were asked to indicate whether various items thought to be important areas of concern and interest to employees constituted high or low priorities for their workplace unions. They were then asked to indicate whether each item *should* be a high or low priority for their unions. The intention is not only to examine members' beliefs about what issues unions should focus on, but also to see whether union members identify a "priority deficit" between the importance they and their workplace unions attach to particular issues. We should note that, depending on the issue, between 17 percent and 28 percent of union members did not know whether a given issue was or should be a priority for their unions. Therefore, a considerable number of members may be unaware or uninformed of union activities and priorities. For the present analysis, "don't knows" are omitted.

Unions are perceived by their members to prioritize the following items in descending order: pay and conditions, working in cooperation with management, the future of the company, changes concerning employees' jobs, "family friendly" or flexible work practices, training, and individual employment contracts. The rank ordering of what *should* constitute union priorities is substantially similar to that of the perceived ordering of existing union priorities. There is, therefore, little or no demand among rank-and-file union members for any reordering of union priorities, at least with respect to those items examined here. That said, however, members report that unions are giving insufficient attention, and should give greater voice, to certain issues. In particular, a "priority deficit" is most evident in regard to training and to family-friendly and flexible working conditions.

These results would seem to suggest that unions are doing a good job representing members' interests with regard to pay and conditions and cooperating with management—the priority deficit is smallest in these two items—but that they "must try harder" to prioritize and give voice to the need for employee training and family-friendly policies. Thus, union members expect their representatives to concentrate on more issues.

Preferred Union Role

Finally, this study allows us to examine the kind of role, if any, employees would like to see unions perform in their workplace. All respondents were asked to indicate which of three statements came closest to their view. Thirteen percent preferred that unions play no role in their workplace; 29 percent chose the option that limited unions' role to collective bargaining and grievance handling; the majority (58 percent), however, indicated that they would like unions to extend their role beyond collective bargaining and develop cooperative relations with employers to improve organizational performance. Further bivariate and multivariate statistical analyses revealed that union members were significantly more likely to believe that unions should have a role in the workplace. Also, echoing the discussion of union bargaining priorities above, union members were more likely to want unions to develop a cooperative relationship with employers. Older workers, too, favored a collaborative union posture, as did employees in manufacturing and in finance and the business services sector.

Nonunionized Employees' Views of Union Voice

Almost two-thirds of employees in Ireland are not union members. They are present in unionized and nonunionized workplaces. This is the first time it has been possible to examine their views of unions, their reasons for not joining a union, and their willingness to join in the future.

Why Do Employees Not Join Unions?

As well as being important in its own right, this question is also important in considering whether union density decline in Ireland is due in large measure to the postures of employers and whether, in the face of their opposition to union organization, there remains among employees a significant unsatisfied and unrealized demand for union voice. Of course, it could also be otherwise, that employers' views of unions are shaped by their employees' own preferences for remaining outside union membership. In other words, union recognition is eschewed by employers in deference to workers' own preferences and perceived interests.

Only 24 percent of nonunion members employed in unionized companies had ever been asked to join a union. The remainder (76 percent) had never been approached to consider union membership. The present analysis is confined to a consideration of the views of the former, who were *decidedly not* union members. The principal reasons they chose not to join a trade union were because they preferred to deal with issues or problems on their own and directly with management (80 percent) and they trusted their employer to take care of its employees and, as a consequence, saw no need to join a union (50 percent). Objections to unions in principle or to the manner in which unions voice worker interests did not feature very prominently as factors dissuading people from joining unions. Neither was the cost of union membership an important consideration. Notwithstanding their decision to remain outside union membership, the vast majority (79 percent) reported that they would vote for continued union representation, "if an election was held today to decide whether employees at your workplace should continue to be represented by a trade union." In sum, while nonunion members in unionized workplaces may not see any direct benefit for themselves in joining a union and prefer using direct-voice mechanisms, they were nonetheless supportive of the principle of union organization and would vote to ensure its continuance. They were thus tolerant of other employees' voice preferences; their personal views of unions did not extend to a blanket opposition to union voice.

Nonunion employees in nonunion companies were also asked of their reasons for not being union members. The number involved here, though, is small, as again the questions were confined to those who refused an approach to join a union. There are some similarities in the responses, although a larger spread of reasons is perhaps evident. Again, a preference to take up issues with management directly (57 percent) and the absence of a need to join a union given management's care for its employees (51 percent) figure prominently. Similarly, respondents did not possess any fundamental objections to unions in principle (22 percent), but many did see unions as being too confrontational in their dealings with employers (41 percent). There was also a perception that being a union member might damage a person's career prospects (47 percent).

Would Nonunion Employees Join a Trade Union?

Nonunion employees were also asked whether they would be prepared to join a union in the future, if asked. In the case of respondents in nonunion workplaces, the question drew a distinction between two scenarios, one where management agreed to support union organization and another where managerial support was not forthcoming.

In unionized workplaces, a little over 40 percent of nonunion employees indicated a willingness to join a trade union. The propensity to unionize in nonunion workplaces is striking, and it is especially marked in situations where management offers its support for union representation. In such circumstances, almost two-thirds of respondents (64 percent) indicated that would join a union if asked. This figure drops substantially, however, to 28 percent in situations where management is not prepared to support union organization. Nevertheless, that so many employees, even in the absence of employer support, would be prepared to join a union suggests that there is a significant "representation gap" in Ireland. Thus, as in the United States and the United Kingdom, a critical factor in facilitating union membership and organization is employees' perception of their employer's support for independent representation (Freeman and Rogers 1999; Gallie 1996).

These responses allow us to estimate the level union density might rise to in Ireland if those currently not in unions were to join. Using the level of union density found in the UCD Employee Voice Survey, if one assumes management support for union organization and if all those employees who said they would join a union did, union density in Ireland would rise to 71 percent. In the absence of management support, union density would rise to 56 percent.

Which Workers Might Join?

It is also possible by use of regression analysis to examine which employees currently working in nonunion workplaces might be more likely to join a union if given the opportunity by their employer. On examining the relative likelihood of different occupational categories joining unions as compared with managers (the reference category), it was found that two broad groups—professional/associate professional/technical staff and clerical/service/sales staff—are more willing to join a union. Perhaps surprisingly, craft workers show the lowest relative likelihood of joining. The position of operators is perhaps less clear-cut with a p value of 0.055. Thus the occupations—craft workers and plant operators—most often associated with union membership are now among the least likely of nonunion employee groups to countenance union membership. It will be recalled, too, from the analysis of the QNHS data from 2000 to 2004 above, that the decline in density among craft workers was the second highest overall, that the decline among employees in clerical, services, and sales positions was among the smallest, and that union density increased marginally among associate professionals and technicians. Perhaps surprisingly, employment status exerts no influence, nor does whether workers were union members in the past.

What does stand out, however, is that workers in workplaces where the climate of management-employee relations is perceived to be poor are more favorably disposed toward joining a union. Finally, the nationality of a firm would appear to exercise little if any influence on nonunion employees' willingness to join a union.

In summary, we find a variety of reasons for nonmembership in unions. Many nonunion employees in unionized workplaces have never been approached to consider union membership. These workers have never considered explicitly the merits of joining or not joining a union. For those employees who did deliberate on joining a union but decided not to, the principal reason was that they preferred to deal with management directly to address any concerns, believing that their employer would act in good faith and in their interests. Objections to union membership and representation were rarely informed by some fundamental principle or deeply held opposition to unions. Indeed, many nonunion employees appreciated the value of union voice, if not for themselves, then at least for others. Consider, for example, the high proportion of nonunion workers in unionized workplaces who endorsed union representation in their workplaces for those employees who sought it. Notwithstanding the general endorsement of unions by substantial numbers of nonunion employees, many others, particularly in nonunion workplaces, consider unions to be too adversarial in their dealings with employers. Others, too, are of the view that union membership would damage their career prospects. Such views are likely, in part at least, to be informed by employers' views of unions. So it is that employers' postures toward unions are a critical factor in mediating employees' decision to join a union. If Irish employers were seen by their employees as supporting union recognition, many more workers would be prepared to join a union, to the extent that current union density would (in the most optimistic scenario) double to around 71 percent. In the absence of employer support, many Irish workers see little practical benefit in joining unions or are fearful of the consequences if they do join. The evidence indicates that there is a considerable amount of unsatisfied demand for union voice among employees in Ireland.

How Do Employees Regard Nonunion Voice Mechanisms?

The discussion now turns to examine the incidence, and employees' views, of nonunion voice practices, both indirect and direct.

Presence of Nonunion Voice Practices

First, respondents to the UCD Employee Voice Survey were asked whether there was an "employee committee or association in your workplace which represents you and your co-workers in dealings with management but which is not a trade union?" What stands out is how rare such employee consultative committees (ECCs) are in Ireland in comparison to the other countries examined in this book. Only 14.6 percent of employees said that an ECC was present in their workplace. Such committees were marginally more numerous in unionized workplaces than in nonunion establishments. They were considerably more evident in the public sector and the commercial public sector where union density is high. In the private sector, employees in foreign-owned companies were considerably more likely to report their presence as were employees in larger workplaces.

Respondents were asked how ECC members were selected. Almost two-thirds (64 percent) said that ECC members were elected by fellow employees; in nearly a quarter of cases (24 percent) they were nonelected volunteers; in 10 percent of cases they were appointed by management; in only 1 percent of cases were they nominated by a trade union. As to ECC effectiveness, substantial numbers of employees were positive: 19 percent believed ECCs were very effective and 58 percent, quite effective. In contrast, 19 percent said their ECC was not very effective and 4 percent, not at all effective. Views differed little between employees working in unionized and nonunionized workplaces and also between union and nonunion members.

The NCPP/ESRI/UCD Survey examined the incidence of direct task participation mechanisms.[3] The reported incidence of such initiatives appears modest, certainly when set alongside that reported by employers in previous studies (cf. Geary 1999). Thirty-eight percent of respondents indicated that direct task participation practices were present in their workplaces. When coverage is taken into account, over 70 percent of employees participated in these arrangements. They were more widespread in large workplaces: 23 percent of employees in the smallest workplaces (with 1–4 employees) reported the existence of such practices, in comparison to 49 percent of employees in workplaces of one hundred or more employees. Involvement in direct task participation was found to be related to occupational category: professionals and managers were much more likely to report the presence of, and their involvement in, such arrangements than were unskilled manual workers. There was also a striking difference in their reported incidence as between union members and nonunion employees, 46 percent and 32 percent, respectively (O'Connell et al. 2003).

The UCD Employee Voice Survey also inquired whether other forms of direct employee voice, in particular mechanisms that seek to provide for justice and fairness, were present in the workplace (table 4.3). The vast bulk of re-

---

[3] These were taken to involve arrangements that "involve staff directly in the way in which work is carried out on a day to day basis." Examples included work teams, problem-solving groups, project groups, quality circles, and continuous improvement groups.

TABLE 4.3
The presence of direct employee voice mechanisms in unionized and non-unionized[a] workplaces

	Percentage of employees			
	Present in workplace	Have used it	Perceived as being very or quite effective	N weighted
Your manager has always said his/her door is open and you are welcome to come and talk things through at any time	83.4 (80.5)	61.7 (67.3)	90.5 (95.0)	743 (657)
A formal grievance or appeal procedure involving multiple stages (i.e., if you are not satisfied with what your immediate manager thinks you can appeal to a more senior manager)	57.4 (31.7)	18.5 (16.7)	61.5 (88.2)	730 (643)
A formal appraisal or review process that allows you to discuss your work and concerns on a regular basis with your manager	56.5 (42.4)	61.6 (67.0)	84.2 (91.8)	742 (651)
A formal mentoring system[b] where you can talk things through with your mentor if need be	42.1 (29.4)	54.1 (65.7)	96.8 (95.1)	713 (625)

Source: UCD Employee Voice Survey 2005.
[a]The figures for employees in nonunionized workplaces are provided in parentheses.
[b]This was defined as a colleague or superior who is assigned to an individual employee to offer guidance and advice in matters relating to their work and career.

spondents reported the presence of an open door policy. By comparison, the other three voice mechanisms—a formal grievance/appeal procedure, an appraisal/review process, and a mentoring system—were less evident. While there was little difference in the reported incidence of an open door policy in unionized and nonunionized workplaces, the differences in the reported presence of the other three direct-voice mechanisms is of note: roughly half of the employees in unionized workplaces said they were present in their workplace compared to only about a third of employees in nonunionized establishments.

Employees in nonunionized workplaces were more likely to report that they had used these direct-voice mechanisms than had their counterparts in unionized workplaces with one exception, the grievance procedure. In general, employees seem to have been satisfied with the manner in which these voice systems function. The notable exception was the grievance/appeal procedures, where over a third of employees in unionized workplaces believed that they had not operated effectively. This was the highest recorded level of dissatisfaction with the four direct-voice mechanisms examined in the survey.

Grievances and the Voice Mechanisms Used by Employees

The survey then focused specifically on the issue of how employees sought to have particular grievances or concerns addressed. First, respondents were asked whether they had experienced any of a list of ten grievances; where they had, had they sought the assistance of a manager, a trade union, an employee committee, or perhaps a lawyer? In the case of some items—not being paid a fair wage, having to regularly work in excess of forty-eight hours a week, and not having a say in day-to-day work decisions—almost one in ten employees stated that they had been unfairly treated by their employer. Other forms of ill-treatment, such as racial and sexual harassment, were less widespread (0.9 percent and 0.3 percent, respectively). Overall, the reported incidence of grievances is comparatively low by international standards; to this extent, Irish workers seem to be a relatively contented lot (cf. Freeman and Rogers 1999; Gospel and Willman 2005).

Most employees go to their manager to seek their help in addressing grievances, and many respondents report that their manager was helpful. There are, though, some notable exceptions. Comparatively few employees would appear at ease in going to their manager with grievances relating to long working hours and, in the case of employees in nonunionized workplaces, the failure to pay the national minimum wage (NMW). In regard to such grievances as bullying, long working hours, and unfair treatment, management was seen as not having done enough to address employees' concerns. It is of note, though, that on the whole managements in unionized workplaces were seen to be more sympathetic and to have done more to seek redress for aggrieved employees.

Turning to the issue of whether employees in unionized establishments view the union as an important voice mechanism, the most striking finding is that many employees (in most cases up to 50 percent) do approach their workplace representatives for help, especially with respect to not being paid a fair wage, not being paid the NMW, and not having a grievance addressed. But with respect to other grievances—bullying, unfair treatment by a manager, and lack of say in the workplace—comparatively few employees approach their union for assistance; instead, they go directly to their manager. One other finding stands out: grievances relating to long working hours. Only a third of unionized employees take this concern up with management, and only 18 percent go to their union for help. In nonunionized workplaces, four out of every ten employees said they approach their manager. Thus, this grievance goes largely "unvoiced" and unheard in the Irish workplace.

In summary, representative nonunion voice mechanisms, such as employee consultative committees, are rare in Irish workplaces. From the available data it is difficult to assess whether such committees are being used by employers to supplant or complement unions as a voice mechanism. However, the former would seem unlikely, as, in most cases, ECC members are elected by employees, and they are also more evident in strongly unionized sectors of the economy. Direct-voice mechanisms are more evident in unionized workplaces and are generally perceived by employees to have worked well, although dissatisfaction with grievance or appeal procedures is more pronounced among employees in unionized workplaces. Although some unionized workers are prepared to approach their union representative when they have a grievance or have been ill-treated at work, this is not always the case. Questions are thus raised as to whether employees view unions as an appropriate or perhaps an effective voice mechanism for resolving certain grievances at work.

Preferred Voice Routes

We turn to the voice "routes" employees would ideally prefer to use, assuming all such options are readily available, to resolve a range of possible grievances. My intention is to examine whether employees would prefer to go directly to management or have some intermediary voice mechanism act or mediate on their behalf, namely a trade union or an employee committee (defined as a committee that represents workers' interests but that is not a trade union). The preferences of unionized and nonunionized employees differ markedly. The former show a greater reluctance to approach management directly, particularly regarding pay increases, unfair treatment, and fears surrounding job security. These areas are the mainstay of union representation, and generally two out of every three unionized employees would prefer to seek union assistance in these matters. Roughly one of every ten nonunionized employees would ideally seek the help of a union in matters relating to unfair treatment, sexual harassment, and fears about job security. In general, both unionized and nonunionized employees are more likely to want to go directly to management with issues relating to training and promotion.

Few respondents indicated that they would prefer to seek the assistance of an employee committee. Earlier we learned that 17 percent of unionized employees reported that such a committee was present in their workplaces and that it was rarely used to resolve grievances. Putting these findings together, it might be observed that unionized employees, at least, have little appetite for collective voice mechanisms that do not involve union representation. In contrast, when nonunionized employees are prepared to countenance a collective voice mechanism they do not seem to show a consistent preference for union representation over an employee committee—either mode of collective voice might be used. There are some differences in regard to specific items, but it is difficult to discern a consistent pattern to their preferences. The vast bulk of nonunionized employees, though, prefer to go directly to management to resolve any grievances or concerns.

What Is Being Done for Employee Voice?

Having considered the various employee voice mechanisms used in Irish workplaces, and employees' views as to their effectiveness, the discussion now turns to the various initiatives and postures adopted by unions, employers, and the state to give shape and influence to employee voice in Ireland in recent years.

Unions

Irish unions manifestly face significant challenges in maintaining and expanding their voice and influence within the workplace. They have pursued a number of initiatives. The first was to seek an extension of "social partnership" to the level of the workplace to ensure that where unions had been granted recognition their presence and influence could be more securely rooted and guaranteed. Unions' advocacy of the principle of establishing cooperative relations with employers at the workplace level under the rubric of workplace partnership represented a significant shift in union orientation; not only was this an attempt to install an "articulated" or "integrated" system of employee representation (from the national to the workplace level) but it was an explicit acknowledgment that the principles underpinning the once-dominant adversarial model of union voice may no longer be appropriate for the changed business circumstances and the challenges presented by employers' actions. Although endorsed by the Irish Congress of Trade Unions and by large affiliated unions, it remains a matter of dispute whether local branch officials and workplace activists are at ease with this revision of union workplace orientation, either because they are ideologically opposed to any such recasting of union strategies or because they are confronted by employers who have little understanding or sympathy for union involvement in company decision making. In the face of such opposition, the priority that individual unions and their officers place on partnership varies considerably.

The second was to argue for legislative provision for union recognition and employee voice. This strategy took a dual route: first, unions have pursued with increasing vigor legislation to permit workers guaranteed rights to union representation and recognition; and second, unions have advocated the enactment of individual employment rights—not conditional on union membership—such as a universal right to information and consultation, as well as independent representation, on the heels of the European Directive on Information and Consultation (Geary and Roche 2005, 188). With respect to the former, the compromise reached to date under the aegis of social partnership has been to establish a union "right to bargain." A series of proposals, subsequently enshrined in legislation in 1999 and 2004, give greater powers to the Labour Relations Commission and the Labour Court in resolving disputes in companies where employers refuse to recognize unions or allow for union representation. The legislation does not, however, go as far as to institute mandatory provisions for union recognition as were enacted in the United Kingdom under the Employment Relations Act of 1999. Nonetheless, the first rulings from the Labour Court suggest that the provisions of the legislation constitute a form of "arms-length collective bargaining" or "shadow recognition," and have been generally welcomed by trade unions (Dobbins 2005a). Thus, for example, in some cases the court has directed companies to apply national pay awards negotiated under national wage agreements and, in other cases, companies have been required to adopt the prevailing wage rates and conditions of employment in their sector. Although some commentators have been sharply critical of these developments, and employers and their representative organizations have expressed their reservations and worries, the number of workers affected by the court's rulings has been modest, and they are, in the main, confined to small and medium-sized enterprises. Large nonunion multinational corporations have, as yet, remained outside the reach of these provisions. Most independent commentators are agreed that the direct effect of the legislative provisions on unions' fortunes has been modest.

Third, a further response has been to campaign for the better enforcement of worker rights and the rectification of perceived inequities in the labor market. Many of these campaigns have focused on providing a union voice for immigrant workers whose number has increased greatly since Ireland opened its borders to workers from the new EU accession states. Allegations of exploitation of immigrant workers, job displacement, downward pressure on wage rates and rising income inequality, and charges of a general "race to the bottom" figured prominently in union postures preceding the recent talks between the social partners and government to agree to a new national social partnership agreement. The ICTU's attempts concentrated on the establishment of a new enforcement regime to include a larger and better resourced labor inspectorate, new legislative procedures for governing collective redundancies, and, most contentiously, legislative provision to enforce sectoral wage norms.[4]

---

[4] The new agreement, titled Towards 2016, which was agreed since writing this chapter, has made provision for dedicating significantly more resources to ensuring compliance with employment rights. A new Statutory Office of the Director for Employment Rights Compliance is to be established, the number of labor inspectors is to be trebled, penalties for non-compliance have been strengthened and new administrative resources are to be made available to meet a government commitment to address cases expeditiously.

Other related initiatives involved campaigns for workers' rights that would have existed outside traditional bargaining domains; for example, the introduction of the national minimum wage and the advocacy and strengthening of legislation to prevent bullying in the workplace. Yet other campaigns have focused on broader equality and social justice issues, such as the provision of affordable social housing, child-care arrangements, old-age provision (including pensions), and new immigration policies.

Finally, unions have initiated new recruitment drives (Dobbins 2005b). ICTU's new strategic plan, for example, places recruitment and union organization as the number-one priority for the Irish trade union movement. The president of the ICTU, Peter McLoone, has called for unions to make available their strike and contingency funds to finance a new recruitment campaign. It is envisaged that that such a fund would be managed by the ICTU and would be used for general promotional purposes as well as for targeting specific sectors where unions have been traditionally strong but have lost significant numbers in recent years (Higgins 2005).

Employers

At the outset, the general observation can be made that, while employers and their principal representative organization, the Irish Business and Employers' Confederation (IBEC), have publicly endorsed the importance of enhancing employee voice in the workplace, they have shied away from supporting explicitly detailed provisions that might prescribe representative forms of voice over direct forms of employee voice. Consider the 1997–2000 social partnership program, Partnership 2000, which was the first to promote an extension of partnership to enterprises and workplaces through a national framework agreement. The objectives of "enterprise partnership" were to include the enhancement of the enterprise's prosperity and success; the engagement of all stakeholders' ideas, abilities, and commitments; and the creation of a basis for arrangements for discussing major decisions affecting the organization's future (Partnership 2000, 62). Reflecting the wide diversity of employer approaches to employee voice, the agreed definition of partnership was broad and general and allowed for both representative participation and direct employee participation; no unitary model or institutional arrangement was agreed to or advocated. Firms, employees, and their representatives were encouraged to tailor partnership arrangements to the circumstances of their own firms and workplaces. No attempt was made to prescribe the areas that might be encompassed by partnership. Subsequent social partnership programs also followed this approach, endorsing voluntary nonprescriptive arrangements and broad indicative agendas for the promotion of partnership and employee voice in firms and workplaces (Geary and Roche 2005).

The EU Directive on Information and Consultation has the potential to constitute the single greatest innovation in recent times in Irish employment relations in general, and in making provision for employee voice in particular. There are a number of notable aspects to employers' response (Geary and Roche 2005). First, the IBEC did not agree to an ICTU request to enter national-level talks with a view to formulating a framework agreement for the transposition of the directive into national legislation. Central to the IBEC's posture is the wide variety of positions and sharp differences of view across and within unionized and nonunionized firms as to how the directive ought to be transposed into Irish law. Different perspectives on the directive, as for workplace partnership, reflect the emergence of a highly differentiated system of employment relations in Ireland based on firms' diverse nationalities, business sectors, and competitive strategies.

Thus, the IBEC argued for a legislative framework that would permit individual employers the scope to determine their own specific employee voice arrangements. To have argued for, and pursued, a shared solution reached on the basis of compromise with a union position would likely have sparked challenges from a significant section of the IBEC's membership. Guided by these apprehensions, the IBEC moved instead to enter bipartite talks with the government to shape the legislation in a way that best met its requirements.

The State

As noted earlier, the absence of a general statutory system of employee voice has marked Ireland's industrial relations system apart in Europe. Traditionally, the state's posture regarding employee voice has been to defend and champion a voluntarist industrial relations regime. In practice, the state has tended to act pragmatically, and its predisposition toward favoring voluntarism has often been tempered by a preference that employers permit employees access to union voice when requested, to the extent that the state encouraged incoming foreign-owned companies to fall in line with prevailing voice practices and to grant union recognition to their workforces. However, beginning in the mid-1980s, as competition between nation-states intensified to attract inward investment, this injunction was effectively abandoned, and foreign-owned companies were permitted greater scope to establish their own voice practices, which may have made no provision for union voice.

In recent years, the government, in its role as a social partner and employer, has agreed with and supported the broad objectives of "enterprise partnership." This has resulted in the introduction of partnership arrangements in the public services from the late 1990s. Extensive formal partnership arrangements were put in place in the civil service, health, and local government sectors. The advent of such arrangements represented the most significant change in voice processes in the public service in half a century. Successive public service pay agreements have sought also to provide incentives for the establishment of partnerships and the handling of joint programs of change on a partnership basis (Geary and Roche 2005).

With respect to the private sector, while the government has supported workplace partnership, it has adopted a largely exhortative and noninterventionist position. Consistent with this, the National Centre for Partnership and Performance (NCPP), established initially by the government under the national agreement, Program for Prosperity and Fairness, operates as a voluntary catalyst for partnership and employee voice.

The introduction of European legislation in the area of employee voice has presented the Irish government with a different set of challenges. The wide variety of voice preferences used in Irish workplaces, as noted above, together with an economic development strategy that is heavily dependent on inward investment, has reduced the state's steering capacity to regulate changes in voice practices except in the most general or minimalist of fashions. In response to employer lobbying, the legislation which transposes the EU Directive on Information and Consultation into Irish law permits employers considerable freedom to determine their own preferred voice practices, including the scope to use direct employee involvement arrangements. The unions have argued that the government has missed a significant opportunity to enhance employee and union voice at the workplace level and has adopted a minimalist posture in deference to employers' concerns and objections. Far from constraining the voice preferences of employers, it is very likely that the legislation will add to their capacity to develop what Streeck (1997) has termed "privatized" forms of employee voice.

The Prospects for Employee Voice

In this chapter I have sought to provide an account of the status of employee voice in the Irish workplace. Drawing on data from two recent large-scale employee surveys, it has been possible for the first time to examine Irish employees' experiences of and views about different forms of employee voice. The following observations are highlighted in summary before considering the prospects for employee voice in the future:

1. Irish employees have high expectations of the level of voice they expect from their employers. These aspirations, however, have not always been met. The evidence points to a significant gap in perceptions between management and employees as to the level of influence that workers are permitted in the workplace.

2. Employees also have high expectations of those who seek to act as voice intermediaries for them. Although many union members assess their union representatives highly as "voice personages" and in general remain favorably disposed toward unions, they expect more of them, particularly in respect of training and family-friendly policies. Commitment to unions is closely linked to the bargaining effectiveness of unions and, where they exist, the success of partnership arrangements with employers. Many workers say that union membership has become more important to them in recent years and very few are likely to quit being members in the coming years.

3. A majority of employees report that they would like to see unions embrace a cooperative productivist orientation in their dealings with employers in place of an adversarial arms-length approach.

4. With regard to nonunion employees' views of union voice, it is important to distinguish between those who are employed in unionized and nonunionized environments. Although both groups report that they decided against membership because they prefer to take up problems or concerns directly with their manager, and in turn trust their manager, the latter were more likely to view unions as confrontational and feared that joining a union might damage their career prospects. Few, though, had any fundamental objection to unions. Many nonunion employees would be prepared to join a union if their employer indicated a willingness to support union organization. If this prounion sentiment was realized, it could translate into a union density level of around 71 percent, twice the current level. Such evidence suggests that a significant representation gap exists in Ireland.

5. As for nonunion voice practices, employers have introduced a variety of direct and indirect arrangements. Although employee consultative committees are not a prominent feature in the Irish workplace, employees commonly report the existence of particular direct-voice mechanisms. For instance, open door policies are widely used. Formal grievance/appeal procedures and appraisal schemes also exist in many workplaces, although formal mentoring systems are less evident. In broad terms, employees are content with the manner in which these voice systems operate, and on many issues workers, including unionized workers, choose to go directly to management to resolve problems. Employees, too, seem happy with the way they are treated by management, or at least record having comparatively few grievances. Grievances about long working hours, however, go largely unvoiced in both unionized and nonunion workplaces. In contrast, direct task-participation practices that permit

employees a say in decision making with respect to their own jobs are notably less common. A little over a third of employees report that their employer had introduced teamwork and other such practices that involve staff directly in how their work is performed.

6. Finally, what do workers want? Well, they want more voice. They would like the option of joining a union. Many, including unionized workers, prefer to voice at least some concerns and interests directly to management. They want unions to work cooperatively with management and address workers' interests beyond the narrow confines of the wage-effort nexus.

Irish workers thus place a high store on the opportunity to exercise voice, and they expect a lot of management and unions. There remain two questions: Will these expectations be met or dashed in the future? And by what means will employees' interests and concerns be voiced?

The prospects for the future of union voice at the workplace level are not propitious. Many employers establishing new operations are at best indifferent, and at worst hostile, to unions. Some, particularly those from the United States, have introduced human resource management practices, including direct-participation arrangements, that are designed, sometimes explicitly, to protect the nonunion status of the enterprise. In such circumstances, many employees do not feel secure in seeking union representation. In addition, employees' interests have become increasingly diverse and difficult to aggregate; their preferences for modes of representation vary, too. Specifically, the issue is whether workers' interests as traditionally conceived—confined to job-related issues and the wage-effort nexus—and represented can continue to be prioritized over a "newer" bargaining agenda to include areas such as training, influence over work decisions, and family-friendly policies. The findings as documented in this chapter highlight the existence of a sizeable priority deficit; the demand for a more vociferous union presence on these matters has not yet been met. This represents a significant challenge for unions. Consider the last item. To the extent that workers—male and female—must reconcile the competing demands of work and home life, unions are forced to address and represent a wider range of workers' interests. Nor can the difficulties associated with voicing the other aforementioned interests be underestimated. Although employers might accommodate union influence over wages and conditions of employment, a voice agenda that includes having a say over the organization of work, training, and a greater say generally in company decisions is often seen to represent a significant challenge to managerial prerogative, and may be rebuffed. A solution might be sought through the adoption of alternative representative postures and, in particular, a cooperative partnership-based approach to employment relations. Although there are undoubted difficulties here, there are definite benefits: principally, such an approach would resonate favorably with members' (and nonmembers') preferences for the adoption of a more cooperative posture in union dealings with employers, and it might help to erode the negative image—as perceived by many nonunion employees at least—that unions accord undue priority to adversarial bargaining.

The pursuit of a qualitative voice agenda through a partnership approach might help to unite an otherwise disparate union membership and prove attractive to nonmembers. To the extent that unions continue to give priority to traditional worker interests and adversarial bargaining they risk further membership contraction and marginalization.

The difficulty, however, for unions is that the circumstances of employees are not uniform. Some workers still complain of poor wages and conditions of employment. To the extent that such conditions exist, traditional adversarial voice may win more favor with employees. Thus, partnership cannot be prescribed as a universalistic solution. The challenge for unions is to devise representative strategies that not only align and integrate the diverse interests of their membership but also to decide between adversarial bargaining and cooperative partnership-based approaches, or indeed what combination of approaches might be advocated and pursued.

The second challenge for unions is to give voice to those employees in nonunion companies who seek union representation but whose employers are not willing to countenance union organization and recognition. To accomplish this, unions will have to organize employers. How might this be achieved? The two strategies pursued by unions (or at least the compromises reached) to date regarding workplace partnership and the right-to-bargain provisions have had limited success thus far. A statutory mechanism providing for union recognition may be necessary. This is certainly the preferred aim of the ICTU. And it may prove helpful, but it is unlikely to be a panacea (as shown in the chapter on the United States). Such a provision may constitute a double-edged sword: it may enable employees to win recognition from a reluctant employer, but it may also aid employers to mobilize workers to campaign for union derecognition.

The ICTU's recent request of unions to redirect and devote more resources (from their strike funds) to recruitment and organization has its perils, too. More resources dedicated to recruitment risks a reduction in resources assigned to serving the needs of existing members and, as Willman (2004, 83–84) has emphasized recently, the interests of cooperating employers. Here the interests and preferences of employers are key and are unlikely to be ignored by unions. In an Irish context, much may well depend on the size of Irish unions' "war chests"; where these are substantial, no such cross-subsidization may be necessary, but otherwise the subsidization costs incurred may be considerable. Thus, as Willman stresses, while the decline in union density can largely be accounted for by outside factors, the prospects of renewal and growth in union voice are endogenous to unions—and the strategic choices for future action are complicated by the economics and politics of union organization.

What of employers and the state? Both parties have worked closely with unions at a national level. A succession of triennial social agreements has ensured that all parties share in the decision-making process regarding a wide range of economic and social issues. Unions have found it difficult, however, to successfully exploit that position to win support for embedding and ensuring unions' place as a voice mechanism in firms and workplaces. Three specific items that are important to unions and are seen to be critical to enhancing their workplace voice—statutory union recognition, union-based partnership arrangements, and the transposition of the EU Directive on Information and Consultation—have been opposed and significantly recast to appease employer and government objections. The "promise" of the first two has been significantly neutered, and while it may be premature to make any bold statement about the third, there can be little doubt that the government has gone a considerable distance to accommodate employers' concerns. Thus, the hoped-for "promise" of the EU directive, too, may have been stolen. The upshot is that employers are free in large part to develop their own "privatized" versions of employee voice. And here their preferences are clear. The likelihood, then, is that in organizations where unions are absent or weak, employees' request for representative voice will not be met and direct-voice arrangements will predominate. Where this occurs, it is probably safe to assume, based on the research evidence documented above, that many employers will indeed introduce direct-voice mechanisms, but with low and narrowly circumscribed decision-making authority. However, where employers confront strong unions with the ingenuity and organizational capacity to exploit the promise of the new EU directive, direct-voice arrangements may not come to supplant representative-voice mechanisms.

Chapter 5

Australian Workers

Finding Their Voice?

JULIAN TEICHER, PETER HOLLAND, AMANDA PYMAN,
AND BRIAN COOPER

At the start of the twenty-first century in Australia, employee voice is at best unstable and perhaps even in crisis. In 2005, union density in Australia was less than 23 percent of the workforce and had been declining since the 1980s. The decline has been particularly pronounced in the public sector and in the traditional "blue collar" heartlands of union representation, such as manufacturing. Central to the decline in union representation and, by implication, union voice, has been an increasingly hostile political climate in which neoliberal ideology has provided the rationale for ongoing legislative innovation at the national level. However, for most of the period since the 1980s, the government did not hold a majority of seats in the upper house (Senate), and this tempered the pace and extent of legislative change in a range of areas including industrial relations. Thus, the Workplace Relations and Other Legislation Amendment Act 1996 (Cth.) 1996 (WRA), which drew its inspiration from New Zealand's Employment Contracts Act 1991, was diluted in order to secure its enactment, and subsequently, many attempted amendments were defeated by the Senate.

This situation changed in October 2004 when the Liberal-National government led by Prime Minister John Howard was reelected with a majority in both houses of the national parliament. In July 2005, the government outlined sweeping industrial relations changes under the catchy title of Work Choices (Teicher, Lambert, and O'Rourke 2006). The passage of the Workplace Relations Amendment (Work Choices) Act 2005 was rapid, receiving royal assent on 14 December 2005. The most contested changes resulting from the passage of the legislation are the move from a federal to a unitary system of industrial relations; curtailing the safety net of minimum conditions that apply to workers covered by both agreements and awards of industrial tribunals; stripping the national industrial tribunal of key powers, including in dispute resolution and the setting of minimum wages; exempting businesses with fewer than one hundred employees from unfair dismissal laws; increased penalties for industrial action and the subsequent elevation of employer power; and further restrictions and undermining of the traditional legal rights of unions (right of entry, freedom of association) (Dabscheck 2006). Together, these features of the new act constitute a radical and historic dismantling of Australian social democracy, overturning one hundred years of a unique tripartite system. As Teicher, Lambert, and O'Rourke (2006) argue, the new act breaks with a tradition of equity and fairness, and dramatically erodes employee and union rights.

In this chapter we analyze employee voice in Australia in light of the industrial relations changes introduced over the last decade. We ask: What voice do workers have, and what do they desire? How closely do employee preferences and regulatory practice match? What are the implications of these findings for unions, employers, and government? The discussion demonstrates that changes to employee voice processes in Australia have been complementary: that is, union and nonunion voice practices do not operate as substitutes. Notwithstanding this fact, unions still face significant challenges in the recruitment and organization of workers, and these have been intensified by the recent legislative changes. On the one hand, employees report positive attitudes and satisfaction with unions, and the survey results indicate substantial organizing potential among young workers and the low paid. On the other hand, union voice is hampered by a lack of reach in the private sector and an inability to convince workers to join. These problems are likely to be exacerbated in the ever more hostile legislative environment created by the Work Choices Act, which challenges unions to respond strategically in order to preserve and extend employee voice in all its forms. In turn, employers need to consider the ongoing benefits of complementary voice regimes and how mutual gains in the employment relationship can best be achieved. The challenge for governments is twofold: to come to terms with the positive role of formal union voice, particularly in combination with informal voice channels, and to rise above partisan agendas and recognize that employee voice is both an economic imperative and a cornerstone of Australian society.

The Institutional Context

Governance of industrial relations in Australia is complicated by the federal system of government. The Australian Constitution enshrines a division of powers between the two levels of government (national and state) by granting the national government only those powers that are specifically enumerated. Additional powers have been ceded to the national government by the states since the inception of Australian federation in 1901. Unusually, the legislative power over industrial relations can be exercised concurrently by the two levels of government, though the Work Choices Act is predicated on a fundamental rereading of the Australian Constitution. Until 1988, regulation of industrial relations at the national level relied almost exclusively on the industrial relations power in the constitution, but subsequent amendments have increasingly relied on the "corporations power."[1] Significantly, the Work Choices Act invokes the corporations power to underpin the national unitary system of industrial relations.

Following the formation of the Australian federation in 1901, the states and the national government enacted industrial relations legislation based on the view that society expected Australian governments to strike a balance between the rights of management and labor. The creation of a highly interventionist and protective system of compulsory conciliation and arbitration, and the special status given to unions, was designed to both shift that balance in the direction of labor and to provide a mechanism to minimize socially divisive conflicts. In principle, a registered union gained exclusive rights to represent specified groups of workers and to use the arbitral system to gain an "award" regulating wages and conditions of employment. This was a system that preferred and encouraged union voice as the mechanism for settling and avoiding industrial disputes. As this system evolved over the course of the twentieth century, there was increasing focus on centralized determination or coordination of wages and conditions (Howe 2005).

However, the importance of conciliation and arbitration and of unions as a representative voice for workers has waxed and waned over the last century. Since the 1980s, the arbitral model has been in decline as workplace-based

---

[1] Section 51 (xxxv) of the Australian Constitution, the industrial relations power, allows the federal government to conciliate and arbitrate for the prevention and settlement of industrial disputes extending beyond the limits of any one state. Section 51 (xx) of the Australian Constitution, the corporations power, allows the federal government to control and regulate certain corporations, including trading and financial corporations, on a national basis, and provides the legal foundation for the Corporations Law. The constitutional validity of the Work Choices Act has been challenged in the High Court of Australia by every state and territory—particularly the use of the corporations power to replace separate state and federal jurisdictions with a single national system. Various unions have also lodged a challenge to the constitutional validity of the Work Choices Act. The case was heard on 4–11 May 2006. A decision on the challenge was not expected until late 2006. In a radical but predictable rereading of the Constitution on 14 November 2006, The High Court of Australia, by a 5-2 majority, dismissed collective state and trade union challenges to the constitutional validity of the Work Choices legislation. The decision therefore upholds the Commonwealth's reliance on the corporations' power as the basis of the new legal framework, centering regulation on industrial relations between constitutional corporations and employees Australia-wide. The High Court also rejected the challenges to the central features of the Work Choices Act and to particular legislative provisions (Public Information Officer, High Court of Australia 2006).

agreement making has increased (e.g., Davis and Lansbury 1998; Hancock 1999). This shift has been driven by the perceived imperative for increased labor market flexibility and national economic competitiveness (Teicher and Bryan 2002). Initially this process occurred through institutional innovation at the national tribunal, the Australian Industrial Relations Commission (AIRC), and then moved to legislative innovation.

The process of legislative innovation gained pace with the Industrial Relations Reform Act 1993 (Cth.), which heralded the most far-reaching changes to industrial relations since the introduction of the arbitral system in 1904 (McCallum 1994). The act enshrined enterprise bargaining as the primary form of wage determination by shifting the responsibility for agreement making to the workplace and reorienting the arbitral model to the more limited function of providing a safety net of wages and employment conditions. Other significant changes included the introduction of nonunion enterprise agreements, a legislated right to strike, and good-faith bargaining provisions (Naughton 1994).

The election of the Howard Liberal-National government in 1996 was a major turning point. Its legislative changes were predicated on the view that labor market flexibility and increased competitiveness could best be enhanced by decentralizing employment regulation to the workplace and, more importantly, marginalizing third party (union and industrial tribunal) intervention in the employment relationship (Quinlan 1998). The principal changes implemented were simplifying awards (limiting the safety net to twenty allowable matters), restricting the availability of compulsory conciliation and arbitration of disputes, introducing freedom of association provisions and Australian workplace agreements (individual contracts), restricting union entry to workplaces, and restricting the scope for protected industrial action.

While the WRA builds on the legacies of earlier Labor government legislation (Creighton and Stewart 2000), it broke new ground in attempting to marginalize union voice and third-party intervention. The latest phase of legislative innovation in the form of the Work Choices Act heralds the most significant changes to Australia's industrial relations system in the last century. The amendments will undoubtedly ensure that the role of unions and the AIRC are further marginalized, as the making of individual Australian workplace agreements is facilitated and these agreements are moved closer to a system of common law regulation (van Barneveld 2006). This new legislative environment, along with declining union density, raises questions about both the legitimacy of unions as a representative voice for workers and the availability and effectiveness of alternative nonunion and direct-voice mechanisms for Australian employees.

Data and Method

The Australian Worker Representation and Participation Survey (AWRPS) was undertaken in order to explore the changing nature of worker representation, participation, and influence. The AWRPS was based on the 1994–95 Worker Representation and Participation Survey (WRPS) conducted in the United States (Freeman and Rogers 1999), the British WRPS (Diamond and Freeman 2002), and the New Zealand WRPS (Haynes, Boxall, and Macky 2003). One thousand employees were surveyed nationally using computer-assisted telephone interviewing (CATI) techniques. Potential respondents were selected randomly from the residential telephone directory and contacted between October 2003 and March 2004. The interviews were conducted in the evenings. The sample was limited to Australian residents in paid employment of more than ten hours per week who had left secondary school. Self-employed persons and company owners were excluded from the survey, as were mobile, business, and commercial telephone numbers. The sample was stratified by Australian state or territory to reflect the geographical distribution of the population as reported in the Australian Bureau of Statistics (ABS) Census of Population and Housing 2001.

Of the respondents, 59.9 percent were female, and the mean age of the sample was 41.5 years (SD = 11.41). The mean number of hours worked per week was 36.50 (SD = 12.19), with 67 percent working full-time (defined as thirty-five hours or more per week). The majority of respondents (80.8 percent) were nonmanual workers and were born in Australia (77.9 percent). Just under half of the respondents (45.5 percent) reported that they worked in organizations with five hundred or more employees. The mean number of years worked for their current employer was 8.46 (SD = 8.02).

Although our sample over-represents women and nonmanual workers, particularly professionals, it is reasonably representative of the Australian population in terms of demographic characteristics.[2] However, there is overrepresentation in some industries, with a large concentration of our sample in the health and education sectors (33.8 percent compared with 17.2 percent using ABS 2001 Census data). Because of the skew across industries, where appropriate we weight the sample by industry (using ABS 2001 Census data) to compensate for sample nonresponse bias. Unless otherwise indicated, weighted statistics are reported. Tests of statistical significance, however, are based on the unweighted data set.[3]

---

[2] ABS 2001 Census figures show that 45 percent of employed Australians are female and 70 percent work in nonmanual occupations.

[3] We follow convention and set the upper bound at $p < .05$. Some of the associations we discuss meet the more stringent threshold of $p < .01$.

Union Voice

Union Density and Union Reach

Based on the weighted data set, 27.3 percent of the total sample report that they belong to a union, somewhat higher than the ABS estimate of 22.4 percent (ABS 2006). Those younger than twenty-five are significantly less likely to be union members (16.7 percent) compared with people aged fifty-five and over (37.5 percent) (table 5.1). This finding is consistent with data from Canada, the United States, United Kingdom, and New Zealand (e.g., Bryson, Gomez, Gunderson, and Meltz 2004). As in New Zealand (see chapter 6), union density is highest in the public sector: education (50.3 percent), government (44.7 percent), and health (40.6 percent). In the private sector, density is consistently below 30 percent.

TABLE 5.1
Australia: Union reach, density and demand (by selected characteristics)

	Union reach	Existing union density	Representation gap	Potential union density
Gender				
Male	46.1%	30.2%	16.8%	47.0%
Female	43.8	24.9	20.8	45.7
Age				
< 25 years	34.9%	16.7%	29.5%	46.2%
25–34	41.7	22.9	22.5	45.5
35–44	46.8	26.4	18.0	44.4
45–54	47.0	30.5	15.4	45.9
55 years and over	50.1	37.5	13.8	51.3
Employment status				
Full-time	47.3%	30.1%	16.0%	46.1%
Part-time	39.8	21.4	25.0	46.4
Tenure				
< 5 years	33.8%	14.9%	29.0%	43.9%
5–9 years	42.6	25.4	16.4	41.8
10 years and over	65.0	49.3	4.6	53.9
Occupation				
Managers	31.4%	19.9%	19.8%	39.7%
Professionals	65.7	40.9	8.3	49.2
Associate professionals	45.2	30.6	19.8	50.4
Tradesperson	45.7	30.3	15.2	45.5
Advanced clerical/sales	23.1	13.9	21.5	35.4
Intermediate clerical/sales	36.0	15.9	24.4	40.3
Intermediate production	69.5	41.2	19.2	60.4
Elementary clerical/sales	48.4	27.5	24.1	51.6
Laborers	41.3	29.9	26.0	55.9
Industry				
Agriculture/mining/utilities	44.5%	33.2%	8.5%	41.7%
Manufacturing	39.4	23.2	20.2	43.2

TABLE 5.1
Continued

	Union reach	Existing union density	Representation gap	Potential union density
Construction	43.1	29.4	15.7	45.1
Wholesale trade	34.8	21.7	21.7	43.4
Retail trade	39.3	26.8	22.3	49.1
Hotels and accommodation	35.6	13.3	24.4	37.4
Transport	44.1	23.5	20.6	44.1
Communication	44.0	16.0	20.0	36.0
Finance	36.4	18.2	29.5	47.7
Property and business	29.3	19.5	29.3	48.8
Government	83.0	44.7	0.0	44.7
Education	86.1	50.3	2.3	52.6
Health	63.0	40.6	12.7	53.3
Cultural and recreational	27.8	11.1	38.9	50.0
Personal services	7.1	7.1	28.6	35.7
Income (gross $ per week)				
Under 400 per week	30.6%	13.4%	29.2%	42.6%
400 and under 600	39.9	23.5	24.2	47.7
600 and under 800	41.3	25.2	25.1	50.3
800 and under 1,000	55.3	29.3	10.9	40.2
1,000 and under 12,000	63.2	47.3	6.6	53.9
1,200 and under 1,499	57.3	46.0	11.2	57.2
1,500 and over	33.2	22.7	10.7	33.1
Organizational size				
< 20 employees	12.1%	5.8%	28.9%	34.7%
20–99	27.0	16.7	30.1	46.8
100–499	48.8	29.3	16.5	45.8
500 or more employees	67.7	42.4	8.9	51.3
Ethnicity				
Born in Australia	46.5%	27.6%	18.9%	46.5%
Born in other English-speaking country	35.9	24.8	17.9	42.7
Born in non-English-speaking country	42.9	27.5	21.0	48.5
Management attitudes to unions				
Favorable	72.1%	50.1%	8.2%	58.3%
Neutral	50.9	30.2	14.5	44.7
Opposed	33.4	20.7	24.9	45.6
All workers	44.8%	27.3%	19.0%	46.3%

Note: Estimates weighted by industry.

Union reach is defined as the presence of a union at the workplace that an employee can join (Haynes, Boxall, and Macky 2006). Of the total weighted sample, 44.8 percent of respondents report that there is a union at their workplace that people doing their type of work can join. Union reach is highest in education (86.1 percent), government (83.0 percent), and health (63.0 percent) and lowest in real estate (29.3 percent), cultural and recreational services (27.8

percent), and personal services (7.1 percent). Reach is lower among young workers, workers in small organizations (fewer than twenty employees), part-time workers, employees with fewer than five years' organizational tenure, and among employees who perceive that management opposes unions.

That over 50 percent of respondents report the absence of union reach should be a matter of concern to unions. Two factors may explain this finding. First, the continuous decline in density and an associated reduction in membership revenue have undoubtedly reduced the capacity of Australian unions to establish an ongoing presence and recruit in nonunion workplaces. This reduction in organizational capacity is particularly problematic in the growing areas of employment, typically in private-sector services. These are often newer workplaces, such as call centers, in which employees have had little or no contact with unions (e.g., van den Broek 2003). Second, there is evidence to suggest that the WRA has marginalized unions, limiting their representative role, and that the provisions and the antiunion rhetoric of the government have produced increasing employer resistance to third-party involvement in the employment relationship (Peetz 2002; Pyman 2004; Briggs 2004). The AWRPS findings, however, provide mixed support for the importance of managerial opposition in inhibiting union reach, unlike the situation in the United States where managerial opposition is a driving factor (Freeman and Rogers 1999). Of those who responded, 40.3 percent believe managerial attitudes are opposed to unions, compared to 59.7 percent who say they are either favorable or neutral.[4] However, differences in union reach according to employee perceptions of managerial attitudes to unions are statistically significant, ranging from 50.9 and 72.1 percent respectively, where managers are neutral or favorable, to only 33 percent where managers are perceived to be opposed. Overall, it seems more likely that the problem is one of union supply and a lack of efficacy in organizing in Australia, rather than latent managerial opposition.

Unsatisfied Demand for Union Membership: The Representation Gap

The "representation gap" refers to the proportion of the workforce in nonunion workplaces who would join a union if given the opportunity (Freeman and Rogers 1999). As we have seen, the majority (55.2 percent) of the sample did not have a union at their workplace that people doing their type of work could join. This group was asked, "If a union was formed at your workplace, how likely would you be to join?" Table 5.2 shows the percentage of workers in nonunion workplaces who report that they would join a union if one were available at their workplace. Combining the "very" and "fairly likely" categories as a proportion of workers in nonunion workplaces furnishes a representation

---

[4] Note that 21.9 percent of respondents did not answer this question.

TABLE 5.2
Likelihood of joining a union (no union in workplace)

	Percentage of workers in nonunion workplaces	Unmet demand in nonunion workplaces as a percentage of total sample
Very likely	16.9%	8.3%
Fairly likely	21.6	10.7
Fairly unlikely	21.0	10.4
Not at all likely	40.5	20.0

Source: Based on AWRPS Q24, "If a union was formed at your workplace, how likely would you be to join?"
Notes: Estimates are weighted by industry. Excludes "don't know" responses (4.2%). Chi square statistics are calculated using unweighted data. Total unweighted sample N = 1,000.

gap of 38.5 percent of those working in nonunion workplaces, equal to 19 percent of the total sample.[5] Unfulfilled demand for union membership in nonunion workplaces is higher than the 32 percent found in the United States and New Zealand, and slightly lower than the 41 percent in the United Kingdom estimated by Charlwood (2002, 352) using the 1998 and 2001 Workplace Employment Relations Survey data.

If those workers who are very likely or fairly likely to join a union (19 percent of the total sample) were added to the current ABS national estimate of union density (22.4 percent), total potential union density in Australia would be just below 42 percent. As argued in the New Zealand chapter in this book, this estimate must be regarded with some caution because it assumes that all those either very or fairly likely to join would do so if presented with the opportunity. If the measure of intention is based only on those very likely to join a union (8.3 percent of the total sample), the potential union density in Australia is slightly less than 31 percent. The importance of distinguishing between hard and soft support for union joining is highlighted by the high levels of personal indifference toward union representation among the AWRPS respondents. The majority of workers in nonunion workplaces (66.2 percent) believe that a union would make no difference to them personally at the workplace, while only 20.5 percent believe they would be better off with a union. Even among those who express a strong desire to join a union, over a third believes that a union would make no difference to them personally. This high level of indifference poses problems for Australian unions and the expansion of their influence, suggesting an inability to convince workers of the benefits of union voice and, therefore, of incurring the costs of joining. Cregan (2005, 301) found

[5] The presence of a representation gap among Australian workers, albeit not as pronounced, was also confirmed by a 2005 telephone poll that found that among those who were not members of a union, 14 percent of the Australian work-force (or 1,525,000 employees) would like to join a union (Roy Morgan Research 2005). The telephone poll conducted by Roy Morgan Research in October and November 2005 surveyed 1,315 respondents throughout Australia, aged fourteen and over.

similar results in a study of individual attitudes toward union membership in Australia, arguing that the core problem facing Australian unions is their ineffectiveness in persuading most workers that joining costs are worthwhile.

The representation gap varies across several worker characteristics. Statistically significant relationships are identified between the proportion of unmet demand in nonunion workplaces and the variables of age, income, tenure, and perceived management attitudes toward unions. Unsatisfied demand for union membership declines steadily with increasing age. Consistent with the New Zealand and the Canadian data, the representation gap is considerably higher for those under twenty-five (48.9 percent) compared to those fifty-five and over (29.8 percent) (see chapters 2 and 6). This finding is also consistent with a recent Australian telephone poll that identified 33 percent of those twenty-five to thirty-five as wanting to be union members, the highest proportion of all age groups (Roy Morgan Research 2005).

The high levels of desire for union representation among young workers challenge traditional assumptions that young workers are more individualistic and antiunion (e.g., ACIRRT 1999[6]). However, even though young workers are more likely to want to join a union, union density is lowest among this age group and union reach is more difficult. There are two possible explanations for this paradox. First, younger workers may be located in nonunion workplaces that are small and costly to serve and where there is little exposure to union activity, or in workplaces where management is actively opposed to unions; for example, many call centers (van den Broek 2003). This proposition is supported by the low levels of union reach in small workplaces and among workers with organizational tenure of fewer than five years. It echoes Haynes, Vowles, and Boxall's (2005) findings that workplace size and labor market location (small, hard-to-organize firms in service sectors) are the core explanations for the density gap between younger and older workers in New Zealand. Second, assuming young workers do have the opportunity to join a union, the findings may reflect a gap between their intentions and behavior. Reasons for not following through on their intentions to join may include the high cost relative to their income earning capacity, perceived lack of direct personal benefit, and actual or perceived management opposition to unions. The inadequately understood gap between intentions and action poses a major barrier to membership growth.

Average weekly income is significant in determining unmet demand in Australia, as it is in Canada and New Zealand (see chapters 2 and 6). The demand for representation in Australia is much greater for low-income earners. For those earning less than $800 (AUD) per week, the representation gap stands at

---

[6] ACIRRT, formerly the Australian Centre for Industrial Relations Research and Training, is now known as the Workplace Research Centre and is located at the University of Sydney, NSW, Australia.

46 percent compared with 33.7 percent for those earning more. As in New Zealand, unmet demand is more pronounced in the secondary labor market.

Organizational tenure is also significantly related to the representation gap. Workers with tenure of less than five years are over three times more likely to want to join a union (49.2 percent) than those with ten or more years' tenure (13.9 percent). In terms of employees' perceptions of managerial attitudes toward unions, about a third of those who believe management is neutral or favorable to unions are likely to join a union, compared to 41.1 percent of employees who perceive management as being opposed to unions. This mirrors the findings in New Zealand and is not surprising in light of the legislative changes enacted since 1996. It can reasonably be expected that the Work Choices Act, which has been labeled as a concerted attempt to tilt the balance of labor regulation in favor of employers (Stewart 2006), will result in an increase in the proportion of employees who believe that management is hostile to unions.

Infill Recruitment

Some 50 percent of workers report that they have never been asked to join a union at their current workplace, despite having a union that they could join. A similar proportion of employees in unionized workplaces in the United Kingdom (56 percent) say that they have never been asked to join (Bryson 2003). The Australian and U.K. figures are higher than the figure in New Zealand, where only 33.9 percent of employees in unionized workplaces have never been approached to join (see chapter 6). The high level of potential infill recruitment in Australia is surprising. The Australian Council of Trade Unions (ACTU) has pursued an "organizing approach" since its 1993 Congress. Subsequently, the ACTU has aimed to encourage and support grassroots activism, to recruit and organize in nonunion workplaces, and to achieve membership growth in new areas of the economy (ACTU 1999, 2003). Our findings strongly imply that this strategy has not been implemented effectively.

Free Riding

Problems of union supply and reach are exacerbated by the incidence of free riding in Australia. While union members represent 60.8 percent of those who have the opportunity to join a union at their workplace, the remainder (39.2 percent) are free riders who enjoy the benefits of collective action without bearing the costs. The significance of free riding in Australia is demonstrated by the 51.7 percent of nonunion members who cite "no point in joining since I get all the benefits anyway" as a reason that they have not joined a union (figure 5.1). Some 55.6 percent of respondents cite membership fees as a reason for not

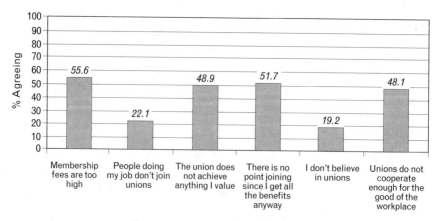

Figure 5.1: Reasons for not joining a union (nonmembers)

Note: Estimates weighted by industry.

joining. Cregan (2005) also found that a cohort of uncommitted workers believed that the costs of being a member were too great.

Two other reasons for not joining a union that are identified by half the respondents are a perceived lack of value (48.9 percent) and a perceived lack of cooperation by unions for the good of the workplace (48.1 percent). The latter finding is consistent with a preference among the AWRPS respondents for cooperative relations between employers and unions. Taken together, these findings suggest that many employees refrain from union membership on the basis of a simple cost/benefit analysis, taking into account monetary constraints, a perceived lack of benefit to the individual, and a predisposition to avoid conflict. Consistent with the New Zealand findings, nonmembership is not related to the presence of nonunion voice mechanisms in the workplace such as a human resources department or joint consultative committees, suggesting that nonunion voice does not act as a substitute for union voice (see chapter 6).

Attitudes toward Union Performance

Union members are very positive about the service they receive from their union, with 87.2 percent reporting that the service represents "good" or "reasonable" value for money. Unionists are most satisfied with the insurance and protection functions provided by unions, with 79.4 percent agreeing that their "union fights hard when employee interests are threatened." These positive attitudes toward unions are comparable to those in a survey conducted in 2002, in which 71 percent of respondents reported that they were "looked after" by their union (ACIRRT 2002). Similarly, in the AWRPS 76.2 percent of union members report that they trust their union and 72.9 percent feel loyal to their union. As Haynes, Boxall, and Macky (2006) note, under a voluntary membership regime high levels of satisfaction and positive attitudes toward unions are not surprising because dissatisfied members are free to leave. In Australia, it is relevant that freedom of choice to join or not join a union was central to the enactment of the WRA and is strengthened under the Work Choices Act, to restrict unions' capacity to engage in a range of tactics that support collective representation of workers' interests (Forsyth and Sutherland 2006). Despite the most recent amendments to the freedom of association provisions, it would be simplistic to assume that informal or group pressure to join a union will cease to exist.

Union-Management Relations

The survey results indicate that union members have a clear preference for union-management cooperation in the workplace across a range of dimensions. A large majority (70.2 percent) agree that unions cooperate with management at the workplace, yet 66.2 percent agree that relations should be more cooperative. A still larger majority (82 percent) of unionists agree that management should cooperate more closely with the union. A similar proportion (70 percent) of members also agree that unions should focus greater attention on helping the organization succeed. This preference for cooperative union-management relations reinforces previous research that found that Australian workers want their unions to be cooperative, without being compliant, and to have a pragmatic understanding of the interdependence of interests in industrial relations (Peetz 1998).

In summary, the AWRPS provides a mixed report card for Australian unions. On the positive side, members are satisfied and positive about the services they receive. There is a high level of latent support for union representation among unorganized workers, and union members express an overwhelming preference for union-management cooperation. On the negative side, unions still face critical challenges in recruiting and organizing new workers. These challenges stem largely from the problem of union reach in many private-sector service industries and among particular groups of workers, ineffective recruitment practices, high levels of free riding, and widespread personal indifference to the perceived value of union membership. At a time when the representative role of unions is being progressively marginalized, primarily through legislative innovation, apathy about the benefits of unionism may prove the greatest challenge to entrenching and extending union representation and influence in Australian industrial relations. Like their U.K., New Zealand, and Canadian counterparts, Australian unions need to increase their efficacy and their ability to convince workers of the benefits of joining, particularly in nonunion workplaces. Because innovation in organizing is increasingly likely to be undertaken with limited resources, and because union and nonunion voice do not act as substitutes, Australian unions may be well advised to pursue the expansion of voice through nonunion options, as has been proposed in the United Kingdom (see chapter 3).

Nonunion Voice

A majority of respondents report access to one or more forms of nonunion and direct-voice arrangements, with 83 percent of respondents being in a workplace with an open door policy to discuss problems with their supervisors and senior management. A smaller yet substantial number of workers report the occurrence of regular staff meetings (60.1 percent), and the presence of a personnel or human resources department or person (48.1 percent). Committees of employees (38.9 percent) and employee involvement programs such as quality circles (35.8 percent) are the least common nonunion voice arrangements reported by respondents.

Consistent with the U.K. and New Zealand data (see chapters 3 and 6), organizational size and perceived managerial attitudes toward unions are significantly related to the presence of nonunion voice arrangements. The presence of a full-time human resources department or person, regular staff meetings, and a committee of employees were all more common in large organizations (500-plus employees). Importantly, employees who perceive that their managers are opposed to unions are less likely to work in places that have an open door policy, regular staff meetings, or employee committees.

Union presence is positively associated with the presence of several nonunion voice arrangements in Australia. This finding suggests that, contrary to intuition, nonunion arrangements complement rather than compete with union voice. The same pattern is also evident in Canada, the United Kingdom, and New Zealand (see chapters 2, 3, and 6). For example, employees who report regular staff meetings at the workplace are more likely to have a union present. Employees who report the presence of a committee of employees that meets regularly with management to discuss issues of common interest or the presence of an employee involvement program, such as quality circles, are almost twice as likely to have a union present.

Overall, 50.3 percent report the presence of a joint consultative committee of some kind in their workplace. Nonunion joint consultative committees, that is, those composed of employees chosen by a method other than a union or staff association, represent nearly half of the sample (46.3 percent). A majority of respondents rate their nonunion joint consultative committees as effective (79.9 percent), indicating that these committees are broadly representative of the views of employees. This finding is consistent with the New Zealand findings that 77.9 percent of employees with a consultative committee report them to be very or quite effective (see chapter 6).

Regression analyses enable us to investigate the effectiveness of different types of voice arrangements more comprehensively. As shown in Pyman et al. (2006), a strong predictor of managerial responsiveness to employee needs, perceived job control, and perceived job rewards is a combination of union, direct, and nonunion representative voice. The combination of direct and nonunion representative voice also predicts employees' perceived control over their jobs and perceived influence over job rewards. Of the different types of direct-voice arrangements, the use of regular staff meetings was found to be the most predictive of managerial responsiveness, job control, and influence over job rewards. In summary, multiple channels of voice are more influential than a single channel, reinforcing the evidence that union, direct, and nonunion voice arrangements are complementary rather than substitutes in Australia. These informal voice regimes can supplement formal union channels, particularly as the latter are marginalized by the Work Choices Act.

Implications for Employee Voice

Unions

In common with unions in many other countries, Australian unions have faced, and continue to face, a difficult environment. Although some of the results from the AWRPS are encouraging for unions, demonstrating the prevalence of prounion attitudes, high levels of member satisfaction, a preference for union-management cooperation (alongside a desire for unions to strongly defend worker interests), and the complementarity of union and nonunion voice mechanisms, it is clear that unions have yet to meet some major challenges. In particular, 50 percent of employees have never been asked to join a union, and a substantial proportion of these would like to join. The potential for infill recruitment and the representation gap among young and low-paid workers are major concerns, particularly in view of the efforts of the ACTU and many of its affiliates (for example, the Liquor, Hospitality and Miscellaneous Union and the Community and Public Sector Union) to reorganize their structures and transform their operations so as to focus on organizing the unorganized. Although our findings demonstrate opportunities for Australian unions to recruit new members, it is also apparent that unions need to review their policies, practices, and strategies. Particular issues that should be considered include the extent to which the challenge of organizing has been taken up by ACTU affiliates, the potential for recruiting in partially organized as well as unorganized workplaces, and an audit of current recruitment and organizing practices by

ACTU affiliates and their success to date. In light of the restrictive Work Choices Act, the need for a review of union recruitment and organizing strategies takes on greater urgency. As Forsyth and Sutherland (2006) note, while the Work Choices Act will inevitably lead to the erosion of wages and conditions for some workers, the legislation also provides opportunities for unions to reestablish their relevance.

Perhaps the larger challenge for Australian unions under the Work Choices Act is the demonstrated indifference of employees toward union representation and the widespread incidence of free riding. Unions need to find ways of attracting workers to the benefits of unionism and convincing them to join, particularly younger workers and new entrants to the labor market who display prounion attitudes. As the data suggest that older workers and workers with greater job tenure are less likely to express an intention to join unions, it appears crucial that recruiting efforts are concentrated on new entrants to the workforce.

As this chapter has shown, legal changes implemented since 1996 demonstrate the continuing importance of legislation for Australian unions. If nothing else, continuing legislative change is likely to exacerbate the difficulties of recruiting in the secondary labor market among lower-paid and less-educated workers; it may also weaken the attraction of union membership as collective bargaining is delegitimized and increasingly replaced by nonunion voice, manifest in individual and nonunion collective agreements and other forms of direct employment relations. From this perspective, unions need to continue their campaign to preserve union voice in workplaces where this is strong and also to preserve union channels in workplaces with dual-voice regimes. In relation to the latter strategy, unions have much to gain from demonstrating to both employers and employees that formal and informal direct-voice practices are complementary. Indeed, unions would do well to capitalize on the present popularity of the partnership concept, arguing that employees prefer union-employer cooperation and hold more positive attitudes toward employers and their jobs when unions are present, yet independent, in the workplace.

Employers

For employers, the AWRPS findings present the paradox that, despite significant challenges, unions remain a principal participant in Australian industrial relations, and their presence in workplaces is positively related to the existence of a variety of individual and nonunion representative voice mechanisms. The rigors of increasing global competition, the rise of human resource management, and a hostile legislative environment have not eliminated employee support for unions. This point is evidenced by our findings on the representation gap and the potential for infill union recruitment. At the same time, it is evident that employers in smaller workplaces and in newer industries in the service sector are more able to avoid union penetration, and that the absence of unions in such areas is likely to be associated with a workforce that sees little value in membership.

In the AWRPS, we find complementarity between union and nonunion voice practices, consistent with other research in Australia and the United Kingdom (e.g., Deery and Walsh 1999; Machin and Wood 2005). Nonunion voice arrangements, including the presence of a human resources person or function and joint consultative committees, are more likely where a union is present. Conversely, where employees perceive that their management is opposed to unions, a range of nonunion voice practices, including an open door policy, regular staff meetings, and joint consultative committees, are less likely to exist. These findings support the notion that part of the labor market is caught in a Dickensian "bleak house" or "black hole" scenario (e.g., Sisson 1993; Guest 1995), characterized by union marginalization and exclusion, adversarial relationships, and a cost-minimization approach to production.

The AWRPS results also suggest that the coexistence of union, nonunion, and direct-voice practices is associated with cooperation between employers, employees, and unions across a range of indicators. For instance, 70.2 percent of union members agreed that unions cooperate with management, while 82.0 percent agreed that the parties should cooperate more closely. This preference for cooperation may provide employers with scope to develop a partnership or mutual-gains approach to managing unionized workplaces in an increasingly competitive environment. Where unions are not present, the priority should be to foster greater cooperation through direct and nonunion representative voice mechanisms.

Government

In common with other advanced Western market economies, since the 1980s a process of decentralization has occurred in Australian industrial relations, with the locus of regulation increasingly shifting to the workplace. Under the rubric of labor market deregulation, the initial focus was on increasing labor market flexibility and national competitiveness (Buchanan and Callus 1993, 4). With the election of the Liberal-National government in 1996, the agenda of labor market deregulation in Australia gained a hard edge: the new focus was on marginalizing unions and industrial tribunals in the process of employment regulation. The enactment of the WRA was the first step in a process of shifting the balance of power from labor to management. As noted above, the 1996 changes were less radical because the government required the support of the minority parties in the Senate to secure the passage of its legislation. In contrast, the Work Choices Act enacted in 2006 represents the most radical recasting of Australian industrial relations in over a century. Further changes are likely with legislation altering protections for independent contractors. As of late 2006, the Workplace Relations Amendment (Independent Contractors) Bill was being heard in the Senate, introduced on 13 September.

In Australia over the last decade there has been significant legislative reform of the workplace-relations system to place a primary focus on agreement making at the workplace. That aside, the government has continually argued that the industrial relations system remained complex and that further improvements were needed to make the system simpler, accessible, and more effective. According to the Liberal-National government, Australia needs a more flexible labor market to maximize economic growth and employment opportunities and to maintain and improve living standards in an increasingly globalized economy (Andrews, 2005). This was the underlying rationale for the Work Choices Act, which increased the volume of the WRA and related regulations to some seven hundred pages of legislative provisions and one thousand pages of regulations.

Under the Work Choices Act, unions and industrial tribunals are pushed to the margins and union voice is undermined without any effort being made to replace formal channels with alternative voice regimes. By way of illustration of the delegitimization of union voice, certain kinds of industrial demands are now illegal and cannot be contained in agreements. These include trade union training leave, the right to union notice boards, work site right of entry for union officials, union involvement in dispute resolution, union picnic days, bargaining fees for nonunion workers, redress for unfair dismissal, limits on the use of independent contractors and labor hire, and skill-based career paths.

Predictably, the Work Choices Act has sparked widespread concern, particularly the government's attempt to use the corporations power in the constitution to override state industrial relations jurisdictions and, in effect, negate the constitutional division of powers. Other areas of widespread concern include the removal of the AIRC's power to set minimum wages by vesting this power in the newly established Fair Pay Commission, which has a directive to give greater attention to economic considerations; the exemption of employees from unfair dismissal protection in organizations with one hundred employees or fewer; and a dramatic curtailment of the safety net of wages and conditions (a reduction to five minimum conditions known as the Australian Fair Pay and Conditions Standard), while simultaneously enabling employers, in certain circumstances, to move employees from awards onto individual agreements without negotiation.[7]

---

[7] The Cowra Abattoir in New South Wales placed itself at the center of the furor over the Work Choices legislation in March 2006, when it sent termination letters to twenty-nine workers, citing operational reasons, and subsequently offered to rehire them on new contracts which included pay cuts

This situation is compounded by the absence of a requirement on employers to negotiate an agreement with employees under Work Choices. An immediate consequence of the Work Choices Act has been that a major constitutional case has been fought in the High Court, and, despite the recent decision on 14 November 2006 (see footnote 1), further litigation is likely. Moreover, the states remain defiant. The five states that retain a separate industrial relations jurisdiction have steadfastly refused to cede their powers to the national government (High Court of Australia 2006).

What level of support does the government's new Work Choices Act find in the results of the AWRPS? The implications for government are quite straightforward. First, support for unions has been remarkably resilient notwithstanding a hostile political/legislative environment, and recent opinion polls suggest that only a minority support the new laws (O'Neill, Kuruppu, and Harris 2006). Second, and relatedly, Australian workers adhere to an overwhelmingly pluralistic conception of industrial relations. Management and unions are regarded as partners in enterprise, but at the same time unions are expected to vigorously support employees' rights. In essence, there is little support for a further onslaught against unions and by implication union voice. Further, the finding of complementarity between the various forms of voice provides some support for the proposition that the hostile legislative environment created by the Work Choices Act may ultimately have an adverse impact on organizational efficiency and effectiveness, by increasing labor turnover, reducing employee trust and commitment and simultaneously heightening managerial prerogative, and impeding information flows at the local workplace level.

Future Directions

Australian employee voice has changed dramatically since the introduction of compulsory conciliation and arbitration in 1904. Since the 1980s, under the rubric of labor market deregulation, union voice has declined and the role of unions and industrial tribunals has been marginalized, particularly through the WRA and most recently the Work Choices Act. At the same time, the inci-

---

of up to AU$180 a week in addition to the loss of performance bonuses (Shaw and Schubert 2006). In July 2006, the Office of Workplace Services, which was set up to oversee the operation of Work Choices, deemed the abattoir's actions lawful on the basis that the financial viability of the company was the primary reason for the workers' dismissal, not their union membership (Colvin 2006). The controversy of this case was compounded by the fact that the abattoir employs fewer than one hundred staff, and under the Work Choices Act, employers with fewer than one hundred employees can terminate employment for operational reasons and avoid unfair dismissal claims. While the government has reiterated that the freedom of association provisions prevent employers from sacking employees entitled to award or agreement conditions for the sole reason of cost minimization, the freedom of association provisions have also been diluted under Work Choices (Shaw and Schubert 2006).

dence of nonunion and direct-voice mechanisms has grown, supported by legislative innovation promoting individual and nonunion agreements. The current legal and political climate in Australia is best described as unstable, as employers, employees, unions, and the government adjust and/or respond to the far-reaching changes contained in the new Work Choices Act.

The AWRPS findings demonstrate that employees desire union-management cooperation and often prefer complementary voice regimes, as opposed to a single channel of voice. Indeed, when measured on the basis of managerial responsiveness to employee needs, perceived job control, and perceived job rewards, multiple channels of voice are the most effective for employees (Pyman et al. 2006). Although the evidence from the AWRPS suggests that union and nonunion voice mechanisms do not act as substitutes, and unions remain a principal participant in the industrial relations system, Australian unions face a number of core challenges. These include free riding, widespread indifference to the benefits of union joining, and a lack of efficacy in organizing. On the other hand, the AWRPS also identifies a range of positive factors for unions, including high levels of membership satisfaction and recruitment potential (latent support for unionism) among employees in the secondary labor market. The challenge for unions, as bargaining and organizing rights are removed, is to capitalize on partnerships and cooperation with employers. In turn, employers may be wise to promote and take advantage of complementary voice regimes and a mutual-gains approach to the management of workplaces. The challenge for the government is clear: to move beyond ideology and ensure that management and unions remain partners in enterprise and that informal nonunion voice regimes do not wholly displace formal independent channels of union voice. It appears that this will be a hard task for the government—the principal changes introduced by the Work Choices Act seek to do the opposite, by shifting the balance of power overwhelmingly in favor of employers.

Chapter 6

Employee Voice and Voicelessness in New Zealand

PETER BOXALL, PETER HAYNES, AND KEITH MACKY

New Zealand is small country with a very tractable legislative framework for industrial relations. The system's pliability is presently helping to narrow the gap between the voice most workers want and the voice they have. New Zealand workers report high levels of employment satisfaction. Nonunion voice options have been developing and increasingly complement unionized voice. Management's use of consultation appears to have grown, not receded, in the more liberalized New Zealand labor market of the last fifteen years and the evidence suggests that it is generally robust.

On the other hand, research shows that a large minority of New Zealand workers would like, but cannot access, traditional representation through trade unions. This "representation gap" is greater among younger and lower paid workers and among workers in smaller organizations and in the private sector. Unions have strongholds in the larger organizations and are readily available to public-sector workers but they have serious problems in reaching the more vulnerable groups of private-sector workers. Although improving union reach into small firms and reducing the incidence of free riding on unionized sites would lift union density, the biggest issue facing the unions is how to become relevant to a workforce in which most people have become skeptical about their value. The evidence presented here suggests, in fact, that both government and unions need to think more innovatively about employee voice.

The Institutional Context of Employee Voice

New Zealand has no state parliaments and no upper house in its legislature, making reform much more tractable than it is in other parts of the Anglo-American world. Since 1990, there have been two substantive reforms of the industrial relations regime: the Employment Contracts Act 1991 (ECA) and the Employment Relations Act 2000 (ERA), both pushed through relatively easily by governments with strong majorities. The ECA dismantled what remained of a system of compulsory, state-provided conciliation and arbitration developed in the 1890s and early 1900s. As in Australia, this system created a structure of "awards" regulating employment conditions across firms and, in certain cases, across industries. The ECA facilitated the large-scale demise (though not the total elimination) of these cross-employer bargaining structures (Boxall 1993, 1997; Whatman, Armitage, and Dunbar 1994). Given the opportunity, employers sought, and achieved, the sort of business-focused bargaining structures they had wanted to enable them to adapt to the liberalization of product and capital markets pursued by the Labour government of 1984–90 as it sought to dismantle the excessive regulation of the postwar period.

Along with decentralization in collective bargaining, most employment contracting shifted onto an individual basis. Thus, the New Zealand employment system is fundamentally a system of individual contracts, albeit still influenced by trends in wage rates and conditions negotiated in the unionized sector (Boxall 1997, 2003). There is also a substantial difference between models of employment in the private and public sectors. Unionization is still typical in the public sector but has become atypical in the private sector.

A high degree of compulsion in union membership was a feature of the New Zealand legal framework prior to the ECA: union membership was, in effect, compulsory for workers whose occupation had historically been regulated by the arbitration system (Deeks and Boxall 1989). This resulted in artificially high levels of union density. Shortly before the ECA went into effect in May 1991, union membership was estimated at 49.9 percent of New Zealand wage and salary earners, with women and hospitality industry workers having higher density than men and those in other industries (Charlwood and Haynes, forthcoming). New Zealand unions fared badly under the ECA. Union density was halved over the first five years of the ECA, having declined by 26.7 percent in 1990–93 and then by a third in 1993–96 (Charlwood and Haynes, forthcoming). The abrupt decline over the first two-and-a-half years of the ECA was concentrated almost entirely in the private and the mixed and nonprofit sectors, and was sharpest among workers in the secondary labor market. The fall was fastest in private-sector services, where the hospitality industry, retail and wholesale, and financial and business services unions sustained 71.4 percent, 50.0 percent, and 39.1 percent falls in union density respectively.

The Employment Relations Act 2000 aims to promote collective bargaining, if not to recollectivize the workforce. It requires "good faith" in employment dealings and provides unions with improved workplace access and bargaining status. In particular, unions have the right to enter workplaces to recruit, enjoy the sole right to be the worker party to collective agreements, and may initiate negotiations for new collective agreements (including multiemployer agreements for which striking, under certain conditions, is now legitimate). Added to the provisions that enhance union rights is an important change affecting individual employees: even though they may previously have signed an individual contract, union membership confers the right to coverage by any applicable collective agreement that may exist (commonly described in union pamphlets as "join the union, join the collective"). However, in retaining voluntary union membership and eschewing compulsory arbitration, the ERA does not represent a return to the highly centralized regime that prevailed before the ECA. Since the advent of the ERA, union density appears to have stabilized at around 21 to 22 percent of wage and salary earners (Haynes, Boxall, and Macky 2006).

Economic Structure and Performance

In terms of scale, two-thirds of the New Zealand workforce is employed in organizations with fewer than fifty employees, including a quarter who work in firms with fewer than five employees (Boxall 2003). At the other end of the distribution, only a quarter of the workforce is employed in organizations with more than one hundred employees. Given the difficulties of raising capital locally, foreign ownership is high in the corporate sector (around 50 percent). As a result of the privatization programs carried out in the 1980s and 1990s, government in New Zealand owns few large trading enterprises. Government activity, however, is dominant in the health and education sectors.

After low levels of economic growth during an intense period of restructuring from 1984 to 1992, the New Zealand economy experienced solid expansion in the 1990s (Conway and Orr 2000). In the eleven years prior to 1992, New Zealand's GDP per capita grew at around 0.50 percent per year against an OECD average of 2.25 percent per year, while in the eleven years prior to 2002, New Zealand grew at 2.25 percent per year against an OECD average of 1.75 percent per year (The Treasury 2004).

Although multifactor productivity has been improving since the major restructuring of the New Zealand economy, the rate of labor productivity growth remains a concern (The Treasury 2004). The comparison with Australia is one that particularly interests New Zealanders. Multifactor productivity growth (at

1.1 percent per year) has been the same in Australia and New Zealand since 1988, but labor productivity growth has been greater in Australia at 2.3 percent versus 1.9 percent (Black, Guy, and McLellan 2003, 22). This is associated with a higher capital-to-labor ratio, which may "reflect differences in the industrial structure between the two countries. . . . The Australian economy has a larger mining and quarrying industry" (Black, Guy, and McLellan 2003, 23), which has much higher capital intensity. Other factors may be excessive investment in the New Zealand property market and small industrial scale (The Treasury 2004).

In effect, New Zealand's economic growth has been "employment rich" over the last ten years, reflected in an unemployment rate of 3.6 percent in late 2005, the lowest of the Anglo-American economies and less than half the average rate in the euro area of the OECD (8.1 percent in May 2004; OECD 2006). The labor market is as hot as it has been since the precrash mid-1980s. Skill shortages and relatively high rates of labor turnover are major concerns for employers (Boxall 2003; Boxall, Macky, and Rasmussen 2003).

Data and Method

The data reported in this chapter are largely based on responses to the New Zealand Worker Representation and Participation Survey (NZWRPS) 2003, a survey of New Zealand workers' responses to and attitudes toward workplace involvement practices, unions, and union-management relations in New Zealand. NZWRPS was based on the 1994–95 Workplace Representation and Participation Survey in the United States (Freeman and Rogers 1999) and the 2001 British Workers' Representation and Participation Survey (Diamond and Freeman 2001), which are reported elsewhere in this book. Questions were modified to fit the New Zealand institutional and demographic context, some new questions were added, and enhancements were made to some attitudinal scales.

NZWRPS involved interviews with employees conducted by telephone using standard computer-assisted telephone interviewing techniques. One thousand New Zealand workers were drawn randomly from residential telephone directories and surveyed between 10 January and 12 February 2003. The sample was limited to New Zealand residents in paid employment of more than ten hours per week who had left secondary school. It was drawn from across New Zealand and quotas for regions reflected the spatial distribution of the population as reported in the Household Labour Force Survey. It was not possible to determine the eligibility of a majority (645 or 59.2 percent) of the 1,090 households that refused to answer the survey, so the response rate was no lower than, and possibly much higher than, 47.8 percent.

The respondent sample is broadly representative of the New Zealand working population. Some 51.1 percent were female, and most described themselves as New Zealand European in ethnicity (77.9 percent), with a further 7.5 percent describing themselves as Maori. Contrasting these observed percentages with those reported in the Household Labour Force Survey (Statistics New Zealand 2003) shows no significant differences for gender or ethnicity. Full-time workers (78.5 percent) were somewhat overrepresented as compared with the total workforce (68.1 percent). In occupational terms, there is a skew toward technicians and associate professionals, who account for 27.2 percent of the sample but represented 10.8 percent of the workforce at the time of the survey.[1] There is also a slight bias in the sample toward the health, social work, and education sectors. The statistics here are based on weighting the data set by occupation and industry to adjust for oversampling. Further details about the survey, including the questionnaire and sample characteristics, are contained in Haynes, Boxall, and Macky (2003). When we discuss key relationships among variables, we focus on those that are statistically significant.[2] Fuller details of statistical procedures can be found in the specific papers that are cited.

Survey Findings

Experience of Work and Demand for Influence

NZWRPS indicates that New Zealand workers are very happy with their employers' performance and their personal experience of work (Haynes, Boxall, and Macky 2003). Almost nine out of ten New Zealand workers say they are satisfied with their jobs overall. Some 86 percent agree/strongly agree that their job is secure, and 70.7 percent see it as part of their long-term career. Popular reports of the demise of the career would seem to be greatly exaggerated in contemporary New Zealand.

These high levels of employment satisfaction are not surprising: NZWRPS was conducted following a lengthy period of sustained employment growth in a relatively benign economic climate. Some 82 percent agree/strongly agree that they trust their employer to keep their promises. Further, 85 percent agree/strongly agree that, in general, relations between employees and management are good. This means they rate relations between management and workers nearly 20 percent better than U.S. workers and 15 percent better than British workers (Freeman and Rogers 1999; Diamond and Freeman 2001). These findings closely parallel the positive picture painted by the government's own sur-

---

[1] Labor force data are drawn from NZ Statistics, Household Labour Force Survey, March Quarter 2003 (HLFQ.SZA3PA–HLFQ.SZA3PZ).

[2] We follow convention and set the upper bound at $p < .05$, but most of the associations we discuss meet the more stringent threshold of $p < .01$ and some $p < .001$.

TABLE 6.1
The "influence gap"

Area over which influence exercised		A lot	Some	A little	None	N	χ^2 (df) sig.
Deciding how to do job and	Have	62.0%	23.6%	9.0%	5.4%	974	309.77
organize work	Want	69.1	26.0	3.7	1.2	969	(9)
	Diff	7.1					.0001
Setting hours including breaks,	Have	46.9	21.8	13.2	18.1	972	740.65
overtime, and time off	Want	57.3	28.8	7.1	6.9	957	(9)
	Diff	10.4					.0001
Deciding pay raises for people	Have	10.4	19.1	14.4	56.0	962	374.16
in work group or department	Want	30.3	38.9	11.4	19.5	963	(9)
	Diff	19.9					.0001
Pace of work	Have	56.9	23.5	9.2	10.4	965	760.63
	Want	66.7	26.3	4.9	2.1	963	(9)
	Diff	9.8					.0001
Deciding how to work with new	Have	42.5	30.0	12.7	14.7	954	683.74
equipment or software	Want	57.5	31.5	6.5	4.4	956	(9)
	Diff	15.0					.0001
Deciding perks and bonuses	Have	9.9	15.3	15.5	59.4	965	337.62
offered to employees	Want	26.9	43.8	11.9	17.4	958	(9)
	Diff	17.0					.0001

Source: Based on NZWRPS Q15, "Using the scale 'A lot,' 'Some,' 'A little,' or 'None,' how much direct involvement and influence do you have NOW in . . .?" and NZWRPS Q16, [If "A lot" in Q15] "Suppose you could have a lot of influence in all areas of work—whether you do now or not. Please tell me how much influence you would LIKE to have in . . .?" [If not "A lot" in Q15] "How much influence would you LIKE to have in . . .?"

Note: Excludes "don't know" responses. Weighted N = 976. Chi square statistics are calculated using unweighted data.

vey of the impacts of the Employment Relations Act 2000 in which "most employees (82 percent) rated current relationships between employers and employees at their workplace as very good (49 percent) or good (34 percent)" (Waldegrave 2004a, 155).

NZWRPS asked how much direct involvement and influence workers exercised over a range of workplace decisions and how much they would like (table 6.1) (Haynes, Boxall, and Macky 2005). Large majorities—from 68.7 percent to 85.6 percent—report that they exercise "a lot" or "some" influence over how they do their work, the pace at which they work, setting hours of work, and working with new technology. Contrasting sharply with this felt control over work dimensions, only 29.5 percent and 25.2 percent say they have "a lot" of or "some" influence over pay raises or perks and bonuses.

Following Freeman and Rogers (1999, 47–51), the "influence gap" for each area is calculated by taking the difference between the proportion of those who want "a lot" of influence and those who report having "a lot" of influence in decision making in that area. The influence gap is smallest, at 7.1 percent, for influence over how people do their work, and varies between 9.8 percent and 15.0 percent for the other aspects of "control over work": the pace at which they work, setting hours of work, and working with new technology. The influence gap is widest in the areas of determining pay raises and deciding perks and bonuses, at 19.9 percent and 17.0 percent respectively. These are, of course, those areas where the interests of employers and workers are most obviously in conflict, and where the traditional role of unions remains highly relevant.

Overall, 75.0 percent of respondents agreed or strongly agreed that they were satisfied with their influence in company decisions on their job or work life, compared to 20.2 percent who disagreed or strongly disagreed. Compared to the workers surveyed in the United States and the United Kingdom (Freeman and Rogers 1999; Diamond and Freeman 2001), New Zealand workers report having, and desiring, higher rates of influence in all areas of decision making (Haynes, Boxall, and Macky 2005). For example, the influence gaps for determining pay raises and deciding perks and bonuses, at 19.9 percent and 17.0 percent, compare to 22.9 percent and 19.7 percent in the United Kingdom and 35.0 percent and 54.0 percent in the United States. Although it seems likely that New Zealanders enjoy more influence in the workplace than either U.S. or U.K. workers, some of this difference may be due to the fact that the New Zealand survey covered workers in all sizes of firms, including very small ones. Job satisfaction is generally higher among workers in small firms where relationships between employers and employees are less formal and where involvement is much more direct (e.g., Beer 1964).

Union Density and Reach

Of those surveyed in NZWRPS, 21.3 percent report being a member of a union (Haynes, Boxall, and Macky 2006). Union density is highest in sectors that are either entirely in the public sector or are dominated by public-sector organizations: education (58.1 percent), central and local government (52.9 percent), and health and social work (38.6 percent). No part of the private sector registers above 30 percent density; manufacturing coming closest at 28.8 percent, followed by finance and insurance at 23.1 percent, and transport and communications at 18.5 percent. The rest of the private sector languishes around 10 percent or less, including such major areas of employment as real estate and business services (7.9 percent), retail and wholesale trade (8.5 percent), and hotels and restaurants (10.2 percent).

Measures of "union reach" (for workers, as opposed to workplaces) are provided by the proportion of respondents who report the presence of a union of some kind at their workplace, and those reporting a union at their workplace that they can join.[3] Over 40 percent (43.2 percent) report having a union of some kind at their workplace, and 38.6 percent report that there is a union at their workplace that people doing their sort of work can join.

The reach of unions is greatest in education and in central and local government, and above average in health and social work, finance and insurance, and manufacturing. It is least in private-sector services: in particular, real estate and business services, retail and wholesale trade, and hotels and restaurants. In most instances where a union is present, the vast majority of respondents can belong to this union if they so desire; the principal exceptions are manufacturing and retail and wholesale, where 14.4 percent and 12.5 percent respectively report being ineligible to join.

Unsatisfied Demand for Unionism: The Representation Gap

Those who have no union at their workplace that they can join, and who are "very likely" or "fairly likely" to join a union if asked, account for 17.8 percent of the total sample (Haynes, Boxall, and Macky 2006). Following the method used by Freeman and Rogers (1999) and adding the 17.8 percent who are very or fairly likely to join to the 21.3 percent of employees who are already in unions gives an estimate of potential union density in New Zealand of 39.1 percent. Those who would join a union if one were formed at their workplace represent 32.4 percent of those working in nonunionized workplaces. This figure is almost identical to the U.S. equivalent of 32 percent for 1994 estimated by Freeman and Rogers (1999, 68) and lower than the 41 to 50 percent for British workers using 1998 and 2001 data reported by Charlwood (2003, 52).

This approach assumes, of course, that those who say they are fairly likely to join (11.5 percent of the total sample) *would* actually join a specific union when, and if, the chance arose. How much of the fairly likely category represents soft support for unionism that would be unlikely to translate to membership is debatable, given that 67.2 percent of those fairly likely to join also reported that if a union was formed at their workplace, it would make no difference to them personally, and a further 8.0 percent reported that they would be worse off. The lowest estimate of potential density would include only the very likely to join respondents (who represent 6.3 percent of the total sample), giving a potential union density of 27.6 percent. If we remove three-quarters of those fairly likely to join from the calculation (i.e., those who think unionism will make no difference to them or make them worse off), the realistic density for unions might be existing density (21.3 percent) plus the very likelies

---

[3] Our concept of union reach should be distinguished from the related concept used by Peetz (1998, 10) to measure the extent to which a job is nonunion, optionally unionized, or compulsorily unionized.

(6.3 percent) plus 25 percent of the fairly likelies (2.9 percent). This gives a more realistic potential union density in New Zealand of 30.5 percent, or a growth of 43 percent in the union roll (Haynes, Boxall, and Macky 2006).

In nonunion workplaces, the representation gap varies across a number of different worker characteristics, though not all (table 6.2). There are statistically significant relationships between unsatisfied union demand and the variables of income, age, size of employing organization, industry, and type of work performed (Haynes, Boxall, and Macky 2006).[4] Unsatisfied demand for union membership is much greater for low-income earners. One in three workers earning less than $10,000 has an unsatisfied demand for unionism as does one in four earning between this level and $20,000. Similarly, one in three under twenty-five years old and one in four between twenty-five and thirty-four have unsatisfied union demand. Size of workplace also plays a role: union density is only 4.7 percent in workplaces with up to twenty workers and one in three would like union representation. The representation gap is larger for the business services, hospitality, and primary sectors than for other industries. It is also largest in the services/sales, clerical/secretarial, and agricultural occupations and smallest in the plant/machine operator and trades occupations. As we noted above, the decline in union density in the period following the introduction of the ECA was fastest in private-sector services. This suggests, alongside the evidence presented here of greater unsatisfied demand for union membership in this sector, that much of the fall in union density immediately following the abolition of compulsory union membership was not due to workers leaving their unions, but rather to their unions no longer being able to organize and service the large numbers who came within their catchments under compulsory membership.

Reflecting the relative strength of public-sector unionism, women have higher union density than men (by 5.3 percent). However, their level of unsatisfied demand for union membership is similar to that of men, and the relationship between gender and unsatisfied demand is not significant (Haynes, Boxall, and Macky 2006). Similarly, the level of unsatisfied demand does not vary significantly across levels of educational achievement, and the level of unsatisfied demand is not significantly different for part-time workers than their full-time counterparts.

Overall, the analysis supports the conclusion that the representation gap is greater in the secondary labor market. The gap declines with income, age, and size of organization. In other words, it is greater among younger and lower-paid workers in smaller organizations in the business services, hospitality, and

[4] The statistics reported here are based on unweighted data. Weighting by industry and occupation generally exaggerates the patterns discussed and therefore does not alter statistical significance from that reported.

TABLE 6.2
New Zealand union reach, density and demand (by selected characteristics)

	Union reach	Existing union density	Representation gap	Total potential density	N
Gender					
Male	38.4%	18.8%	18.4%	37.2%	515
Female	38.6	24.1	21.3	45.4	461
Ethnicity					
NZ European/ Pakeha	37.7%	20.8%	18.5%	39.3%	795
NZ Māori	50.0	28.9	20.0	48.9	90
Other ethnicity	36.5	18.8	31.8	50.6	85
Employment status					
Full-time	39.8%	23.2%	18.9%	42.1%	772
Part-time	34.5	14.3	23.2	37.5	203
Age					
Under 25	16.2%	3.8%	36.9%	40.7%	130
25–34	33.8	15.0	23.9	38.9	213
35–44	41.4	25.3	14.7	40.0	292
45–54	44.9	26.8	15.1	41.9	205
55 and over	53.1	32.0	12.5	44.5	128
Organizational tenure (to nearest year)					
<1	24.9%	11.6%	28.1%	39.7%	249
2	30.3	17.2	24.6	41.8	122
3	40.4	18.2	23.2	41.4	99
4	54.1	18.9	12.2	31.1	74
5	43.9	24.6	12.3	36.9	57
6–10	41.4	22.0	17.2	39.2	186
11–20	58.5	36.4	13.6	50.0	118
21–30	67.5	60.0	5.0	65.0	40
31–40	45.0	25.0	5.0	30.0	20
Education level					
No secondary	21.1%	10.5%	10.5%	21.0%	19
Some secondary	45.2	22.6	18.6	41.2	177
School certificate or equivalent	26.5	13.7	17.9	31.6	117
6th form certificate/UE	37.5	20.8	20.0	40.8	120
Bursary or equivalent	25.0	15.9	27.3	43.2	44
Technical or trade certificate	31.1	19.6	22.3	41.9	148
Tertiary diploma	41.5	20.2	30.9	51.1	94
Bachelor's degree	40.6	26.3	17.7	44.0	175
Postgraduate degree	61.5	30.8	11.5	42.3	78
Income					
Up to $10,000	18.0%	2.0%	36.0%	38.0%	50
$10,001–$20,000	27.5	11.3	24.6	35.9	142
$20,001–$30,000	43.1	19.6	21.6	41.2	204
$30,001–$40,000	38.3	26.2	20.2	46.4	183

TABLE 6.2
Continued

	Union reach	Existing union density	Representation gap	Total potential density	N
$40,001–$50,000	49.6	32.8	16.8	49.6	137
$50,001–$60,000	60.0	36.5	4.7	41.2	85
More than $60,001	34.5	18.7	14.4	33.1	139
Size of organization					
1–20	10.1%	4.7%	32.2%	36.9%	276
21–100	30.8	18.4	19.4	37.8	201
101–500	51.9	18.0	9.8	27.8	133
501 and above	57.4	33.5	14.8	48.3	209
Occupation					
Manager/ professional	44.3%	25.8%	18.6%	44.4%	264
Technical/other professional	46.7	31.4	16.2	47.6	105
Clerical/secretarial	29.2	16.7	24.2	40.9	120
Service/sales	27.1	12.9	30.3	43.2	155
Agriculture	25.9	4.7	22.4	27.1	85
Tradesperson	31.6	17.9	15.8	33.7	95
Plant/machine operator	63.6	38.6	6.8	45.4	88
Manual	40.6	18.8	18.8	37.6	64
Industry					
Agriculture, forestry and fishing, mining and utilities	19.6%	8.7%	30.4%	39.1%	92
Manufacturing	52.7	28.8	8.9	37.7	146
Construction	30.9	8.8	16.2	25.0	68
Retail and wholesale	19.9	8.5	22.7	31.2	176
Hotels and restaurants	22.4	10.2	32.7	42.9	49
Transport and communications	35.2	18.5	18.5	37.0	54
Finance and insurance	53.8	23.1	15.4	38.5	26
Real estate/business services	14.9	7.9	38.6	46.5	101
Central and local government	79.4	52.9	5.9	58.8	34
Education	83.8	58.1	8.1	66.2	74
Health/social work	61.4	38.6	19.3	57.9	88
Community services	35.3	20.6	13.2	33.8	68
Public/private sector					
Private sector	30.0	14.5	21.6	36.1	779
Public sector	73.0	48.5	12.2	60.7	196

Source: Based on NZWRPS Q18, "Is it a union that people doing your sort of job can join?" (union reach); Q19, "Are you a member of this union?" (existing union density); and Q24, "If a union was formed at your workplace, how likely would you be to join?" (representation gap); and demographic questions.

Notes: Excludes "don't know" responses. Columns 1 and 2 are calculated by taking those who answered "yes" to Q18 and Q19 as a proportion of the total workforce for the category in question, and column 3 is calculated by taking those who answered "fairly" likely" or "very likely" to Q24 as a proportion of the total workforce for the category in question. It is not intended to imply that the total workforce was asked Q18, Q19, or Q24.

primary industries. Although unions are doing well in larger organizations and are readily available to public-sector workers, they are having serious difficulties in reaching smaller firms in the private sector where a vulnerable minority of workers would like to be represented collectively.

Why Is There Unsatisfied Demand for Unionism?

What accounts for unsatisfied demand for unionism in New Zealand? In unionized sites, there is some potential for infill recruitment. Some 33.9 percent of workers in unionized workplaces who have never been a member of a union have never been approached to join (Haynes, Boxall, and Macky 2006, 202). The level of unsatisfied demand for union membership in unionized New Zealand workplaces is thus lower than that found in Britain, where 56 percent of eligible nonmembers have never been asked to join (Bryson 2003). Consequently, the potential for infill recruitment is greater in the United Kingdom than in New Zealand.

In-depth analysis of the reasons fewer young people are in unions supports the view that unsatisfied union demand is largely associated with lack of union reach into small, private-sector workplaces (Haynes, Vowles, and Boxall 2005). Union density for New Zealand workers aged twenty-nine years and under is around half that of workers aged thirty years or more. This places New Zealand in the same league as Canada, the United States, and Britain, where union density for youth (16–24 years) is around one-third to one-half that of their older counterparts (Bryson et al. 2004; Gomez, Gunderson, and Meltz 2002), and Australia, where union membership in the 20–24 years age group is around two-thirds that in the 35–54 years age group (Buchanan and Bretherton 1999, 12).

As in other Anglo-American countries, attitudes toward unions do not account for the lower union membership levels among younger workers (Haynes, Vowles, and Boxall 2005). On the whole, the differences between younger and older New Zealand workers' attitudes toward unions are slight or nonexistent. If anything, younger workers' attitudes and willingness to join are more positive than those of their older counterparts. Regression analysis shows that the main reason for low union density among young workers is that they are heavily located in nonunion workplaces, which dominate the service industries and small firms in which they work (Haynes, Vowles, and Boxall 2005). The higher labor mobility of young workers also poses practical difficulties. As elsewhere, age is inversely related to labor turnover in New Zealand: those under thirty are working through a period in the adult life cycle in which attachments to individual employers are naturally more exploratory and provisional (Boxall, Macky, and Rasmussen 2003). They switch employers readily to improve their lot. Hanging on to join, or help form a union, is a much less likely course of action among the young.

What about the impact of management opposition, a major factor deterring union membership in the United States (e.g., Fiorito 2003)? In the main, New Zealand employers do not wage antiunion campaigns or disrupt union organizing. The government's own survey of the impacts of the Employment Relations Act 2000 found that "management views on unions did not appear to be a key barrier to unions accessing employees" (Waldegrave 2004b, 120). In this same survey, only one in ten employees thought their employer opposed unions (Waldegrave 2004a, 149). According to NZWRPS respondents, 29.4 percent of managers oppose unions while 54.7 percent either support or are neutral toward them (Haynes and Boxall 2004). Employer opposition does not appear to be a major reason for union leaving: 52.4 percent of nonunion workers who had been members of a union stated that they had left the union of their own volition, a further 43.3 percent stated that they had left when they changed their job, and only 4.3 percent stated that they had left for another, unstated, reason. Further, management attitudes toward unions are not found to have an independent effect on propensity to join the union in unionized workplaces (Bryson 2006). Overall, it seems likely that individual employer obstruction is a small factor and much less of an impediment to unionization than the fact that the vast majority of bargaining is enterprise or workplace based. In this context, unions simply struggle to exercise all their rights of entry: it is very hard to cover the patch.

How Do Workers See Unions?

The descriptive statistics in NZWRPS suggest that union members in New Zealand are generally very positive about their unions (Haynes, Boxall, and Macky 2003). Large majorities report that they are loyal to their union (85.3 percent), trust the union leadership to keep its promises to members (87.2 percent), and agree that their union fights really hard when important employee interests are threatened (84.8 percent). When asked whether the union leadership has an agenda that they do not share, union members are more equivocal: 24.4 percent agree or strongly agree, 20.0 percent are unsure, and 55.7 percent disagree in some measure. Union members' high rates of satisfaction with their unions are, of course, only to be expected. In a voluntarist regime, dissatisfied members and those unconvinced of the benefits are free to leave.

Regression analysis of NZWRPS data enables us to go beyond these descriptive statistics and test a range of hypotheses on union belonging (Macky, Boxall, and Haynes 2005). Three models of why individual workers join unions are commonly discussed in the literature (e.g., Charlwood 2002; Kochan 1979; Wheeler and McClendon 1991). One model emphasizes the role of threats to worker interests or job dissatisfaction, which prompts a decision to unionize. A second model is purely based on instrumentality or utility: workers will unionize if they expect the benefits of doing so to outweigh the costs. In this case, a sense of threat or job dissatisfaction need not be a trigger. A third model is driven by ideology or personal beliefs.

Using items in NZWRPS that related to these explanations, a set of scales was developed to measure respondent perceptions of the quality of their employment relationship and management and union performance (Macky, Boxall, and Haynes 2005). Scales were also developed to measure their political beliefs and their beliefs about the role and importance of unions. Various control variables were included in the logistic regression, including age, tenure, hours worked, industry, management attitudes toward unions, the degree of nonunion voice present in the workplace, and perceived degree of union membership at one's place of work.

The results provide strongest support to the instrumental model: perceptions of union performance are clearly influential in union belonging (Macky, Boxall, and Haynes 2005). Although some workers who join may be dissatisfied with their employment or may believe that unions have an important role to play, the influence of these factors on the probability of union belonging is mediated through perceptions of union performance. Poor perceptions of union performance act as a circuit breaker between employment dissatisfaction and union belonging. We thus support the central argument in the U.S. literature on the mediating role of union instrumentality in union belonging (e.g., Kochan 1979; Premack and Hunter 1988; Fiorito 2003). There is also some support for the role of political beliefs: people with more left-wing views are more likely to belong to unions. However, the effects of ideology should not be exaggerated. New Zealand union members are fundamentally instrumental, not sentimental.

The data analysis also reveals that some control variables have an effect: union members are more likely to be longer-serving employees and female. They also think that a high proportion of their co-workers are in the union. The results in terms of gender confirm what is now well known anecdotally about the New Zealand union movement. The unions operating in New Zealand's public service, education, and health systems, where women predominate and long tenure is encouraged, now have a disproportionate share of union density. The role of perceptions of union penetration is also not surprising: people are more likely to be members when they perceive that more of their colleagues are. This is consistent with both an instrumental and a social-custom model of trade union membership.

The strength of these pragmatic attitudes is confirmed by the incidence of free riding and poses serious problems for the unions (Waldegrave 2004b). Union members represent 55.3 percent of those who have the opportunity to join a union at their workplace (Haynes and Boxall 2004). Technically speaking, around 45 percent are free riding. This is almost identical to the figure of

46 percent reported by Wyllie and Whitfield (2003) in the government's evaluation of the ERA. There is considerable variation between industries in the incidence of nonmembership within workplaces with a union presence: the highest levels are in construction (71.4 percent) and in private-sector services: retail and wholesale trade (57.1 percent), finance and insurance (60.0 percent), and hotels and restaurants (54.5 percent). In other words, "technical free riding" is lowest in industries where union penetration is highest (Haynes, Boxall, and Macky 2006). Further analysis shows that nonmembership in unionized workplaces is highest at both the lowest and highest levels of income and education, and lowest in the middle range (Haynes and Boxall 2004). That is to say, nonmembership is "U-shaped" by level of income and education. This pattern suggests that technical free riding may be broadly bimodal. Lower-income workers may find the cost of union membership difficult to sustain at any level. On the other hand, high-income workers may feel less need for union representation as a result of their greater job security and labor market power.

Nonmembership was not found to be associated with a number of variables that might be expected to have an impact on free riding (Haynes and Boxall 2004). These variables include the presence of a human resource department or person, the presence of a consultative committee, and the reported willingness of the employer to share power or keep everyone up to date with proposed changes (Haynes and Boxall 2004; Bryson 2006). Furthermore, free riding in New Zealand is more likely when there are few workplace problems and when unions are perceived as less effective (Bryson 2006).[5] This suggests that nonunion forms of worker participation are not primarily playing a role as union substitutes in New Zealand.

What about motives for free riding? The most cited reason for nonmembership is that "there is no point joining since I get all the benefits anyway," with 64.1 percent agreeing or strongly agreeing with this statement. Some 44.2 percent of nonunion workers either agree or strongly agree that "people doing my job don't join trade unions," which suggests that while they may be "passive beneficiaries" of union gains in their workplaces or industries, they ought not to be included among the "calculating free riders." There are a variety of reasons why workers might believe that union membership is inappropriate for people doing their jobs, including supervisory or managerial responsibilities, or occupational identity (see, for example, Milton [2003] on highly skilled technical workers).

In addition, perceived union ineffectiveness and/or a perception that the costs of union membership outweigh any benefits also appears to be an important factor explaining nonmembership in unionized workplaces. Some 43.6

---

[5] The measure of worker problems employed in Bryson (2006) is also employed in chapters 1 and 3 of this book, where it is referred to as measuring "needs for representation or participation."

percent say that unions do not achieve anything of value, and 37.4 percent consider membership fees too high, suggesting that for many the decision not to join is not about free riding but about perceiving union membership as not sufficiently valuable to warrant "purchase." It may be that prospective members do not have an accurate idea of the costs of union membership, or it could be that unions need to review the net benefits they offer. These findings parallel responses to similar questions in Britain (Bryson 2003).

In sum, NZWRPS confirms that the problems the unions face are threefold: they include lack of reach and free riding, but, most seriously, they include indifference or skepticism on the part of the majority of private-sector workers. While not minimizing the problems of reach and free riding, indifference is the biggest impediment to re-unionization in New Zealand.

Workers and Nonunion Voice

The NZWRPS provides the most complete picture to date of the incidence of nonunion voice mechanisms in New Zealand (Haynes, Vowles, and Boxall 2005). Workforce coverage by the range of voice mechanisms follows a similar pattern to that reported in the United States (Freeman and Rogers 1999, 92), and coverage is somewhat higher than that revealed by the BWRPS survey for British workers (Diamond and Freeman 2001, 10). A large proportion of New Zealand workers report that their workplaces have one or more procedures for resolving workplace problems and/or for involvement in decision making. Most (85.9 percent) report that their organization has an open door policy so employees can tell senior management about problems with their supervisors, and around half report that managers in their organizations hold regular meetings with staff (58.0 percent) or that their organization has a personnel/human resource department or person (50.1 percent). A minority (34.6 percent) report an "employee involvement program such as quality circles" in their workplace. Only a very small minority (5.0 percent) report that they do not have access to any of the procedures mentioned.

The key finding, however, is the incidence of joint consultation (Haynes, Vowles, and Boxall 2005). A large minority (39.4 percent) of respondents reports the existence of a committee of employees that discusses problems with management on a regular basis, and a higher proportion (49.8 percent) reports that a committee of management and employees or staff forum meets regularly to consult on workplace issues. At four to five workers out of ten, a greater proportion of New Zealand workers are covered by joint consultation than by collective bargaining, which was estimated by Wyllie and Whitfield (2003) to cover 36 percent of employees.

Consultative committees are relatively commonplace across all types of industry, but there are noticeable associations with organizational size. This is to be expected, with informal voice likely to be most effective in smaller organizations (Kaufman and Levine 2000, 154). It is consistent with the relationship between organizational size and incidence of workplace consultative committees reported in the United Kingdom (Millward, Bryson, and Forth 2000, 109). Having said this, the incidence of consultative committees in workplaces with up to twenty workers is 28.4 percent, and it is nearly 50 percent in workplaces with 21–50 workers. These are small workplaces by international standards, and yet they show a reasonable degree of consultative management.

Consistent with the British and Australian experience (Millward, Bryson, and Forth 2000; Benson 2000), there is an association between joint consultation and unionization: two-thirds of those in workplaces with a union presence report that they have a consultative committee in their workplace, compared to 36.8 percent of those in nonunion workplaces. The association with management attitudes is also significant: consultative committees are increasingly likely to be found in workplaces as managers' reported attitudes to unions become more positive.

How effective is joint consultation in the New Zealand context? When asked, 23.1 percent of those with a consultative committee report them to be "very effective" and 54.8 percent "quite effective." Workers elect or appoint the employee representatives on consultative committees covering 38.4 percent of the workforce, and employee members are "self-selecting" on consultative committees covering 32.0 percent. By comparison, employee representatives are chosen by management on consultative committees covering 26.5 percent of the workforce. Those covered by committees with solely management-appointed representatives are less likely to report them to be effective (64.8 percent) than those covered by committees with representatives selected by other employees only (89.7 percent), unions only (86.3 percent), self-selection (84.6 percent), or a mix of methods (87.8 percent). It is likely that while such committees are often initiated by management, the large majority represent the views of the workforce with significant though varying degrees of autonomy and effectiveness (Haynes 2005).

The impact of unions on the effectiveness of consultative committees depends on how effective the union is. There is no association between the presence of a union and the reported effectiveness of consultative committees (Haynes, Boxall, and Macky 2005). However, a scale composed of responses to a bank of questions about the workplace union's effectiveness was found to be positively associated with the reported effectiveness of consultative committees. Further, when the proportion of employees in the workplace who are members of the union is used as a proxy for union effectiveness at the workplace, a positive association is found between the effectiveness of the consultative committee and union effectiveness.

The effectiveness of joint consultation is also related to management attitudes toward unions (Haynes, Boxall, and Macky 2005). Respondents who report that their workplace management favors unions are more likely to report that the consultative committee in their workplace is very effective than those who report that their managers are neutral toward unions. Similarly, those who say their managers are neutral are more likely to report that their consultative committees are effective than those who report that their managers are opposed to unions.

The overall picture is of a relatively broad array of nonunion voice options in New Zealand with a growing incidence of joint consultative committees. Consultative committees are important because of their potential to provide a worker-oriented voice mechanism, that is, a way in which workers can express concerns about their interests and not simply respond to a management-driven productivity agenda.

Current Voice Initiatives

Unions

As this chapter shows, New Zealand unions have been at a disadvantage for some time. Employing multivariate shift-share methodology, Charlwood and Haynes (forthcoming, 1) find that over the 1990–2002 period compositional change and attitudinal change to the efficacy of trade unions "had almost no impact on union density decline."[6] Rather, the decline in density explained in shift-share analysis is almost entirely attributed to "within-group behavioral change"; this is most likely due in large part to the receding reach of unions in the private-sector services, given that we find that such workers have high levels of unfilled demand for union membership. As Charlwood and Haynes (forthcoming, 11) put it, "The immediate effect of [the ECA] was indirect: it exposed the weakness of those unions that lacked the resources and organizational strength in the workplace to cope with the rapid decentralization of bargaining in the absence of official sponsorship or employer support." Consequently, unionism has become increasingly a public-sector and manufacturing-industry phenomenon, as it is elsewhere. In addition, job satisfaction levels are high and workers' felt need for unionism is low in much of the private sector.

The government's evaluation of the impacts of the Employment Relations Act 2000 shows that the unions have concentrated their recruitment efforts on the larger workplaces and organizations where management performance

---

[6] In this case, shift-share analysis measures the extent to which union membership decline can be attributed to compositional change (i.e., change in the structure of the economy and workforce) compared to within-group behavioral change (i.e., change in the probability of union membership for workers with a given characteristic) and changes in employee attitudes about the efficacy of unions.

is lower and/or management is neutral to union membership (Waldegrave 2004b). This is understandable.

The problem is that further recruitment in the smaller workplaces in private-sector services calls for a more radical response. Applying the "organizing model," where it is the most appropriate approach, is resource intensive, and the unions that need to do it (i.e., those covering low-skilled private-sector workers) are the least well resourced. The success of the newly formed Unite union in recruiting large numbers of younger workers in the private-sector services, most notably the fast food, hotel, and cinema industries, with an innovative mix of radical and traditional tactics, underlines this point. Despite a reported 100 percent turnover in membership per year, Unite had grown to more than six thousand members in May 2006, with a further five thousand that do not pay fees, since it was formed in early 2003 (Cumming 2006; interview with Matt McCarten, 3 May 2006). It employs a relatively low-paid (compared to its more traditional counterparts in the service sector) or volunteer organizing staff to overcome the resourcing barrier, allowing it to charge low fees (with no fees until contract negotiations commence). It also has a militant high-profile campaigning style, emphasizes text-messaging and e-mail for communication with members, and provides basic advocacy services (interview with Matt McCarten, 3 May 2006).

In the absence of such a radically different approach, reorganizing union structures to better cover the secondary labor market is required. Union mergers deliberately constructed across the primary and secondary labor markets would help unions to cross-subsidize recruitment in favor of the latter. This, however, is difficult to achieve because of the interunion politics involved. Even if it is achieved politically, it remains a difficult model in practice because of the problem of sustaining union membership in small workplaces where both rates of business failure and levels of employee turnover are high.

Government

As noted above, the Labour Party–led governments since 1999 have done much to enhance employee voice. They have followed a classical path, enhancing union rights and promoting collective bargaining, and improving New Zealand's compliance with international labor standards (Roth 2001). They have responded most recently to the fact that the return of voluntary unionism has encouraged free riding and somewhat undermined the ability of unions to demonstrate their effectiveness. Recent legislative amendments to the ERA aim to reduce the incidence of free riding by allowing for bargaining fees to be negotiated and implemented subject to a secret ballot. These measures go as far as can be done, short of reintroducing compulsory unionism. They may help to reduce free riding, but, as indicated above, the motives for it are complex and the sort of measures being introduced are cumbersome and likely to have a limited impact.

Employers and Employee Voice

The NZWRPS suggests that a more consultative style of management has been evolving in New Zealand. The incidence of joint consultation is high, encompassing more workers than collective bargaining. The inference from our data is that the general ideology and style being pursued by management is one that increases consultation without encouraging independent worker representation or while remaining neutral about unionism. It is not, in the main, a "bleak house" scenario (Sisson 1993) in which there are few ways employees can express their voice and be treated as important stakeholders. Elements of bleak house clearly exist in the secondary labor market, as the demand for traditional unionism there implies. However, even in small organizations, we see a relatively high degree of consultation, which workers regard as effective. In sum, nonunion voice options are developing and increasingly complement unionized voice.

Key Messages

The first key message that might be gleaned from the New Zealand case is the value of a relatively tractable system of industrial relations in which governments, employers, employees, and unions can experiment and learn. Allowing for some exceptions, the greater freedoms of the more liberal environment have not generally been used by the direct parties in a negative fashion. Management has become more consultative, and ongoing innovation in nonunion voice is enhancing options for employee voice in ways that are not detrimental to unions.

Having said this, the second key message that emerges from the New Zealand case relates to the ongoing representation gap among the low paid, the less skilled, and workers in small firms. This gap seems to have opened up with the abolition of compulsory union membership in 1991. It continues to exist despite the efforts of recent center-left governments to promote collective bargaining and bolster the historical unions. It is now abundantly evident that the unions face serious difficulties in forming strategies to deal with the problem of reach in a decentralized labor market. This suggests that while public policy should continue to do its best to enhance the floor of employee rights and their enforcement through government agencies, it should start to do more to facilitate nonunion voice in small firms. Our data show that nonunion voice is far from absent in small firms and imply that it could grow further. The present government's objectives are very much wedded to promoting union voice. Without undermining this objective, the time has come to think more broadly about the kind of voice options that workers want. A government objective of promoting employee voice including, but not limited to, collective bargaining would be more relevant to the contemporary labor market.

The third key message is that the unions need to think seriously about their performance in areas where they are capable of making an impact. This is something that is difficult in politically constituted tradition-conscious organizations. The key question facing unions is how to become relevant to a workforce, largely in the private sector, that sees little or no benefit in union membership. The workforce differs significantly from what it was like when unions were founded. Orientations to work have become more diverse, worker aspirations have become more developmental, and employers have become more consultative. As Kochan (2003) argues, the tried-and-true methods of organizing around discontent have less traction in this environment. Like government, then, unions need to think more creatively about what workers want. This should begin by questioning long-held assumptions and may lead to strategies and structures that fit better with the diverse needs and wants of current and potential members.

Chapter 7

Employee Voice in the Anglo-American World
What Does It Mean for Unions?

DAVID PEETZ AND ANN FROST

Unions find themselves at a crossroads globally, and those in the Anglo-American countries are no different. Unions in the six countries covered in this book—the United States, Canada, Australia, New Zealand, the United Kingdom, and Ireland—share many common features, draw on a shared heritage, and face a more or less similar set of challenges. In this book, the application of a common research focus across these six countries allows us to take an unprecedented look at those challenges and to examine employee, employer, and union responses to them.

The purpose of this chapter is to draw on the survey results from these six Anglo-American countries to uncover the lessons for unions. The analysis of the series of individual country research projects suggests possible avenues for union reform and remobilization. The findings from the country studies indicate both a number of common outcomes as well as some key differences. Unions, we believe, can draw some important lessons from these data.

Despite falling union density in all six of the countries, we argue that all is not a depressing, bleak way forward for unions in the Anglo-American world. Rather, data from employees surveyed in these six countries are on the whole encouraging. Yes, unions in these settings continue to have problems and face difficulties in organizing new members and gaining access to the vibrant and rapidly growing sectors of the economy. However, there are indications of hope. Workers who are union members continue to value union membership, and significant numbers of nonmembers continue to desire membership. In this chapter we seek to understand how unions might organize new members and contribute meaningfully to shaping workplace practices and policy.

Summary of Data across the Six Countries

In all six countries, union density has fallen over the past decade and a half. These drops range from a mere five percentage points in the case of Canada (roughly 35 percent in 1990 to just over 30 percent in 2004) to almost thirty percentage points in the New Zealand case (from 50 percent in 1990 to 21 percent in 2004) (table 7.1). Current union density in the six countries ranges from a low of just under 12 percent in the United States to 38 percent in Ireland. The other four countries have between one-fifth and one-third of their workers represented by unions (table 7.1). Yet, despite these drops, sizeable numbers of workers in these six countries report a continued desire for union representation.

With the exception of Canada and the United States, data on union density in the Anglo-American countries are somewhat deceiving. In all four cases, unions have a significant problem with free riders. Around 40 to 45 percent of

TABLE 7.1
Union density over time, union coverage, and freeriders, by country

Country	Union density 1990	Union density 2004	Union coverage[g]	Freeriders[g]
United States[a]	16.1%	12.5%	13.8%	9.5%
United Kingdom[b]	39.1	28.8	48.4	44.2
Canada[c]	34.8	30.4	30.4	N/A
Australia[d]	40.8	22.7	44.8	39.2
New Zealand[e]	49.9	21.1	38.6	44.7
Ireland[f]	51.7	34.6	52.5	28.2

Note: Figures are derived from data in the following sources:

[a]All columns: *U.S. Historical Tables: Union Membership, Coverage, Density, and Employment, 1973–2004: All Wage & Salary Workers*, www.unionstats.com (accessed 4 October 2005).

[b]1990: Sneade, A. 2001. Trade union membership 1999–2000: an analysis of data from the Certification Officer and the Labour Force Survey, *Labour Market Trends*, September, 433–44. 2004, including union coverage and freeriders: Department of Trade and Industry, *Trade Union Membership 2004*, HMSO, March 2005, www.dti.gov.uk/er/emar/tradeunion_membership2004.pdf.

[c]All columns: Human Resources and Skills Development Canada, *Union Membership in Canada, 1990–2004*, www.hrsdc.gc.ca/en/lp/wid/union_membership.shtml (accessed 4 October 2005).

[d]1990 and 2004: Australian Bureau of Statistics, Cat Nos 6306.0 and 6310.0. Union coverage and freeriders: Teicher et al., chap. 5 in this book).

[e]1990: Charlwood and Haynes (2005). 2004 and union coverage and freeriders: Haynes et al. (2006).

[f]Central Statistics Office, Quarterly National Household Survey Union Membership, 1994 to 2004, www.cso.ie/releasespublications/documents/labour_market/current/qnhsunionmembership.pdf. Union coverage and free-riders: Geary, chap. 4 in this book.

[g]Union coverage and free-rider figures vary by year: United States (2004); United Kingdom (2004); Canada (2004); Australia (2003/04); New Zealand (2003); Ireland (2003).

all employees working in a unionized workplace in Australia, New Zealand, and the United Kingdom, and nearly 30 percent of those in Ireland, are not members of the union. Union coverage, therefore, is considerably higher than the union density figures suggest (table 7.1).

For nonmembers in unionized workplaces (the free riders), and those employees without union representation because they are employed in a nonunion workplace, unions in Australia, New Zealand, Ireland, and the United Kingdom require a two-pronged response to building membership: organize new workplaces and organize the nonmembers in unionized worksites. In many cases, nonmembers in union workplaces report never having been asked to join the union. This ranges from a low of 34 percent in New Zealand to 76 percent in Ireland. Many nonmembers working in unionized workplaces surveyed in these six countries report they would join the union if asked.

Despite the falling density rates across all six countries and the often significant free-rider problem in several of them, union member satisfaction remains high.[1] In Australia, unions enjoy high, and increasing, levels of approval from both members and nonmembers. In New Zealand, more than 80 percent of the union members surveyed report that they trust their union leadership, are loyal to their union, and believe that the union fights hard for their interests. More than 80 percent of union members in the United Kingdom surveyed reported that they got reasonable or good value from their union dues. In Canada, more than three-quarters of union members surveyed (77 percent) reported they would vote to keep their union if they were asked. In Ireland, 78 percent of union members rate their union as effective. These are all very encouraging numbers for unions.

This positive view of union membership's benefits is clearly also shared by a significant number of workers who do not have access to union membership at their workplace. A serious representation gap exists for these workers. Across the board in these six countries, approximately one-third of workers in nonunion workplaces report that they would vote for a union if an election were held at their workplace today.

What is it that members appreciate about their union and that nonmembers desire? It appears from the survey data that workers in these six Anglo-American countries desire influence in a number of workplace-related areas and believe in many cases that they are not able to have the level of influence that they desire. This representation gap is especially large in the United States, ranging from twelve to fifty-four percentage points depending on the issue (Freeman and Rogers 1999, exhibit 3.5); is significant in Canada, ranging from

---

[1] This may seem obvious since union membership in most of the six countries examined here is voluntary. However, some members may belong to a union because they see a union's protection as a preferred alternative to no representation. That said, though, they could be less than satisfied with that representation.

fourteen to thirty-one percentage points depending on the issue (Campolieti, Gomez, and Gunderson 2004); and is still significant in New Zealand where, depending on the issue, it ranges from a gap of seven percentage points to one of almost twenty percentage points (chapter 6). Workers also continue to desire union representation for very traditional reasons: the wage gains unions negotiate with employers and the protection union membership confers on workers against capricious or unjust treatment on the job.

Moreover, with the increase in the past decade and a half in the number of channels for employee involvement initiated by employers in these six countries, employees see a union presence helping to ensure that not only are employer concerns dealt with but workers' issues are taken into consideration as well. Overwhelmingly, the employees surveyed in these six countries report that they want their workplace representatives to engage cooperatively with management. In Australia, 79 percent of those surveyed agreed or strongly agreed with the statement that unions should give more attention to helping the organization succeed. Sixty-six percent agreed or strongly agreed that unions should cooperate more closely with management (chapter 5). In the United States, employees surveyed reported that they too favored more cooperative labor-management relations, with nearly two-thirds of those surveyed reporting that they "preferred an organization with little nominal power but which had management cooperation to an organization that had more power but [which] management opposed" (Freeman and Rogers 1999, exhibit 3.8). In the United Kingdom survey, employees (both union members and nonmembers) were asked whether they preferred "an organization representing workers that declared its main function as working with management to improve the workplace and working conditions; or an organization that declared its main function as defending workers against unfair treatment by management." The vast majority of both union members and nonmembers chose the former. However, as Freeman and Bryson (chapter 3) point out, detailed questioning revealed that, to workers, cooperation means management sharing power and authority with unions, not some sort of sham whereby management leads and the union cooperates by following. It is thus useful to think about this as workers' desire for each side to engage in reciprocal behavior, where responsibilities and benefits are shared.

In summary, the collection of six Anglo-American country surveys and analyses paints a fairly consistent picture of the state of unions in these settings. First, union density has declined, but appears to have mostly stabilized. Second, in four of the countries (Australia, New Zealand, the United Kingdom, and Ireland) union reach is considerably higher than the union density figures indicate—which highlights a significant free-rider problem. Third, those who are members of a union overwhelmingly report high levels of satisfaction with their union. Fourth, many nonmembers report their willingness to join a union given the opportunity—importantly, this includes nearly a third of all workers in nonunionized workplaces. Fifth, employees in these six countries report wanting a degree of influence over decision making at work that they do not yet have. Finally, the employees surveyed consistently report (with perhaps the exception of Canadian employees) that they desire a cooperative relationship between the union and management at the workplace—but this does not only apply to the union because they also expect management to reciprocate by cooperating with the union to solve workplace problems. Given this background, we now turn to outlining and describing the opportunities these data suggest for unions in the Anglo-American world.

External Organizing

In none of the six Anglo-American countries can unions wait for legislative reforms more conducive to encouraging and building union membership. The political and legal contexts in most of these six countries may not be getting any more negative toward unions, with the exception of Australia, but they certainly do not appear to be becoming actively conducive to union growth. Unions will have to make do and work with what they currently have.

No single issue dominates the reasons why workers in nonunion workplace have not joined unions. Irish data (chapter 4) indicate common reasons include employer retaliation, a belief in benign employer behavior toward employees, belief in the efficacy of individual solutions, belief in the futility of union membership without union recognition, and aversion to union confrontation. Needs, which correlate strongly with desire for unionization, are not evenly distributed. Some nonunion workplaces will be almost impossible to organize because workers' perceive their needs to be largely met, but even in the United States about a third of nonunion workers believe the majority of their co-workers support unionization (chapter 1). These points suggest that for unions to break into nonunion workplaces requires identifying issues of concern to workers, focusing on those workplaces where needs are significant, demonstrating the efficacy of collective solutions, building up the strength to obtain recognition and prevent employer retaliation, and demonstrating a capacity for an ongoing relationship with the employer that is not founded simply on confrontation.

In thinking about new organizing, unions have several fronts on which they need to attack: organizing new workplaces and segments of the labor force they have traditionally overlooked; developing new methods of reaching out to workers; and piloting new forms of membership.

Across several of the employee surveys, young workers show a disproportionately high level of desire for union representation but a correspondingly low level of membership. It is likely that this is due to the kinds of employers for whom they work and the kind of employment they likely have. Youth tends to be concentrated in small workplaces, often working part-time or in casual or temporary jobs, and having much higher turnover rates than their older counterparts. Moreover, these workers are more likely to be vulnerable to more powerful employers and to be taken advantage of. Perhaps lower expectations, associated with low job tenure and the lack of investment in the job that this implies, explain their lower level of reported needs (chapter 1). Young workers also tend to have weakly formed attitudes—they'll record high "don't knows" on union questions—and low job tenure, which make their demand for unionism volatile and subject to change through experience. All these factors conspire to make them more difficult for unions to organize and, at the same time, easier to lose. First contact with these workers is critical in shaping subsequent attitudes toward unionism.

Unions will need to develop new models of organizing to get to these workers and workplaces. Whether this is via a sectoral focus on industries in which young workers predominate (fast food or retail, for example), or via a focus on particular employers (such as McDonald's), the other key component to a successful union strategy will be conveying to these workers the message about how to organize. Young workers are likely not to know their rights in the workplace or how to form a union. Some unions, such as the United Food and Commercial Workers in Canada, have created a separate youth department in which they deploy youth organizers (who are also young themselves) to organize workplaces from the inside as well as to educate young workers about their rights (Gunderson, Ponak, and Taras 2003).

Data from Canada, New Zealand, Australia, and Ireland also suggest that considerable unmet demand for unionism, or for voice generally, is in small organizations. Here it is most costly for unions to organize and also most important for members to be self-sufficient because of the high unit costs to unions of serving members in small businesses. It is an area that has been largely untouched by organizing campaigns in recent years. Formal structures such as works councils are least appropriate in small businesses, which are largely run along informal lines (Callus, Kitay, and Sutcliffe 1992). Compared to their peers in larger businesses, employees in small businesses are more likely to prefer directly dealing with management, though this does not mean that they are intrinsically opposed to collective representation over wages or even grievances (chapter 2).

Considerable unmet demand for unionism also exists in the secondary labor market generally (chapter 6). Again, these workers are more costly to organize (they are harder to find and to aggregate), and some may be less inclined to unionism (because of their lower attachment to the labor market), but the relatively high representation gap tells us that employee attitudes are not the main problem, and the rapid growth in unions such as the SEIU (Service Employees International Union) in the United States and LHMU (Liquor, Hospitality and Miscellaneous Union) in Australia suggests that these workers are not impossible to organize. What it does indicate, though, is that unions need very different approaches in small businesses and for secondary labor market workers. For these workers, for example, particular emphasis on developing networks across organizations, including through use of new technology, and providing the education and training to enable them to effectively stand up for themselves are actions that could be considered.

Unions focused on external organizing can also look at new techniques for reaching out to workers. Innovations in the use of Internet technology in particular are noteworthy. The AFL-CIO's Working America has created a coalition of community networks to promote social justice actions as well as unionization, making use of the Internet as a basic tool (chapter 1). Likewise, the SEIU's Purple Ocean links up grassroots organizations to participate in mass actions (for example, campaigns against changes to overtime laws), but without collective bargaining. The LabourStart website in New Zealand has been a platform for global activism (Price 2004). In the United Kingdom, the public-sector union, Unison, has a site for working students. Australian unions offer Workers Online, a news and information source for workers. Effective use of technology now appears to be critical for unions no matter where.

The main focus of some of these forms of outreach is on member recruitment as a first step to organizing, as advocated in effect by Kochan (chapter 9) who suggests that unions "will need a mix of social capital, service, professional networking, and community union models. The days of relying on dissatisfaction and protection from lousy employers has reached its end." Although organizing is a key element in effective large-scale recruitment in nonunion workplaces, rather than something that comes afterward, there are alternative routes that may need to be pursued when unions are unlikely to unionize a workplace in a reasonable amount of time. Along these lines, unions in the United States are beginning to look to new forms of union membership as a way to overcome the need for majority representation within a workplace. Some unions have begun to offer associate memberships and to create organizations of workers separate from their places of work. Washtech, the loose affiliation of high-tech workers at Microsoft, is an example of this sort of organization. Creating quasi-membership for nonmembers through web-based organizations is most relevant in the United States and Canada, where being in a nonunion workplace is synonymous with being a nonmember of a union. Through such associate memberships, unions can offer such workers access to collective resources and services without having to engage in collective bargaining. Eventually, though, unions will have to find ways to transition these members from virtual to real membership by using them to organize at the workplace.

Another method of outreach, instead of setting up quasi–community-based organizations, is to develop coalitions of interest with community groups and other nongovernmental organizations. Although community organizations—such as the Industrial Areas Foundation, which pioneered many of the same organizing principles as are now pursued by "organizing" unions—do not have the scale to provide effective voice at the workplace for workers (chapter 1), engagement with them by unions would provide an opportunity to leverage resources, support, and political pressure to be used on recalcitrant employers and governments.

Internal Organizing: Responding to Free Riding

In addition to organizing externally, by bringing union representation to workers in nonunion workplaces, unions in Australia, New Zealand, the United Kingdom, and Ireland face a considerable free-rider problem in the workplaces where they represent workers. Approximately two-fifths of all those covered by a collective agreement do not belong to the union.

The presence of free riders creates two problems. First, unions serving workers who do not support them financially by paying dues face a potential drain on their finite resources. Second, unions do not enjoy the same clout with management that they would if they had higher levels of membership in the workplace. Data from the New Zealand worker survey support this argument. In settings with a high degree of union membership, workers report greater levels of satisfaction with the influence they have at work (chapter 6). A focus on organizing free riders is important to ensure continued union strength and stability.

Free riders give a number of reasons for not joining. Up to two-thirds of those asked about their decision not to join the union at their workplace in Australia and New Zealand report that there is no point—they get the benefits of union membership anyway. In Ireland, three-quarters of nonmembers in unionized workplaces report that they simply have not been asked to join the union. Another large proportion of free riders claim that people doing the kind of job they do don't join unions (somehow union membership is not appropriate for them). About a quarter of the free riders surveyed in Ireland, New Zealand, the United Kingdom, and Australia simply reported that they disliked unions in principle, they didn't believe in unions, or that unions didn't achieve anything they valued. These three types of responses—get benefits anyway, people like me don't join, and I don't like unions—suggest three different avenues for unions to pursue with these potential members.

Canada, alone among these Anglo-American countries, has solved this problem. Through the imposition of Rand formula union security clauses into collective agreements, unions are ensured that even those who choose not to join the union pay for the services and benefits they receive from it. The financial health this brings to unions helps substantially to reduce the incidence of "frustrated nonmembers" who would rather be in a union (whose numbers are quite high in Australia, New Zealand, the United Kingdom, and the United States) by making it easier for unions to organize and effectively represent their members. Of course it does so at the expense of creating "unwilling conscripts" into unions. It is remarkable, however, that even in Canada the number of "unwilling conscripts" to unions (4 percent of all workers) is around one-third the number of "frustrated nonmembers" (12.5 percent of all workers) (chapter 2); and, overall, the number of people whose preferences do not match their situation is lower in Canada (16.5 percent) than in Australia or New Zealand.

Can Rand-style solutions be found in other jurisdictions? The Taft-Hartley Act in the United States makes Rand-style clauses illegal in the twenty-two states that have enacted right-to-work legislation. More positively for unions, recent amendments to labor legislation in New Zealand now allow bargaining fees (payment for union services as distinct from membership) to be negotiated and implemented subject to a secret ballot vote (chapter 6). Attempts in Australia to introduce similar fees have met with legislated resistance from the state. An alternative method might include "social obligation fees"—provisions that require all employees covered by the agreement to make a contribution to a voluntary organization of the employee's choice. Employees would no longer be able to free ride on union gains, yet there would still be no compulsion to join the union.

In the end, however, rather than relying on legal or institutional changes to rectify this situation, unions must rely on their own actions. Aside from promoting norms that discourage free riding, a focus on active recruiting within the unionized workplace is a simple first step. As mentioned above, many nonmembers in unionized workplaces—often as many as half or more—report not having ever been asked to join the union. A more involved second step is to focus on making the union a relevant institution in members' daily work lives. Several successful examples of how to organize internally come from unions operating in U.S. right-to-work states. Unions such as the Communications Workers of America have had considerable success operating with high membership rates in such states. By using a strategy that integrates political action, internal organizing, and the development of interorganizational linkages, the CWA has been able to grow, continue to represent its members effectively, innovate, and respond to environmental complexity (Katz, Batt, and Keefe 2003). For example, the CWA pursued growth through internal organizing in the former Bell affiliates, member-to-member organizing across companies, and mergers with other unions to gain better presence in the information-services industry. Moreover, the CWA has used novel contract language to secure card-check recognition and employer neutrality in new organizing (Katz, Batt, and Keefe 2003).

Organizing and the Requirements for Collectivist Behavior at Work

To organize in nonunion settings and to bring free riders into the union, unions will have to deal with differences in individuals' general orientations toward collective approaches to solving their workplace problems. Several of the worker surveys show that broadly expressed orientations—as measured by answers to questions such as "I prefer to deal with problems on my own" (Ireland); "working with others is usually more trouble than it is worth" (United Kingdom); and "would you feel more comfortable dealing with management yourself, or would you feel more comfortable having a group of your fellow employees help you deal with management?" (Canada)—do not usefully explain union involvement. Rather, a preference for specific collective institutional solutions is a function of experience with unionism (chapters 2 and 3).

The desire for collective or individual solutions is not something that people are born with. It is something very specific to context. Given this, unions must strategize about what is needed to develop and maintain collectivism (Peetz 2004). First, for collective behavior to exist and succeed there must be some identified collective needs (chapter 3). Second, there must be some collectivist attitude among potential members of the group, which requires a common social identity, cooperative values, and a belief that collective action is effective (Bandura 1997). Third, there must be some sort of coordinating capacity between members of a collective and mobilizers of action among those members. This logic is supported by data from the United Kingdom worker survey showing that workplace problems are fewer where unions are stronger (chapter 3).

Thinking about collectivism this way suggests several matters for unions that want to organize successfully. A key issue is building a sense of collective identity among union members that includes promoting norms that encourage collective behavior, developing social capital among members (Jarley and Johnson 2003), and encouraging union members to cooperate with one another—and not just with the employer. At the same time, unions need to ensure that this work is not undone because the cooperative behavior of members is subverted by the free riding of nonmembers (Crouch 1982; Olson 1965). Unions will also have to ensure that employees perceive that their union membership brings with it power and a sense of ongoing involvement in a collective that is providing real benefits (Bandura 1997; Crosby 2005). To deliver these real benefits, unions in turn will have to ensure workplace leaders have the skills required to coordinate members' behavior, mobilize them when necessary, and manage an ongoing relationship with the employer with simultaneous elements of conflicting interest and cooperation (Crosby 2005). None of this is new to unions, but it does suggest that unions will need sophisticated strategies, highly trained workplace representatives, and considerable resources to ensure that this vitally important work gets done.

Unions and Workplace Voice

A large proportion of workers surveyed in these countries indicated their desire for some form of cooperation between workers and management. In the United States the vast majority of union and nonunion members desire a workplace-based organization that is jointly run by employees and management (chapter 1). Seventy percent of Australian workers surveyed reported wanting unions and management to cooperate to resolve workplace issues (chapter 5). Similarly, a majority of workers surveyed in the United Kingdom favor legislation that would require employers to meet regularly with employees or their representatives to take up issues that affect the workplace and working life (Diamond and Freeman 2002, exhibit 20). In all cases, employees report wanting a working relationship between workers or their representatives and the employer in which formal decision-making mechanisms grant employees real influence. Where this occurs, employees report higher overall job satisfaction (Ireland), a higher incidence of high-commitment work practices (Canada), and overwhelmingly rate the committees as effective (Australia and New Zealand).

Employees surveyed in these six Anglo-American countries desire a relationship that involves ongoing involvement and negotiation with the employer throughout the period of the collective agreement that resolves conflict and recognizes and works on areas of common interest. However, true cooperation—genuinely reciprocal behavior—is a fine balance. On the one hand, cooperation is not simply acquiescence to management's agenda. Nor, on the other hand, is it a series of ongoing conflicts with management. In fact, in getting to cooperative workplace relations and an eventual alignment of interests, employees want management more than unions to shift their position. Australian union members are more vigorous in demanding that management cooperate more with unions (82 percent) than that unions cooperate more with management (66 percent) (chapter 5). A similar pattern exists in New Zealand. Yet, despite calling for more cooperation, workers almost unanimously want unions to continue to vigorously defend their interests (chapters 5 and 6). Indeed, union members in Australia are more willing to take conflictual action against the employer when they perceive their union to have been cooperative (Peetz 1998).

So what institutional form should these formal channels of worker and management information sharing and decision making take? What do workers report that they want? Employees report that they want to have joint consultative committees in which workers have real power. In New Zealand, committees for which employees select their representatives, worker representatives volunteer, or some mixture of methods (but not management appointment of worker representatives) enjoy effectiveness ratings twenty or more percentage points higher than committees to which management appoints worker representatives. Forty-five percent of workers surveyed in the United States would choose an institution that elected employee representatives and relied on an outside arbitrator to resolve disputes with management as their first choice for representation at work. A majority of nonunion workers surveyed in the United Kingdom want some form of formal workplace representation, with 29 percent desiring a works council and another 27 percent desiring a works council *and* a union. Not only are workers reporting that they do want real voice and influence on the job, they are also reporting that they know when they do not have it. Data from the Irish survey show that the incidence of workplace consultative committees is low (14 percent of workers surveyed had one in their workplace). In most cases, employee representatives are merely informed of upcoming changes by management with no input into decision making. With this limited and highly circumscribed form of voice it is no surprise that Irish workers report little influence at the workplace.

Capability Development

Given workers' high levels of desire for engagement and real cooperation (not acquiescence) with management over workplace decision making, unions need to prepare themselves to deal effectively in this context. Perhaps the first hurdle to overcome is the need for effective reciprocal behavior. The desire for cooperation is nothing new. It reflects the inherently contradictory nature of the employment relationship that has existed since the foundation of capitalism— workers and employers simultaneously have conflicting interests over the distribution of income and power, but their immediate interests coincide in as much as the survival and prosperity of the employing organization is necessary for employees' job security and wage growth. Moreover, daily overt conflict is not a pleasant experience for either party.

Many of the prerequisites for true cooperation are no different now than they were a century ago and are not necessarily inconsistent with a traditional union strategy based simply on organizing and collective bargaining. Chief among these is trust: despite conflicting interests, parties can still have a fundamentally reciprocal relationship if they believe they can trust the other party—that the other party speaks the truth and keeps its word. A second prerequisite for meaningful cooperation is mutual recognition: parties cannot behave reciprocally if one seeks to deny or prevent the existence of the other. And while the practice of most U.S. employers and a substantial number of Australian, British, and Irish employers has been to do precisely this to unions, there is nothing about developing internal union capabilities that seeks to deny the legitimacy of employers or management. The best way for a union to ensure that cooperation is between equals is through strength and an effective mobilized presence at the workplace (Boxall and Haynes 1997). A common theme throughout the worker surveys is that workers want to see that their union has sufficient clout to get things done. They need to be able to see that the union has the ability to maintain recognition from the employer, using collective action where necessary, and that it is able to secure changes from the employer that are in workers' favor. As we saw in the United Kingdom (chapter 3), needs are lower where unions are taken seriously by management and good relations exist between the parties.

The second important step is finding a way for unions to be increasingly open and responsive to worker needs. In the six country surveys, workers report wanting the ability to influence decisions and behavior not only of their employer but also of their union. In the United Kingdom, unions' biggest weakness is their perceived lack of openness and accountability (chapter 3). Australian evidence also shows how crucial members' perceptions of union democracy are in shaping the desire to stay in a union (Peetz 1998; Peetz and Pocock 2005). Workers expect their unions to both notice employee problems and do something about them. This means they want two-way communication and a reciprocal relationship with their union. The survey data also show the problems unions experience when they treat the union-to-member relationship as a remote transactional service relationship. Successful changes in union strategy are moving away from this traditional transactional, servicing approach.

A third important step is setting out a worker agenda for workplace change. If the union is to engage with management on behalf of its members it must have some set of goals it is trying to reach. Workers, too, need to know that the union's agenda is one that is sensitive to and aware of their issues. This cannot be managed, however, if the union office is imposing its views on what members in the workplace should be doing. Rather, members at the workplace need to be empowered and allowed to advance an agenda that reflects their needs. Obviously, individual workplaces cannot be allowed to depart significantly from overall common union objectives or to identify too strongly with employer interests at the expense of their own collective interests. Thus, the union organization must play a role in shaping workplace-level expectations. This can be done through information sharing, the giving of advice, and keeping in contact with the workplace—a practice more effective than one that relies on rules and dictates. The Canadian Auto Workers union provides a good example of a union skilled in balancing this tension. Local unions within the CAW have developed autonomy, activism, and vibrancy. This is combined with national union-developed policies based on primary research and transmitted through a forum where national and local-level leaders meet to debate, discuss, and argue over issues of relevance to the union's members. The result is a union that operates democratically, provides workers with a voice in the workplace, and promotes democratic causes in the broader society (Frost 2000). Doing this has enabled the CAW to keep a union agenda for change in front of its members so that the employer's agenda does not take precedence and become workers' only point of reference.

Once a union has an agenda that is relevant to members and supported by them, it needs a way to advance this agenda in the workplace. This requires investments in internal organizing at the workplace to empower members to do things for themselves rather than rely on the union office to do it for them remotely. For this strategy to be successful, the union must be able to construct or build up existing workplace structures and develop workplace networks, including an active delegate structure, engaged workplace committees, and dynamic local leaders. In between periods of activism focused around negotiating new agreements, union-based networks among members can maintain enthusiasm for unionism (Jarley and Johnson 2003). Through this, the union will be able to develop workplace activism among the membership more broadly. The workplace-based union will then be supported by the union office through an organizer with the provision of training and information, and some servicing functions.

Training for local union leaders to engage with management effectively becomes important. This includes not only the elected union executive at the workplace but also the broader network of stewards or delegates. This training and development will be most successful if it encourages workers to take responsibility for interacting with their management counterparts, to know what they want and tactics for going about getting it—and not to simply sit back and rely on "the union" as some off-site institution to deliver it to them—and to realize that *they* are the union and that it is through their own activism that the union is able to achieve its objectives.

A Summary of the Lessons Learned

Unions need to reinvent themselves while still maintaining their traditional core mission of representing employee collective interests in the workplace. Organizing, both internally and externally, will remain the key to achieving this objective. However, how unions go about organizing will be the challenge they now face. They need to appeal to workers who traditionally have not been their members and to workers who face a different set of constraints at work: part-time employment, contingent employment contracts, and high turnover. Only a few unions have made the major changes internally that are needed to succeed in the new environment.

Once organized, new members must then be brought into the union as active and involved members. Internal union democracy is important to workers; they want a say in the governance of their union and about the direction the union pursues vis-à-vis their daily life at work. Unions require the active involvement of their members, which is not simply conflict with the employer or a burst of activism when a new agreement is negotiated. Rather, active involvement of members encompasses effective participation of members in ongoing structures and processes of consultation and workplace governance. In workplaces where such institutions (such as joint labor-management committees or works councils) exist, they can be promoted by unions, staffed with active members, and eventually deliver benefits to workers in the firm.

However, to be effective in this new context, unions will require a new set of capabilities. Constructing a union vision for workplace change and ensuring it is communicated effectively to members is central to shaping how worker representatives engage with management in the workplace. The ability to cooperate with management from a position of strength is also a key requirement. Without strength, worker interests are often ignored. Yet, the random overuse of union power may end in conflict with management—something the worker surveys repeatedly said workers do not want. Finally, having a vibrant network of union-trained member activists within the workplace will help unions in at least two critical ways. First, it will make engagement with the employer on the union's agenda much more likely. Second, where a free-rider problem exists, it will help to build the union within the workplace.

There are enough similarities across these six Anglo-American countries in context, institutions, and competitive environment to make learning from one another not only possible but highly practical. All unions are not the same. Freeman and Bryson (chapter 3) point out that unions differ in their policies and practices in ways associated with effectiveness. Frost (2001) similarly documented differences in union responses to the need for workplace restructuring and linked these various strategies to divergent outcomes—some successful, some not. Going forward, it will be important to identify how successful unions have maintained the activism and involvement of their members at the workplace over time. How unions address new organizing and design innovative ways to attract new workers should also be monitored.

The challenges before unions are significant: new employment relations, often hostile employers, and less than accommodating policy regimes. Despite this, workers in these six Anglo-American countries are reporting a continued desire for collective representation and for formal involvement in decision making in their workplaces. Unions are well placed to fulfill these roles. A process of renewal through an ongoing commitment to organizing, both internally and externally, and a careful consideration of how best to engage proactively with members, and on behalf of members with the employer, will ensure that unions remain vibrant institutions in these countries.

Chapter 8

Why Should Employers Bother with Worker Voice?

JOHN PURCELL AND KONSTANTINOS GEORGIADIS

The Anglo-American voice project reveals some remarkably similar trends across the six countries. There are, inevitably, variations, with different levels of change, different proportions of employees in unions, and a variety of forms of voice, but five common trends are evident. First, there has been a widespread and consistent decline in union membership, especially in the private sector of these economies. The most recent data in the United Kingdom show little sign that the decline has stopped, expect perhaps in larger firms (Kersley et al. 2005).[1] The proportion of establishments with ten or more workers with no union members present grew from 57 percent in 1998 to 64 percent in 2004. Union recognition fell from one-third of workplaces in 1998 to 27 percent in 2004, with coverage of collective bargaining in terms of the number of employees shrinking from 53 percent to 48 percent. Second, the use of collective bargaining as a means of determining terms and conditions of employment, the sine qua non of industrial relations in the middle years of the twentieth century, has declined in all countries in the private sector. In the United Kingdom in 2004 in this sector, pay was unilaterally set by management in 79 percent of

---

[1] The 2004 Workplace Employment Relations Survey is the latest in a series of large-scale surveys, first started in 1980, of employment relations in the United Kingdom. The previous survey was in 1998 and allows for comparisons with changes since then. The 2004 survey was undertaken in 2,295 workplaces with five or more employees with a separate survey of 991 worker representatives in these establishments and a survey completed by 22,451 employees.

workplaces, whether on site or at a higher level. Third, there has been a marked growth in all countries in employers' use of direct forms of employee involvement. These types of voice mechanisms, which involve employees without representative intermediaries, usually cover such practices as briefing systems or communication chains, quality circles or problem-solving groups, meetings with all employees (town hall meetings), types of team work giving employees some discretion, employee surveys, and other types of upward communication and regular information sharing. In the United Kingdom, the 2004 data show that there has been a further modest growth in direct involvement, continuing the trend established twenty years ago with workforce meetings and/or team briefings now being almost universal (82 percent in the private sector and 96 percent in the public sector). Fourth, the development of indirect forms of employee voice, in which worker representatives meet with management, such as employee forums, works councils, or joint consultative committees (JCCs), varies significantly, but JCCs are much more likely to be found in workplaces or enterprises where unions have a presence. The exception to this trend is the United States, where it is legally more difficult to establish such bodies. The 2004 British data show that the incidence of JCCs has fallen, especially in smaller establishments, after a period of growth, to just 14 percent compared to 20 percent in 1998. Meanwhile, in multisite firms, higher level JCCs have also declined slightly from 27 percent to 25 percent (Kersley et al. 2005).

In sum, unions are in decline, employers commonly use direct-voice systems, and some, always a minority, also use indirect mechanisms. Whether despite, or because of, these trends, the final, major conclusion is that workers are unequivocal in all countries in experiencing a gap between the type of voice they want to have at work and what they get. Yet, while more voice is wanted, this is far from nascent adversarialism or a desire to return to old-style industrial relations. The desire for cooperative relationships between management and labor is as true for union members as it is for nonmembers, including those who would join the union if they had the opportunity and those who believe the union is not for them.

What all this means for employers is that they are not likely to face aggressive demands for more voice from their employees. The situation is very different from the time when strikes were often used to force union recognition. Indeed, the trend lines suggest that the need for such a "forced" employer response to meet worker voice needs will continue to diminish. About the only circumstances in which employers may be forced to provide employee involvement opportunities is when they are compelled to do so by legislation. This is happening in the United Kingdom and Ireland as a result of the EU Directive on Information and Consultation, but even here there is a wide range of options for employers, including doing nothing. Thus, while workers ideally want more voice, there is little evidence that they have the capacity, or inclination, to turn aspiration into reality. The future of employee voice is largely in the hands of employers. Why should they bother? In this chapter we suggest four dominant reasons and assesses the evidence so far available for each, with particular reference to the United Kingdom, but drawing comparable material from other countries where possible. We pose the following questions:

- Does employee voice contribute to improved organizational performance?

- Does employee voice provide a successful means for dealing with employee problems or causes of grievances?

- Is employee voice an effective means of reducing demand for unionization, the union substitution effect?

- Do employers increasingly implement employee voice because it is more socially desirable or necessary to do so?

Does Employee Voice Contribute to Improved Organizational Performance?

The rhetoric is, at times, deafening. For example, in justifying the U.K. adoption of the EU Directive on Information and Consultation, which gives employees rights to be informed and to be consulted on key employment issues, the government stated:

> It is expected that there will be substantial economic and social benefits from the legislation over time. Effective employee information and consultation systems are a key enabler of high performance workplaces. . . . Employers should see gains from a better informed, more motivated and committed workforce. This should lead to a greater ability to react rapidly to opportunities and threats, and a lower staff turnover, thereby ultimately enhancing a company's productivity. . . . Given the nature of these benefits it is hard to quantify them. However, we estimate that they are in the order of magnitudes of hundreds of millions of pounds over a ten year period (DTI 2004, 2).

Gospel and Willman (2003b) note in their review of the background issues to the directive that there is no justification for this assertion of a voice-performance link. This is a little harsh, but certainly the evidence is thin or at least questionable. There is some evidence of a positive outcome effect from the use of direct forms of involvement and especially when this is combined with indirect JCC types of voice systems, for example in the automobile components sector in Europe (Sako 1998) Vandenberg, Richard, and Eastman (1999) found in the insurance industry in North America that employees' perceptions of involvement in decisionmaking in terms of their power, information provision, rewards, and knowledge of the business was related to performance outcomes seen in employees' intentions to quit and the company's return on equity.

There is, however, surprisingly little research directly focused on the relationship between organizational performance and the adoption of direct, indirect, and combined (both direct and indirect applied in unison) types of employee voice. There are a number of reasons for this. There is little agreement on what constitutes employee voice. Some researchers, mainly from the United States, focus exclusively on direct forms; others, more often from Europe and antipodes, cover both types, while a few make unionization central to their study. A further problem is that it has proved very hard to isolate the influence of voice systems per se from other workplace initiatives such as those found in high-performance work systems (see Godard 2004) or high-involvement work systems (Pil and MacDuffie 1996). For example, Appelbaum et al. (2000) include "opportunity to participate" as one of the three dimensions in high-performance work systems in the three manufacturing sectors they studied. The others were generating worker ability and providing worker motivation. The combination of ability, motivation, and opportunity was associated with positive outcome effects. From an employer's perspective, then, it is not possible to assert unequivocally that there is strong evidence showing that employee voice improves performance. "Not proven" would be a better judgment, but more thoughtful employers might also note that voice opportunities combined with other features of good business practices can have, as Vandenberg et al. express it, "mutually reinforcing attributes" (1999, 305).

This less than positive conclusion about the direct effect of worker voice on performance may also be explained by the problem of measuring performance and the way performance outcomes, such as return on equity, are so remote or distal from workers' experience of participation. This familiar problem in research on the link between human resource management and performance is often referred to as the "black box problem." The need is to show how human resource management, or in this case employee voice, could be linked to performance by exploring the causal chains between the adoption of types of employee voice, workers' experience of them, and the way they are linked to or associated with positive attitudes about work. These positive attitudes toward the job, and commitment to the organization, are then predicted to lower the intention to leave and to be linked to positive behaviors and thence to performance. Once we model the causal chain linking policy, including voice, to performance, the fulcrum is the effect of the employees' experience of the practices on their attitudes and subsequently on their behavior, seen in the performance of the task and in discretionary activity, sometimes referred to as "going the extra mile," and in their willingness to stay with their employer (Purcell and Kinnie 2006). This suggests that, instead of jumping straight to a search for proof that employee voice has a positive performance outcome effect, it is more useful to see whether workers' experience of forms of employee voice is linked to their work-related attitudes. These would typically include affective organizational commitment, job satisfaction, and levels of discretion employees report having in their jobs.

We use the United Kingdom WERS 1998 data drawn from 2,186 workplaces and twenty-five thousand employees to explore whether direct forms of involvement, indirect systems such as JCCs, and both combined is associated with such "positive" attitudes. There is a clear affirmation of such a link. In our analysis we use a tight definition of voice systems that included their being embedded in the organization. That is, they have a degree of permanence and a regularity of use. We find that 68.1 percent of workplaces with ten or more employees had direct-only arrangements and 26.6 percent had dual systems (both direct and indirect). The incidence of indirect only (e.g., JCCs) was so low (five workplaces only) that it had to be excluded from further analysis. Only 3.3 percent of establishments had no voice arrangements reported by the management respondent. Merging both the managers' and employees' surveys and controlling for financial participation, the presence of a range of human resource policies normally associated with high-commitment management, and both company and workforce data, we evaluated the relationship between the existence of types of voice and employee attitudes toward aspects of work and the working environment. A clear, significant relationship can be seen, with organizational commitment (three questions, alpha = .84), intrinsic job satisfaction (three questions, alpha = .76), and job discretion (three questions, alpha = .78)(see table 8.1). In all three models, both direct and dual systems of voice have positive associations with these employee attitudinal variables. If we separate out the effects of direct and indirect voice, then it is clear, from the perspective of the employee, that access to direct voice is more powerful in influencing attitudes than access to indirect voice. This is not surprising since indirect representation is, by its nature, more remote. The effect of the dual systems was almost 10 percent stronger than the effect of direct systems for all dependent variables.[2] Therefore, in line with previous research, the existence of dual-voice systems was found to have the strongest link with employee attitudes.

In sum, employers wanting definitive proof that employee voice improves organizational performance are likely to be disappointed. If, however, a longer-term perspective is taken concerning the quality of working life and work-

---

[2] Since all the relationships are significant at the same level, we can directly compare the size of the standardized beta coefficients.

TABLE 8.1
Relationship between presence of voice systems and employee attitudes

	Organizational commitment	Job satisfaction	Job discretion
Direct only	0.185***	0.123***	0.182***
Dual	0.209***	0.132***	0.210***
R^2	0.117	0.102	0.112
F	34.628	31.068	33.197
N	22,871	22,986	22,920

Source: WERS 98 data base (see Cully et al. 1999).
Notes: *** $p < 0.001$. For controls used in regression analysis, see endnote 3.

related attitudes, then the evidence so far suggests that the use of voice systems has positive effects, especially if dual systems are used. These, in turn, can be expected to feed through to more proximal indicators of organizational effectiveness such as quitting rates, absenteeism, and worker performance in those areas in which their behavior has a direct impact, such as quality.

Does Employee Voice Provide a Means for Dealing with Employee Grievances?

The research into the representation gap looks at worker needs or problems and assesses the extent to which different voice arrangements appear to meet or satisfy these needs or stop them from erupting. The evidence is clear. For example, Freeman reports that in the United States "needs differ by human resource policies. Workplaces with open door policies to deal with group problems have 30 percent fewer needs compared to workplaces without such policies. . . . the presence of a human resource department raises the number of problems modestly." (chapter 1 in this book). Bryson and Freeman (chapter 3), using two sources of data, WERS 1998 and the British Workplace and Representation and Participation Survey (BWRPS) find much the same results in the United Kingdom:

> The BWRPS asked workers about an open door policy, joint consultative committees, a grievance system, and a human resource department. Regression analysis of the number of needs/problems on the presence of these practices (and other determinants of needs/problems) shows that joint consultative committees and open door policies reduced the number of needs, while the other two had little or no effect. The WERS . . . re-

gression analysis shows that regular meetings with management and the presence of quality circles reduce the number of workplace needs.

Given these findings, it would seem to be sensible for employers to adopt voice regimes to reduce worker needs or problems. Voice systems can allow needs or problems to be expressed and dealt with and can help minimize the causes of the problems. The use of open door policies, meetings with the workforce, and quality circles or similar problem-solving groups in direct involvement, and JCCs in indirect schemes, seem particularly effective. They should note, too, that the mere presence of a human resource department is not effective in this regard. What is required is the creation of voice systems, especially a combination of direct and indirect methods. It is the establishment of voice arrangements that has an impact in addressing worker needs, not a human resource department following the dictates of Ulrich (1996) to be "an employee champion." Employees need their own champions and the means to express their views.

Why might the creation of voice systems have this effect of reducing worker needs? We examined the data to explore the extent to which employee relations had been given more prominence by workplace management when they had direct or dual-voice systems in operation compared with the year before the survey. The evidence is consistent, showing that in those British workplaces that have embedded direct forms of voice, and especially in those with dual arrangements, managers report that employee relations is more often taken into account in goal setting, decision making, and supervisory roles, and more information is provided to employees (table 8.2).

These data show how dual forms of voice are particularly influential in the higher-level activities of goal setting, decision making, and providing information. This helps to explain why dual systems consistently outperform direct-only means of employee voice. Between 1998 and 2004 direct involvement

TABLE 8.2
Aspects of the management of employee relations and types of employee voice

	Supervisors' responsibility for employee relations matters	Importance of ER in setting goals and objectives	Amount of information provided to employees	Amount of employee influence in decision making
Direct only	0.222**	0.378***	0.294***	0.138*
Both direct and indirect	0.225*	0.528***	0.479***	0.264**
R^2	0.107	0.182	0.161	0.139
F	4.852	9.033	7.771	6.523
N	1822	1828	1828	1826

Source: WERS 98 data base (see Cully et al. 1999).
Note: * $p < 0.05$, ** $p < 0.01$, *** $p < 0.001$

continued to grow in the United Kingdom, but indirect forms declined. If employers want to deal with worker needs effectively, they need to use both methods. As we have shown, this is associated with positive attitudinal outcomes.

For its part, direct involvement is important in influencing the nature of the relationship between employees and their managers. We were able to obtain workers' judgments of "how good their managers were" at keeping everyone up to date with proposed changes, allowing for comments on changes, responding to suggestions, treating employees fairly, dealing with workplace problems, as well as their views about the overall quality of employment relations (six questions, alpha = .92). Although these issues were positively related to the presence of direct and dual-voice systems in the workplace, direct systems of voice were particularly important. Of course, in a cross-sectional survey of this kind, it is impossible to say whether direct-voice systems influenced management behavior as perceived by employees, or whether "good" managers were more likely to introduce voice systems. What we can say is that they are correlated.

The effect of indirect voice is seen in information flows. In comparing direct-only, dual, and no-voice systems in terms of four different types of information provided by management, it can be seen that there are significant differences between companies that use these different approaches with regard to the regularity of information provision about investment plans, staffing plans, and the financial position of the whole organization and the establishment (table 8.3). It is more likely that regular information is given to employees when dual systems are in place, less likely when direct-only forms exist, and even less when none exist.

In sum, there is very clear evidence that the existence of direct and indirect-voice systems has the capacity both to limit the number of issues or problems listed by employees as matters they want resolved and to deal with them when they arise. Employee voice matters to employees and it should matter to employers concerned with worker well-being and the social life of the enterprise.

TABLE 8.3
Extent to which management regularly provides information by type of voice system (Percent of establishments)

	Investment plans	Financial position of establishment	Financial position of whole organization	Staffing plans
No voice	23.9%	31.0%	30.3%	33.8%
Direct only	53.6	67.8	67.7	60.1
Dual	66.2	84.7	77.1	76.4
All	56.2	71.4	69.9	63.9

Source: WERS 98 data base (see Cully et al. 1999)

Dual-voice systems have this beneficial effect because they appear to give more weight to matters of employee relations in workplace decision making and in the way managers lead and interact with employees. Dual voice is also linked to the provision of information, which is symptomatic of greater transparency and accountability. Employee satisfaction with communication has consistently been shown to be related to higher levels of organizational commitment (Kinnie et al. 2005).

Is Employee Voice an Effective Means of Reducing Demand for Unionization?

Union substitution occurs in a number of ways. Employers sometimes create nonunion representative systems with or without direct involvement in the hope that the desire of workers to join unions will dissipate. On union sites, the creation of nonunion representative methods is sometimes used to restrict union negotiations to a narrow agenda related to the annual (or less frequent) pay round, thereby reducing the scope for solidaristic action. It may also help persuade the union to enter into a "partnership" or more cooperative relationship in order to broaden the scope of issues included in joint discussions, but not necessarily joint regulation, and may encourage free riding.

An informed human resource manager could not fail to draw powerful conclusions from the research reported in this book on the value of nonunion voice systems in reducing the demand for unions. This manager would note that in all Anglo-American countries, with the notable exception of the United States, employers are largely neutral about unions. Relatively few are overtly antiunion, and these tend, in the United Kingdom at least, to be in smaller stand-alone workplaces that are sometimes owner managed or, as in Ireland, in some U.S.-owned multinational corporations. This neutrality implies willingness to work with unions if required but often a preference not to. If unions are seen to "cause" problems, this nonunion preference will be reinforced. Our informed manager, who reads that in British unionized workplaces "union members reported . . . 4.69 problems, while nonmembers reported 3.26 problems, [and] at nonunionized workplaces, members reported 5.04 problems, while nonmembers reported 2.95 problems" (chapter 3) would be likely to want to find ways to discourage union membership. This view would be reinforced when he or she reads that "on-site union representation engenders greater critical awareness on the part of workers and perhaps increases voice-induced complaining" (Bryson 2004, 235). The use of direct and indirect-voice systems may be one of the most effective means of union substitution from an employer's perspective, since they appear to be effective in dealing with workplace issues.

Bryson, in his careful analysis of the WERS 1998 data, concludes that "in general, non-union voice is more effective than union voice in eliciting managerial responsiveness in British workplaces, and direct voice is more effective than representative voice (whether union or non-union)" (2004, 234). He notes that, in delivering benefits to employees, the combination of nonunion representative voice with direct voice is "more effective than any other voice regime" (Bryson 2004, 234). In so doing, the number of problems or issues falls and desire for unionization dissipates. Bryson and Freeman suggest (chapter 3) that "over half of nonunion workers would not want unions if works councils were widely available." Very similar conclusions are drawn elsewhere:

United States. "Conditional on the number of needs, 'progressive' human resource practices, such as employee involvement programs and open door programs, are associated with lower worker desire for unions. Regression analysis shows that EI participants are ten percentage points less likely to say they would vote union in an NLRB election than workers in firms without EI programs, holding fixed the number of needs that workers report" (chapter 1 in this book).

Canada. "Employers in Canada have increasingly tapped into employee voice in a direct fashion through various mechanisms: employee involvement schemes, work teams, quality circles, suggestion schemes, nonunion grievance systems, and problem-solving groups. . . . This is part and parcel of the trend toward 'progressive' human resource management." (chapter 2)

Such a preference for nonunion voice channels, especially nonunion employee forums or JCCs, can be explained in many ways and by using a variety of ideological lenses. Taking the perspective of those employers who are neutral or opposed to unions, one reason for their preference is the different nature of the relationship with nonunion employee representatives compared to that with union shop stewards. For example, our informed human resource manager would take note of findings concerning the election or appointment of employee representatives. In 52 percent of nonunion sites with employee representatives, these either "volunteered" or were appointed by management. Where this occurred, "managers were much more likely to regard the committee as being 'very influential'" (Cully et al. 1999, 101–2). Evidence from WERS 2004 provides some clues as to why this might be so. Managers and representatives, both union and nonunion, were asked about the level of trust between them. "The proportion of workplaces in which both parties agreed that they could trust the other . . . was much higher in respect of management/non-union relationships (64 percent) than management/union relations (31 percent). Trust was one-sided in 46 percent of workplaces with union representatives and 29 percent of workplaces with nonunion representatives" (Kersley et al. 2005, 16). It is possible, on the basis of the published data, to explore this one step further. Two-thirds of managers said that they trusted their union shop stewards, but three-quarters said they trusted the nonunion representatives where they existed. Reversing the position, only 44 percent of union stewards trusted their managers compared to 81 percent of nonunion representatives. Managers are much more likely to trust union shop stewards than the shop stewards are to trust management, a gap of 20 percent. By contrast, more nonunion representatives trust their management than are trusted by them!

Managers are much more likely to be working in relatively low-trust adversarial environments when dealing with union shop stewards than when they are interacting with nonunion representatives. And they are likely to see more of union stewards than nonunion representatives, since only a quarter of shop stewards work less than one hour a week on employee relations matters compared to three-fifths of nonunion representatives (Kersley et al. 2005, 14). When they do meet union stewards, it is more likely that they will be dealing with disputes. Three-quarters of union shop stewards report spending time dealing with discipline and grievance matters, while only 44 percent of nonunion representatives do so. There is a paradox here. Union shop stewards have relatively low levels of trust in management and spend more time in dealing with disputes and other employee-relations matters than nonunion representatives, yet they are less effective at resolving issues as reported by employees. One possible reason for this is that, with the exception of grievance handling, nonunion representatives discuss a wider range of issues with their management than union shop stewards do (table 8.4). In particular, issues associated with recruitment and selection, training, and performance appraisal are noticeably more often the subject of joint discussions with nonunion representatives. In short, the evidence is that employers tend more often to create the type of high-trust partnership relationship with nonunion representative bodies than they do, or are able to do, with unions and their elected representatives.

The evidence, then, is clear for those managers wanting to find ways of reducing union impact and membership and of avoiding recognition. The use of nonunion voice systems in employee forums, such as JCCs, matched with direct forms of involvement, are pretty effective forms of union substitution. But there are costs. Effective employee involvement means giving greater priority to employee-relations matters and a willingness to discuss a wide range of issues with employee representatives as well as allowing the time and providing the resources for direct-voice systems to work. Merely adopting the structures of employee voice is not enough. There needs to be commitment and man-

TABLE 8.4
Topics handled jointly by management and worker representatives.
(Percent of establishments with employee representatives)

	Union representatives	Nonunion representatives
Pay and conditions	68.2%	71.9%
Recruitment/selection	52.6	61.2
Training	58.6	70.2
Systems of payment	54.4	61.2
Handling grievances	86.1	74.2
Staffing	64.8	67.9
Equal opportunities	63.7	63.1
Health and safety	83.6	87.6
Performance appraisal	49.2	64.7

Source: WERS 98 data base (see Cully et al. 1999).

agerial responsiveness to workers' needs to make nonunion voice systems effective.

Giving priority to union substitution is slightly perverse since it elevates the union "problem" to the dominant issue at a time when unions in all countries are in decline. In any case, managers who are opposed to unions are also likely to oppose voice arrangements that is, all forms of employee representation and the sharing of governance. In Australia, for example, it was found that "where employees perceive that their management is opposed to unions, a range of nonunion voice practices, including an open door policy, regular staff meetings, and joint consultative committees, are less likely to exist" (chapter 5). Such employers are now clearly in the minority. This is reinforced by the common findings in this book that voice systems are much more likely to be found in workplaces where unions already have a presence. This complementarity has more to do with the growth of new forms of managing employment relations than with rather dated, zero-sum games between management and unions. Nevertheless, the position is clear. Managements that want to avoid unions will often find that the adoption of nonunion employee voice channels will be effective. This form of competition with unions in providing benefits to employees has been a common feature of sophisticated employer response to unionization for many years (Bain 1970).

**Do Employers Implement Employee Voice Because
It Is More Socially Desirable or Necessary?**

A final explanation for why employers adopt worker voice is that it reflects changing employer, and societal, attitudes toward employment relations and the management of the human resource. Institutional pressures to encourage employers to create employee voice channels have been growing. Using DiMaggio and Powell's (1983) classic framework of mimetic, normative, and coercive pressures toward organizational isomorphism, we can observe evidence of all three forms of pressure to develop employee voice systems. First, as the institutions of industrial relations that developed in the first half of the twentieth century are dismantled (Purcell 1995), new approaches have emerged. There is little evidence of a return to the unfettered management prerogative. This is clear in New Zealand (chapter 6) where there has been a remarkable growth in consultation and the evidence suggests it is "generally robust." Here the complementary nature of worker voice with trade union presence is very apparent. Two-thirds of workplaces with a union presence reported the existence of a consultative committee compared with just over one-third without unions. In workplaces where managers' attitudes to unions were positive the incidence of consultative committees was greater. In Australia too (chapter 5), nonunion arrangements were found to complement rather than to compete with union voice.

These trends suggest that new normative pressures are emerging that are likely to influence management decision making. Beliefs and values about what behavior is socially legitimate, including employee voice, and evidence of them, filters through into accepted practice. This is, in all probability, a part of wider changes in corporate values concerned with social responsibility and stakeholder pluralism (Goshal 2005).

A particularly interesting example of institutional pressures for isomorphism is taking place in the United Kingdom and Ireland. Unlike their Continental counterparts, neither country has historically provided workers with formal legal entitlements to information and consultation. This has now changed with the adoption of the Information and Consultation Directive, which came into force, in the main, in 2005. The enforcement mechanisms clearly add to the coercive pressure for the introduction of employee voice systems.

The traditional approach in the United Kingdom, rather like other Anglo-American countries, was the adoption of a voluntary system within the workplace and an assumption that unions, where recognized, were the legitimate voice of employees. In the 1980s and 1990s, as various EU directives were introduced that required some form of consultation with employees (e.g., in layoffs and company mergers or takeovers), successive governments maintained this union-based position. If a union was recognized, it should be consulted. If there was no union in the workplace, then the directive would appear not to apply, at least in the requirement for collective consultation. The European Court of Justice, in a succession of judgments, found the lack of consultative rights in the growing number of nonunion workplaces unsatisfactory. It changed the requirement for consultation from an exclusive right given to unions, where they are recognized, to a universal right provided to employees. By the late 1990s, it was established that all employees had the right to elect representatives who had to be consulted by their employer in particular circumstances. This was not a general provision but was restricted to one-off consultation dealing with redundancies and mergers and a few other circumstances. In addition, large international companies are now required, if asked by a small minority of their employees, to establish a European works council with directly elected representatives from each European country where they have 150 or more employees. This shift in public policy from a reliance on unions to universal rights enjoyed by all employees has been fundamental in shifting the parameters of the debate on the need for, and value of, voice arrangements.

In April 2005, this was taken considerably further and may well mark a watershed in British and Irish employment relations. The Information and Consultation of Employees (ICE) regulations apply to all enterprises with 150 or more employees, and after April 2007 to those with 100 or more employees, and by April 2008 to the lower threshold of 50 employees. Three-quarters of all workplaces will fall within the scope of the directive. In brief, the directive establishes the rights of employees to receive information about their employer's business situation. In addition, employers have an obligation to inform and consult on likely developments relating to employment and an enhanced obligation to inform and consult about decisions likely to lead to substantial changes in work organization and contractual relations. Consultation must be in good ("appropriate") time and with a relevant level of management, and, in regard to substantial changes, the consultation must occur "with a view to reaching agreement." Once 10 percent of the workforce ask for, and thus activate, these rights, the employer must establish appropriate voice systems (normally elected representative bodies) and thereafter inform and consult. Any scheme must be in writing, must cover all employees (including managers), and must be endorsed by the workforce, for example, in an election or a ballot. An employer can preempt the statutorily enforceable regulations by designing and implementing an equivalent type of voice system, with or without unions. Providing this is endorsed by the workforce or their representatives, such a "pre-existing agreement" is difficult to challenge in the courts: a classic voluntaristic solution under the shadow of legislation.

What is important here is not the details but the way in which the directive's introduction marks a change in the attitudes of employers and of most, but not all, unions to the desirability of employee voice systems, which can be either union or nonunion based or both. A new normative order is being established, much as it seems to be developing in Australia and New Zealand. Once the EU directive was approved in 2002, the British government worked jointly with the federal body of trade unions, the Trade Unions Congress, and employers, the

Confederation of British Industry (CBI), to work out how the provisions would be applied. This is the first time that such a tripartite approach has been used successfully. In part, this reflects a change in lawmaking to a procedural orientation in what is termed "reflective law," in which "the preferred mode of intervention is for law to underpin and encourage autonomous processes of adjustment" (Barnard and Deakin 2000, 341). In other words, rather than the law establishing rules (stop at the red traffic light), the design gives scope for considerable choice provided that fundamental principles are met. The principle here is the right of employees to be provided with information and to be consulted on issues, plans, and progress. How this will be done is up to the parties in the light of their circumstances. If an employer does nothing even though the minimum of 10 percent of the workforce asks for ICE, standard or default provisions can be imposed. All this tripartism is a very far cry from the bitter battles over worker directors in the 1970s and over the Thatcher antiunion legislation of the 1980s and 1990s.

Given trends in the growth of voice systems, especially direct types of involvement, the legislation, and the unique way it is designed, is now more likely to be accepted, pushing as it is at a partially open door. For example, evidence from the CBI in 2004, covering large employers, showed a growth in both direct involvement and indirect schemes for informing and consulting employees. Of their respondents, half said they had already introduced a scheme compared to 40 percent two years earlier. A further 69 percent said they intended to introduce permanent mechanisms for informing and consulting employees (CBI 2004). Although there is a frequent gap between good intention and action, this does seem to imply that large employers are getting the message about the desirability of allowing for employee voice.

The ICE regulations are a clear example of a "coercive" isomorphic pressure, since ultimately lack of compliance can be tested in the courts. More interesting is the way in which ICE has been endorsed by both employer and union federal bodies, as well as by many employers' associations. Most notable has been the support of the Engineering Employers Federation, which has a 110-year history of opposition to most pro-worker initiatives in industrial relations. The professional body for human resource managers, the Chartered Institute of Personnel and Development, is not noted for its support of collectivism, but it too has produced supportive guides to the legislation. These guides, and others produced by consultants and law firms, have model agreements and case studies of best practice, all adding to mimetic isomorphism. None of this will be successful unless there is a groundswell of changing attitudes to new forms of employment relations embodying a variety of types of employee voice.

How far the directive will further encourage change in employer and trade union views on the value of encouraging employee voice is impossible to say. It is instructive to note the New Zealand experience of an extensive growth in representative bodies that now cover around half of workplaces. Boxall and his coauthors note that "the general ideology and style being pursued by New Zealand management is one that increases consultation without encouraging independent worker representation or while remaining neutral about unionism. . . . even in small organizations, we see a relatively high degree of consultation, which workers regard as effective" (chapter 6). This adoption of a management style favoring employee voice is evident in Australia, Ireland, Canada, and in a different way in the United States.

So What Should Employers Do about Worker Voice?

Appeals to economic rationality as the basis for company management to adopt employee voice systems are not likely to be successful. We have noted how the evidence for the link between direct and indirect systems of employee involvement and organizational performance is patchy. This is not to say that there is no positive outcome but rather that it has not been proven. The real purpose of involvement is to give employees a voice in the affairs of the organization in which they work and which employs them. Once the focus is placed on the employees' experience of having a voice, the outcomes are much clearer and much more positive. One justification for employers' adoption of voice mechanisms is that the use of direct, and especially dual, systems of involvement is associated with higher levels of affective organizational commitment, job satisfaction, and latitude to make responsible decisions in their jobs.

Employee voice systems have been shown to be effective in reducing or minimizing the number of concerns and problems employee experience at work. The evidence from the United States and the United Kingdom is very clear here, and shows that employee voice has positive effects on employee perceptions in a way that human resource departments, on their own, fail to do. This positive outcome for employee voice can be used by employers as an effective means of union substitution if they are prepared to make voice systems effective and meaningful to employees. In effect, employers can use employee voice systems as a means of competing with unions. The evidence is, however, that a much higher adoption of voice systems is found in organizations that already deal with unions than in those that do not, emphasizing the complementarity of unionization and employee involvement. Put another way, the type of employer that opposes unions tends also to oppose employee voice, especially indirect forms that require the election or appointment of employee representatives. These types of employers are a small, and declining, minority. There is some evidence that employers are increasingly accepting employee voice systems as part of social legitimacy (Boxall and Purcell 2003), perhaps in line with wider moves toward corporate social responsibility and stakeholder pluralism

(Goshal 2005). This acceptance of a normative position favoring employee voice is evident in New Zealand and Australia. It is likely to be reinforced in the United Kingdom and Ireland as the recent European law on information and consultation begins to have an effect. The Chartered Institute of Personnel and Development believes, for example, "that over time the legislation will help promote more productive employee relations through improved dialogue in the workplace and increased employee involvement" (Willmott 2006, 4).

In the end, the answer to the question "Why should employers bother with worker voice?" cannot be answered rationally in economic terms. Rather more powerfully, answers come through changing social attitudes about social inclusion, coping with change, and the need for social legitimacy. These are not exclusively forces confined to employment relations, but most certainly reflect wider, near universal requirements for greater transparency, openness, accountability, and responsiveness, whether in financial accounting, business-to-business relationships, or consumer relations, and beyond that into public affairs. Such easy rhetoric is not to be confused with reality. Representation gaps still exist in all countries. Employers who want to gain the maximum value from voice systems would do well to note that all the evidence points to the need for direct, face-to-face exchange with employees at their work stations and in groups. This needs to be complemented with consultative forums where representatives of the employees meet with senior management to engage in meaningful dialogue about the management of the enterprise.

Chapter 9

What Should Governments Do?

THOMAS A. KOCHAN

What role does government policy play or should it play in providing employees a voice and representation at work and in employment relationships? There is a lot we can learn from the rich comparative data in these chapters. I have not seen a more helpful and more comparable body of data on this topic since the publication of the Industrial Democracy in Europe studies conducted in the 1970s (IDE 1981).

Why Should Governments Care?

Before we ask *what* governments should do, we need to ask *why* governments in democratic societies and free enterprise economies should care about worker voice and, particularly, about the declines in unions, the major instrument of worker voice of the twentieth century. Let me suggest four reasons.

First, the decline of unions diminishes the quality of our democracies. That is why freedom of association and the right to engage in collective bargaining has been recognized as a fundamental human right for all workers by the United Nations (Freeman 1999). Democracies thrive when a plurality of interests engage in political discourse and have to achieve a balance across their respective interests. When workers lack an effective voice in political debates, important questions are not asked, assumptions are not challenged, and options are not considered that are vital to the interests of workers and their families. Although things have not deteriorated to this point in most of the countries in this study, they have in the United States. This was most clearly visible in recent (1990 and 1994) presidential elections. Labor issues, and indeed all workplace issues, were downplayed or avoided by even the Democratic candidates for fear of fomenting "class warfare" or of being viewed as being in the pockets of a "special interest." The separation of Britain's New Labour Party from the British labor movement is a lesser example of the same phenomenon.

Civil society also suffers as labor becomes marginalized. In the United States today there are no major national forums for labor and business and government leaders to discuss issues of national importance or to build the personal bonds that can be called upon in times of crisis. So when the national crisis triggered by September 11, 2001 occurred, the administration in power rejected the suggestion that business and labor leaders be called on to work together as they had been in past crises and wartimes.

There is another even more basic reason why democracy is diminished when workers lose their voice. Workers want a voice at work! Every survey that has asked questions about this since the birth of the behavioral sciences (at least as far back as the Hawthorne Studies in the 1920s) has documented this fact, as do the surveys reported in these studies. The existence of a "representation gap" observed in each of the surveys means that these societies are not supplying as much voice as workers want.

Second, decline in worker voice means a decline in the power of workers to gradually improve wages, hours, and working conditions in ways that historically have helped move working families into the middle class. A simple comparison in the United States makes the point. From the 1940s through the 1970s, General Motors was the largest employer in the United States. It and the United Auto Workers set the standards for improving wages and benefits that other companies in its industry, and to a lesser extent across the economy, were then pressured to match or follow in some fashion by other unions and by labor market competition. Today, the absence of a similar countervailing power at Wal-Mart, the largest employer in the United States, has the opposite effect. As we have seen in recent retail negotiations, Wal-Mart has set in motion a downward spiral to meet its lower wage and benefit standards. The same is true as unions have lost membership density in industries as diverse as telecommunications, airlines, trucking, auto supply, and meatpacking.

Third, not only have *average* employment standards stalled or declined, inequality in wages and benefits has also increased as worker voice has declined. It has been a quarter century since Freeman and Medoff (1984) demonstrated that unions reduce inequality. Thus, it should not be surprising that inequality has increased by most measures in the United States over the last twenty-five years as unions and union power have declined.

Fourth, a modern knowledge-based economy requires a high level of trust and cooperation at work. Teamwork, networking, information sharing, high levels of commitment, and good customer service cannot be built and sustained if the workforce is frustrated, tense, and lacks trust in management or in one another. Thus, it is not only worker voice per se that society has a stake in supporting but a workplace climate and set of relationships that support high trust and cooperative relations among employees and among employees, supervisors, professionals, and executives that can solve problems and improve customer service and productivity. Thus, governments cannot be agnostic as to the forms of employee voice that evolve in their societies. A government that lets the raw swings in power dictate the amount and form(s) of worker voice and representation is destined to pay the price in an underperforming economy and high conflict–low trust employment relations equilibrium.

Does Government Policy Matter?

Some skeptics might ask whether government policy has anything to do with worker voice. Isn't there a market for labor that would allow those workers who want a voice to find jobs that offer it and avoid those that don't? And, in an economy where labor is subject to international as well as domestic competition, isn't the decline in labor's power and worker voice simply the consequence of an increase in competition in the labor market? So would government policy make any difference?

These are fair questions. There is no doubt that government policies enacted in the first half of the twentieth century in Canada, the United States, Australia, and New Zealand supported union growth. There is also equally little doubt that the Thatcher policies in Britain in the 1980s and the dismantling of the arbitration systems in New Zealand and Australia in the 1990s contributed to union decline in those countries. Although it is more difficult to show cause and effect, there is also no doubt in my mind that a significant portion of the decline in unionization in the United States in the past quarter century is due to the inability of workers to gain union membership in the face of illegal and legal employer opposition tolerated by the lack of effective enforcement and remedies for illegal conduct found in the National Labor Relations Act. So it is clear that, at least historically, government policies have, at different points in history, acted to strengthen and weaken unions. That experiment has been run. We have yet to run the alternative experiment over whether governments can influence a restoration of worker voice that is well matched to the needs of the modern workforce and economy. Below I outline the principles that I believe should guide the design of that experiment.

What Can Governments Do?

Having considered the security screeners' critical role in national security, I have concluded that collective bargaining would be incompatible with national security interests. I have therefore issued an order today that precludes collective bargaining on behalf of screeners.
Letter from ADMIRAL J. M. LOY, undersecretary of transportation for security to airport screeners, January 9, 2003

It is clear that governments can make the problem worse by taking actions that further weaken worker voice and/or increase the adversarial climate in a country. The George W. Bush administration chose to do this in its first term. Among other things it ended labor-management partnerships in the federal sector and in construction. A more blatant example is embodied in the above quote taken from the head of the Transportation Security Administration to airport security screeners explaining why the government unilaterally took away their rights to collective bargaining. Apparently, this administration's labor policy is to either promote adversarial labor relations or, where it can, eliminate independent representation entirely. This is the wrong direction for policy. The Howard government in Australia is moving in a similar fashion. The other countries included in this study continue to have labor movements and political party coalitions with sufficient power to limit such actions. But these examples point out that government can indeed do serious harm to worker voice and representation.

Just as governments can do harm, I believe they can also do good. Let me suggest four principles for a modern policy to support worker voice and representation, each of which is suggested by the evidence presented in these studies.

Allow a Variety of Forms of Representation to Coexist in a Complementary Fashion

A dominant theme in the chapters in this book is that the diversity of preferences and needs of employees and workplace characteristics gives rise to the need for different forms of voice and representation. Prior generations of industrial relations scholars were fond of saying and writing that the economy and workforce were too diverse for one shoe size to fit all. They used this metaphor to argue why collective bargaining made more sense than government regulations of employment conditions. They argued forcefully that parties closest to the problems of the workplace could fashion solutions that best fit their particular needs. Although this is as true today as ever, today's diversity takes us a step further in suggesting that no single form of representation fits all needs. So collective bargaining and union representation in its traditional form are still needed and wanted in some circumstances and need to be available as options. In addition, the workforce is asking for complementary forms of participation and representation that promote cooperative approaches to problem solving and in some cases for direct, individual approaches to dealing with workplace issues. Governments in all countries studied in this book except for the United States seem to accept this principle and have taken various steps to allow alternatives to emerge. It is time for the United States to learn how to do this as well.

This principle is more controversial than it may seem at first glance, especially in the United States. Union leaders fear competition. Managers fear multiple channels of representation and, at least in the United States, prefer to retain unilateral authority to decide on the form and scope of participation and/or representation at *their* workplaces. Yet this is what workers are and have for years been saying in these surveys—one shoe size does not fit all!

The central challenge in allowing multiple forms of voice and representation to evolve lies in making them serve as complements rather than substitutes. The data presented here suggest that collective bargaining and consultative forums such as works councils, sectoral councils, internal responsibility systems, and more direct forms of employee participation can indeed complement each other. Two conditions appear to be necessary for this to happen. First, labor representatives need to engage in these different forums and processes in a proactive fashion and develop the skills and capabilities needed to make them effective. This result (the need for union representatives to be proactive) is consistent with findings from prior studies of the relationship of unions and works councils in Europe (Rogers and Streeck 1995; Turner 1998). Second, management must be kept from using them to undermine or avoid unions. This leads us to the second principle.

Enforce Employee Choice and Mute Employer Opposition to Representation

In a democratic society employee freedom of association should mean just what it implies. Employees should be the ones to choose whether and how to be represented free of coercion by employers (or unions). This is a tall order, more so in the United States than perhaps in other countries where, as these chapters indicate, employer opposition to unionization or other forms of voice and representation is more muted, either by the political culture of the country and/or by more vigorous enforcement of labor law.

Clearly, these studies show that the United States is the outlier in terms of government policy, employer opposition to unions, and the relationship of union and nonunion forms of voice and representation. Other nations have succeeded in creating an environment in which worker rights to unionization are respected and enforced, employer opposition to unionization is muted or more moderate, and union and nonunion forms of representation are complements rather than substitutes. Moreover, with the possible exception of Australia, none of the other countries have government policies that are producing greater adversarial relationships at work at the moment, as has been the case in the United States under the George W. Bush administration.

Promote Cooperative Forms of Voice and Representation

The data from these studies show not only that employees prefer cooperative over confrontational relationships at work, they see strong and effective union representation and a cooperative relationship with management as mutually reinforcing and effective. Several of the chapters, particularly those on Canada and New Zealand, suggest that the combination of union representation, works council or informal participation, and effective human resource management is the most effective combination. The Canadian policy of promoting sectoral councils along with internal responsibility systems for monitoring and enforcing safety or other workplace policies and employee rights provides a useful model. Even in the United States, as David Weil (2004) has shown, unions can enhance the enforcement of statutory rights. Moreover, two decades of research on high-performance work systems in union and nonunion settings have documented the economic benefits associated with high-performance or knowledge-based work systems that include opportunities for workers to have a voice in how work is done (Ichniowski et al. 1996). If we add effective due process and dispute-resolution processes to this mix, the package becomes even more complete.

In summary, the data in these studies reinforce a fundamental and enduring principle of industrial relations that has guided labor and employment policy in most democratic countries for many years. Employment relations are inherently mixed motive in nature (Commons 1934; Walton and McKersie 1965). Therefore, we need a balance in which employees have a voice to express their interests and to negotiate compromises where they conflict with management and to pursue cooperative mutual-gains solutions wherever possible. Respect for the former increases the scope and potential effectiveness of the latter. Rejection of the former makes the latter impossible or a sham.

If governments take the steps proposed here will they close the representation gaps observed in the data reported in these country studies? Would they provide the mix of voice and representation best suited to the needs of the today's workforce and economy? Standing alone, I believe the answer is no. My simple reading of history suggests that this will only happen if unions and professional associations embark on a complementary set of changes to modernize their recruiting and representational models. They will need to provide a variety of services, support cooperation with management, increase the reach of unions to young workers and employees in smaller establishments, and provide for a continuity of membership services as employees move from job to job, in and out of the labor force, and through their career-and-family life cycles.

Encourage Unions and Associations to Develop New Recruitment and Representational Models

Today's workers, as the data from these studies show, are at least, perhaps more, instrumentally oriented in their approach toward unions than workers of prior generations. Ideology will not lead many to organize. Relying on dissatisfaction as a motivating force to join unions will narrow the band of potential union members to the most disgruntled and disenfranchised. Unions need to provide a positive vision, strategy, and set of services that workers see as valuable and as effective.

The data are especially clear on one point. Unions need a recruiting strategy that reaches a larger number of unrepresented members. The biggest reason most workers don't join unions in all these countries is not employer opposition, not an aversion to unions, but the fact that they are never asked or given an opportunity to do so! In part this reflects the outmoded organizing model of unions. It is most problematic in countries such as the United States and Canada that continue to adhere to an exclusive-representation majority-rule model of representation in which it takes a 50 percent majority vote or indication of support to bring representation to one additional worker. Moreover, by tying membership to a specific place of work, this same worker may need to be reorganized several times in his or her career. So unions and associations need a recruiting and representational model that allows individuals to join and to retain their membership for their full working lives, even as they move from job to job or in and out of the labor force (Kochan 2004).

If unions are to have a future they will need to invest in strategies to reach younger workers and workers in smaller establishments and then to hold on to them when they move to other jobs. To do so they will need a mix of social capital, service (instrumental), professional networking, and community union models. The days of relying on dissatisfaction and protection from lousy employers has reached its end.

Will This happen?

Will the mix of government actions and labor union strategies needed to restore worker voice and close the representation gaps happen? I think the answer will vary across the countries in these studies. As the authors point out, and as has been documented before (Bruce 1989), public policy changes on labor issues are easier to achieve in parliamentary systems like those in all the countries other than the United States. Moreover, Ireland and the United Kingdom have the European Union as another transnational government forum in which policies like the European Works Councils Directive and other social and economic directives serve to discipline domestic politics and employer behavior. Thus, we are likely to see more incremental expansions of worker voice and acceptance of alternative representational arrangements in these countries than in any of the others in the study.

As the consistent outlier, however, the United States is not likely to follow suit without a cataclysmic set of events that produce a shift in the political environment, government, and union strategies and structures. If we wait for such a day of reckoning, the task of building more cooperative forms of workplace representation that still maintain their independence will be all the more difficult. Out of such crisis would likely come a more adversarial and militant form of union strategies than those the economy and the workforce need and want. I hope the United States does not wait. It would be better to get on with the task now than to have to pick up the pieces later.

Conclusion

What Workers Say in the Anglo-American World

PETER BOXALL, PETER HAYNES, AND RICHARD B. FREEMAN

Our project has analyzed worker preferences for workplace voice across the major advanced Anglo-American economies. This book carries forward the idea that motivated Freeman and Rogers's (1999) *What Workers Want:* to identify what workers seek in voice at their workplace and to gauge the extent to which labor institutions deliver that voice. Comparing workers' desires for representation and participation across six English-speaking countries that share much in common, the book identifies similarities and differences in the attitudes of workers and in the experience of countries. The similarities reveal potential "universals" in workplace labor issues. The differences point to innovations and reforms that could conceivably be transported across country lines and improve the ability of unions and management to deliver the representation and participation that workers want in areas where the voice systems are unsatisfactory.

In this chapter, we offer our view of the main lessons from the volume for labor and management and public policymakers. We begin with a broad summary of what workers have in terms of voice institutions and what they say they want and then give our answers to the four sets of questions posed in the introduction.

How Fares Worker Voice?

Table concl.1 describes the state of worker voice in the Anglo-American world in the early 2000s. Rows one and two of the table document that unionization has declined throughout the Anglo-American world. Outside the public sector, unions are no longer the "default" option for worker voice in any country. In only one country—Ireland—is *private*-sector union density above 20 percent. Yet Ireland experienced the largest fall in private-sector union density among the six countries in the nine years to 2003 (seventeen percentage points), so this is hardly a success story for unions. Like Australian unions under the Labour government's wage accords of the 1980s (Kenyon and Lewis 1992), Irish unions have discovered that centralized wage setting in the Anglo-American world does not stem workplace union decline and may exacerbate it. Even where unions play a major "social partnership" role in national policy determination, they still need to help workers in the workplace to maintain support.

Our surveys show comparable patterns in the occupational and gender composition of trade unionism among the countries. In the private sector, the strength of the unions has historically revolved around higher-skilled craft workers or large concentrations of plant and equipment operators. Union density fell in part because the traditional trades and industrial sectors have diminished as technology has substituted machines for human muscle and skill, and because mass production jobs have shifted to low-cost developing countries. It also fell because deregulation of industries has weakened the potential for firms in the large manufacturing and transportation sectors to pass on union wage increases to consumers. At the same time, unions have organized broad swathes of the public sector. The public sector has large work sites, which are easier to organize than smaller, often volatile private- sector workplaces. In the fast-growing professional occupations, teachers, nurses, policy advisers, and even administrators are organized in the public sector but not in the private sector. For example, in Ireland, "managerial and professional employees in the public sector are four times more likely to be in unions that their counterparts in the private sector" (chapter 4). The decline of male-dominated craft and industrial unionism and the rise of female-dominated public-sector unionism have essentially eliminated the gender gap in union membership.

The Worker Representation and Participation surveys help us go beyond documenting trade union decline to identifying disequilibrium in the market for employee voice, be it union or nonunion voice. The surveys measure the "representation gap" for trade unionism: the proportion of workers in non-union workplaces who want union representation but do not have it. Row 3 of the table shows that a sizeable minority of workers in all countries fit into this

TABLE CONCL.1
Employee voice in the Anglo-American world: An overview

	United States	Canada	Britain	Ireland	Australia	New Zealand
1. Union density, 2004	12.5 percent	30.4 percent	28.8 percent	34.6 percent	22.7 percent	21.1 percent
2. Density trend in the private sector: 1995–2004 (% of private sector wage and salary earners)[a]	Fell from 10.4 percent to 7.9 percent	Fell from 22.2 percent to 18.0 percent	Fell from 21.6 percent to 17.2 percent	Fell from 45 percent to 28.2 percent (2003)	Fell from 25.1 percent to 16.8 percent	Fell from 19.8 percent (1996) to 12 percent
3. Unfilled union demand (% of workers in nonunion work-places)	32 percent (would vote yes in a union election)	25 percent (would prefer to belong to a union)	10 percent very likely to join and 26 percent quite likely to join a union	63.7 percent likely to join where management is willing to support union organization but only 28.1 percent where management is not willing	16.9 percent very likely to join and 21.6 percent fairly likely to join a union	11.4 percent very likely to join and 21.0 percent fairly likely to join a union
4. Influence gap (% who are not satisfied with their overall influence)	22 percent	25 percent	28 percent	15.1 percent[b]	24.8 percent	20.2 percent

	Town hall meetings; employee involvement committees	Sector councils; Employee involvement committees	Joint consultation committees; quality/problem-solving groups	Teams/problem-solving groups; employee consultation committees	Joint consultation committees; quality/problem-solving groups	Joint consultation committees; quality/problem-solving groups
5. Main types of formal nonunion voice						
6. Management attitudes toward union voice	Hostile in unionized companies; varies from hostile to skeptical in nonunion companies	Skeptical	Mainly tolerant	Largely tolerant	Mainly tolerant	Mainly tolerant
7. Union attitudes toward nonunion voice	Hostile	Tolerant	Skeptical	Tolerant but wary	Tolerant	Skeptical
8. Political climate for unions	Highly polarized	Neutral	Supportive	Supportive	Hostile	Supportive
9. Trend in voice regulation	In crisis	Stable	Stable	Stable	Unstable	Stable

aDensity figures reported in the frirst two rows were compiled with the assistance of the country analysts and do not necessarily appear in each chapter.

bDisagreed with the statement that their "manager/supervisor involves me in decisions about my work."

group. Some of this support for trade unionism can be viewed as soft in the sense that workers are saying they want unions without considering the costs it would take to unionize their workplace and make unionization succeed (Kaufman 2001). But the costs of organizing depend critically on the particular characteristics of the existing regulatory regime. What is soft support for unions in the United States can be strong support for unions in, say, New Zealand simply because organizing nonunion workplaces is so difficult in the United States. Further, if more workers who say they want unions were organized, union movements and the political voice of labor would be strengthened.

The country analyses also demonstrate that many workers want greater influence in the workplace (table concl.1, row 4) but show that the "satisfied with influence" gap is smaller than the union representation gap. The lower influence gap reflects management's development of modes of direct communication with workers and their involvement of workers in solving quality and production problems (table concl.1, row 5). In every Anglo-American country except the United States, public policy allows management to provide alternative forms of *representative* voice in which workers can discuss their employment concerns. As a result, outside the United States, nonunion representative voice now often complements rather than substitutes for union voice, and, even where it substitutes, it does so because workers are generally happy with it. The trend to a more diverse set of direct and nonunion representative voice practices fits with the preferences of many workers.

The last four rows of table concl.1 summarize the state of voice representation in the different countries and our assessment of the success with which the systems of voice have delivered to workers the representation or participation they want at the workplace. The ability of a voice regime to deliver desired voice depends on management, labor, and the institutional structure within which they operate. The desires of workers for voice can be undermined by management's hostility to unions (row 6) or by legal regulations or unions that thwart nonunion voice (row 7). The all-or-nothing adversarial nature of the U.S. labor-relations system, which gives firms the incentive and tools to defeat union organizing efforts and gives unions reasons to fight nonunion channels of voice, delivers a double whammy to worker desires for voice. Management opposition to unions is lower in other parts of the Anglo-American world, although U.S. companies have to some extent exported it to Ireland (chapter 4). Outside the United States, unions, including those in Canada, generally either accept or support nonunion channels of voice.

The national political climate (row 8) can compound these problems. In the United States, employers can stop labor-law reform favorable to workers, while unions can stop reforms designed to promote nonunion mechanisms of voice (Kaufman 2001). The result is a system of providing voice that is in crisis (row 9). U.S. labor laws and institutions, established to secure union voice on a democratic and independent basis, have failed workers. Australia, where in 2006 the government seeks to privilege individual contracts over collective contracts against the desire of many workers and employers, also risks failure in delivering the voice that workers want. In the other Anglo-American countries, national politics are generally supportive of diversity in employee voice, and labor policies seek to enable, rather than obstruct, union organizing and to let workers decide the fate of trade unions.

Critical Findings

Going beyond the broad overview, but abstracting from the details in country or topic chapters, we now interpret and summarize what the surveys tell us about the four sets of questions posed in the introduction. We seek to draw the key arguments in this book together into a set of bottom-line findings that we believe should guide efforts to improve worker representation and participation in the Anglo-American world.

Union Representation Gaps

Question: To what extent, if at all, do workers want greater union representation than they have at their workplaces? Are some groups of workers more frustrated in their ability to gain union representation than others? Are some workplaces or sectors more prone to frustrated union demand?
Answer: Many more workers want traditional, union-based representation than are organized. Unfilled demand for unionism is greatest among workers who are vulnerable or who have severe workplace problems.

A fundamental objective of this project was to establish the extent of frustrated demand for unionism across the Anglo-American world. Country by country, the surveys find a union representation gap. The gap was measured at one in three nonunion workers in the United States in the WRPS and as high as one in two nonunion workers in succeeding surveys in the United States. As much as one-third of workers in nonunion firms in the United Kingdom, New Zealand, and Australia also express frustrated demand for union representation. The gap varies from one in four in nonunion Canadian workplaces to two in three in nonunion Irish workplaces when management is perceived as supportive. As noted, some of this support is soft and unlikely to translate into actual union memberships once workers perceive the costs and benefits of joining a specific union given potential management opposition. Nonetheless, a sizeable minority of workers in the Anglo-American world cannot obtain the traditional union representation they want.

The surveys also identified the types of workers whose desire for unionism is most likely to be frustrated. These are workers who objectively seem to be in greatest need of collective labor protections—young workers, lower-income workers, and workers who report many labor problems at their workplace.

That the union representation gap is large among youth challenges the orthodox wisdom that young workers have become more individualistic and antiunion. In fact, the differences between younger and older workers' attitudes toward unions are slight, with, if anything, younger workers being more favorable and more willing to join unions than their older counterparts. The problem for young workers is that their prounion attitudes do not readily translate into union representation. Young workers have a high propensity to quit their jobs, which makes them a fast-moving target for slow bureaucratic trade unions (Haynes, Vowles, and Boxall 2005). Unless unions develop novel forms of low-cost membership and ways to retain the interest of highly mobile workers as they move across workplaces, membership levels among the young are unlikely to rise. The need for unions to develop new models of organizing young workers is stressed by both David Peetz and Ann Frost in chapter 7 and by Tom Kochan in chapter 9.

That the union representation gap is large among workers facing many workplace problems runs against the view that modern human resource practices and government regulations have largely eliminated the need for unions to challenge management power at the workplace. Employee involvement and open door programs reduce the desire for union representation in the United States (chapter 1), but there is still a significant number of "sick workplaces" with high levels of problems. It shows that "the greater the number of workplace needs, the more likely are workers to favor unions or other forms of worker organization independent of management." Similarly, in the United Kingdom, needs vary across workplaces and are highly positively related to desire for stronger forms of representation. Both chapters show that most workers report that their workplace has few, if any, serious problems while a small number report many problems.

The U.S. and British picture is confirmed by the Irish evidence that "employees working in workplaces where the climate of management-employee relations is perceived to be poor are more favorably disposed toward joining a union" (chapter 4). Size of workplace is not necessarily the factor here—there are many small workplaces where employers and workers experience high levels of mutuality, as implied by the Canadian finding that workers in "larger and presumably more impersonal work environments" had a greater desire for union voice (chapter 2). The key factor is the incidence of employment problems.

In sum, our surveys indicate a representation gap in every part of the Anglo-American world. This should convince unions, employers, and governments that the market for traditional unionism is far from saturated. Workers still seek unionization as a rational response to an employment environment where they perceive wages and conditions and standards of treatment as poor or un-fair. Unmet demand for unionism is strong among low-income workers, among the young, and among those who find themselves in "sick workplaces"—those that generate many problems for workers.

Worker Attitudes toward Representation Generally

Question: In the broadest possible terms, how do workers feel about the different ways their interests are represented in their firm? What can unions, in particular, learn from worker desires for representation and assessment of the effectiveness of institutions to meet those desires?

Answer: Worker needs for representation vary in important ways. No single mode of employee voice, such as unionism, can fit the needs of all workers.

The surveys show that most private-sector workers in better paid, more highly skilled jobs are relatively indifferent to what unions offer. In Australia, for ex-ample, two-thirds of nonunion workers believe that a union would make no difference to them personally (chapter 5). Even among those who express a strong desire to join a union, over a third think a union would make no differ-ence to them personally. Leaving aside the United States, where union contracts typically make a huge difference to pension and health benefits, indifference to what unions achieve is strong in the Anglo-American world. The majority of private-sector workers favor self-reliance in the labor market. In Canada, for example, approximately six out of ten workers prefer direct over collective forms of voice (chapter 2). And, whether they want unions or not, workers have nuanced views on which issues they prefer to address collectively and on which issues they prefer to address the problems themselves.

Our finding of "nuancing" in worker needs raises a serious issue for unions, whose traditional bargaining program has been to seek the same deal for all workers rather than personalizing their services to meet more variegated in-terests. As a result of this, across the Anglo-American world, workers see union voice as more relevant to the classical conflict areas of pay and benefits than to job design and career development. The British survey shows that workers' de-sire for unions to protect them does not mean they want unions to help on "is-sues of career promotion" (chapter 3). The Irish survey shows that "both unionized and nonunionized employees are more likely to want to go directly to management with issues relating to training and promotion" (chapter 4). Further, nonunion employee representatives in the United Kingdom engage management on a broader agenda than do union reps, for instance on ques-tions of recruitment and selection, training and performance appraisal (chap-ter 8). Many highly educated workers believe that they personally must advance their careers and that traditional unions cannot usefully or practically mediate this process.

This means that to renew membership, unions need more "products" than one-size-fits-all membership linked to collective bargaining. Since the circumstances of employees are not uniform, union services should not be uniform either. The need for traditional unionism to organize discontent in sick workplaces will not lead to a mass return to trade unionism in current economic and labor market conditions (Kaufman 2004) nor to unions adding as much value to the well-being of workers and firms as they could. Union renewal in the private sector requires unions doing something *new*. The challenge for union leaders is to find a way to deliver union services that does not depend on organizing around discontent at a specific workplace, as Tom Kochan argues (chapter 9). In the United States, this means finding ways to reach workers who value union services but for whom the union cannot deliver the collective contract (Freeman and Rogers 2002a).

The situation is more complex in the four Anglo-American countries where there is a major free-riding problem at organized workplaces: the United Kingdom, Ireland, Australia, and New Zealand. In these countries, union membership remains voluntary even where unions have bargaining recognition, and many workers who benefit from collective representation do not join the local union. About four out of ten workers in unionized British, Australian, and New Zealand workplaces are free riders, while 28 percent of workers in unionized Irish establishments are nonunion. This differs from the United States, where most workers join their workplace union even in right-to-work states, and in Canada, where the Rand formula requires that workers in an organized workplace either join the union or pay dues to a charity (chapter 2).

Why do unions have such a large infill problem in these countries? One reason is that unions have not actively solicited membership at many organized workplaces. Thirty-four percent of nonunion workers in unionized New Zealand workplaces say that they had never been invited to join the relevant union. In Britain and Australia, the comparable figures are around half of eligible nonmembers (see chapters 3 and 5). In Ireland, three out of four workers who say that they might join have never been invited (chapter 4). One likely reason is that full-time union officials, who should be helping to build effective workplace networks, spend nearly all their time representing workers in collective bargaining and in the implementation of collective contracts. Many unions lack programs to get local members to sell their co-workers on the value of membership and need better methods for assessing what matters to potential members. In chapter 7, David Peetz and Ann Frost discuss the importance to unions of fostering internal voice and building structures and cultures in which members in workplaces have greater say and exercise greater responsibility.

Whatever the reason, the "organizing" approach that many unions espouse has fallen short of the rhetoric. This disjuncture between strategy as formulated and as implemented cries out for reform. Unions in these countries have a high level of passive membership with individual members largely untouched by union communications or asked to help organize others at their workplaces. National bargaining that delivers wage and other outcomes without workplace campaigns, as in Ireland, and formerly in Australia and New Zealand, seems to erode union strength at the local level. Arguably, unions in these countries should first "organize the organized" before embarking on campaigns to organize workers outside the existing union sector.

The surveys show also that free riding is not simply a matter of opportunistic or morally reprehensible behavior. Some 30 percent of free riders in Britain consider union fees too high, and 28 percent consider that people doing their sort of job don't join unions (chapter 3). The latter group is as high as 55 percent in Australia (chapter 5). Analysis of the New Zealand data on free riding shows that nonmembership in unionized workplaces is "U-shaped" by level of income and education, highest at the lowest and highest levels of income and education, and lowest in the middle range (chapter 6). One interpretation of this pattern is that lower-income workers find the cost of union membership difficult to sustain, whereas higher income workers feel less need for union representation as a result of better job security and labor market power. To attract both groups, unions will need to change from their mode of delivering a single "product" to one that meets a greater variety of worker needs.

Worker Attitudes toward Participation and Styles of Voice

Question: How do workers feel about employer-driven forms of influence? Are these forms more effective when complementary with unionism? How well do they work independent of unionism? What styles of engagement with employers do workers seek?
Answer: By and large, workers endorse the growth of management-driven forms of involvement and show a strong preference for the expansion of more cooperative styles of voice.

The surveys show that employee involvement systems, such as quality circles and other forms of small-group problem solving, have become commonplace in the Anglo-American world (row 5 of table concl.1). These management-driven forms of involvement, at the workstation or in off-the-job problem-solving groups, are designed to serve employer goals of improved productivity and flexibility. However, our data suggest they increasingly meet the desire of workers to be involved in the things most directly relevant to them. In the United Kingdom (Diamond and Freeman 2001), the United States (Freeman and Rogers 1999), and New Zealand (chapter 6), the smallest influence gaps that employees report relate to how they do their work, signifying gains for workers from having a greater say in work methods and production processes. Similarly, in Canada, some 61 percent of workers report "high influence over workplace decisions" (chapter 2).

There is a major debate among labor specialists regarding the ways in which new forms of work organization affect workers. Some researchers see new forms of teamwork and employee involvement as creating net gains for workers (see, for example, Appelbaum et al. 2000), while others see them as likely to create more stress (see, for example, Godard 2004). Our data indicate that workers, in the main, report favorably on these institutions.

The data in this book also show that outside the United States nonunion modes of voice and participation are widespread. In Canada, where firms can set up nonunion worker organizations, around 14 percent of workers are in such company "nonunions," with no objection from the Canadian union movement (chapter 2). In unionized workplaces, moreover, there is a growing complementarity between union and nonunion representative voice systems. In Australia and New Zealand, consultative committees are more prevalent when unions are present (chapters 5 and 6). Our surveys show that workers regard these systems as providing real benefits, rather than being talk fests or management-dominated shams. In Ireland, where the incidence of joint consultative committees is lower, nearly four out of five workers rate them as effective (chapter 4). It is therefore not possible to dismiss their relevance and value.

In terms of the sheer variety of worker voice, the United Kingdom is the leading case, due in part to its membership of the European Union. There, "most workers see works councils as complementary to unions," and "the advent of works councils creates an opportunity for unions to expand their influence in the workforce" (chapter 3). As Purcell and Georgiadis explain in chapter 8, many British employers have learned to foster dual-voice systems, combining direct and indirect representative forms. In these establishments, which cover approximately three in ten British workplaces, management takes employee relations issues more seriously in company goal setting, provides employees with a higher quality of information, and involves employees more in decision making than in other firms.

On the basis of the findings in the United States and the United Kingdom, voice practices per se seem more important than human resource departments in determining the quality of employee relations. Simply having a human resource department may not help the firm or workers very much. As Purcell and Georgiadis note (chapter 8), what matters is that human resource specialists facilitate systems of voice in which workers can speak for themselves. Companies that are too small to have human resource departments need to rely on informal, open door policies in which management keeps communication a two-way stream.

All the studies underline the message that workers want more cooperative styles of engagement with management. In Freeman and Rogers's (1999) *What Workers Want*, the majority of U.S. workers, including most union members, wanted an organization "run jointly by employees and management" (x) and saw management cooperation as essential to an effective workplace organization. Workers in other Anglo-American countries have similar attitudes, as Peetz and Frost emphasize in chapter 7 and Kochan underlines in chapter 9. In Britain, workers overwhelmingly favor a worker-based organization that works *with* management to improve the workplace rather than one that simply defends workers against unfair treatment. A major value of cooperation is that it reduces the number of workplace problems (chapter 3). In Ireland, the vast majority of workers want unions "to extend their role beyond collective bargaining and develop cooperative relations with employers to improve organizational performance" (chapter 4). Similarly, in Australia and New Zealand, workers believe in the need for union-management cooperation (chapters 5 and 6). They look to unions to defend them when important interests are threatened but view conflict as nested within a fundamentally cooperative understanding of employment relations. As Peetz and Frost emphasize, they expect both management and unions to cooperate meaningfully (chapter 7).

The implication for union strategy is not that unions should shift to a stance of cooperation in all contexts, but that they should work to enhance the terrain of cooperation where employers readily recognize the union role and work with unions productively. If employers refuse to cede recognition and/or workers have important, unresolved concerns with their pay and conditions, union strategy must involve contestation. The state could potentially "tilt" the field toward cooperation by giving firms and unions that reach cooperative arrangements the right to self-administer labor laws or other regulations. For instance, government agencies could cede the right to monitor compliance with occupational health and safety regulations to management and union groups that work together while spending regulatory resources on workplaces with conflictual labor practices. The Canadian "internal responsibility" system of health and safety committees operates in this manner.[1] In other areas, governments could follow the lead of the U.S. Supreme Court in grievance arbitration, which declared that courts should follow labor-arbitration decisions, barring some egregious activity. States could enact laws that privilege joint labor-management groups to resolve issues regarding labor regulations in ways that do not allow courts or agencies to readily overturn them.

Employee Voice and Public Policy Reform

Question: Are there "institutional rigidities" that render public policy on employee voice ineffective in some Anglo-American countries? What institutional models are more successful in giving workers the voice they seek at workplaces?

[1] http://www.ccohs.ca/oshanswers/legisl/irs.html.

Answer: Compared with the other countries, the United States has a rigid, outmoded system of employee voice that does not protect workers' right to choose the voice options they want and that restricts firms and workers from developing nonunion modes of voice. The Australian government's effort to weaken unions and push workers and firms into individual contracts could potentially create similar problems. The more successful labor regulatory regimes are those that foster diversity and complementarity among the various institutions of voice.

The U.S. model of labor regulation generates the worst levels of worker frustration with their voice opportunities. Why have the other Anglo-American countries done a better job of matching voice institutions to worker desires than the United States (and potentially Australia in the future)? The answer is that they have allowed workers to choose unions more freely and allowed firms to develop nonunion voice practices more freely alongside union ones. They have promoted *diversity* in employee voice and encouraged *complementarity* between union and nonunion modes of voice, thus fostering a closer match between the voice workers have and the voice they want. The contrast within North America between Canada and the United States is particularly noteworthy, since the two countries have applied a common base of ideas in small but critically different ways. The U.S. labor-relations system offers only a "yes" or "no" option of collective bargaining through a union or a default of no collective representation. Faced with a large union wage premium, U.S. management has fought successfully to frustrate worker desires to organize, and with no non–collective-bargaining alternatives, this amounts to fighting for the no-voice option. U.S. unions oppose allowing companies to experiment with nonunion collective voice for fear this would further lower their chances of winning an organizing campaign. Although this could benefit workers overall and might even increase union organizing success (Kaufman 2001), the unions have been unwilling to risk change. The result is that the desire of many workers for some cooperative, unionlike intermediate institution, such as a committee of workers and management, remains an unfilled demand.

The lesson we draw is that government regulation of labor-management relations should promote *a range of forms of employee representation based on employee choice.* As long as workers have a secure right to collective bargaining, public policy should aim to promote flexibility in voice institutions and not simply be concerned with promoting collective representation through unions. Systems like that in the United States in which politicians, employers, and union officials fight a pitched battle between management prerogative and union voice are maladapted in the current economic and social environment.

There are different ways to encourage diversity in representation and participation. The EU model of mandating works councils that have information and consultation rights but do not bargain collectively on wages and cannot strike is one alternative, one with which the United Kingdom has begun to experiment. As Purcell and Georgiadis explain in chapter 8, this entails conferring employees, rather than trade unions, with rights to information and consultation in all enterprises over a certain size. The Canadian model of differentiating between unions and company-sponsored committees is another, as discussed by Campolieti, Gomez, and Gunderson in chapter 2. These options require careful drafting of specific regulations—a process that has proceeded more effectively in the United Kingdom than in Ireland, where, as John Geary explains in chapter 4, there is fear about the possible loss of inward investment.

To be sure, there are complexities in developing a labor system that promotes diversity while ensuring that management cannot frustrate worker desire for union voice nor unions frustrate workers' willing adoption of nonunion voice. But national systems that approach this goal are likely to do best in closing the gap between what workers want in voice and what they have and in encouraging experimentation by unions and firms in developing the voice institutions that best suit the economy.

Worker Voice: Old Lessons and New

The surveys in this book extend Freeman and Rogers's (1999) work by confirming the existence of representation gaps in all six Anglo-American societies. The business of bringing independent representation to vulnerable workers that motivated trade unions in the nineteenth and twentieth centuries is not finished. Frustrated union demand is high among the young and the low paid, and at "sick workplaces" with high levels of problems. These workers need a traditional union organization that secures recognition and contests management decisions and power.

But our surveys also show that most workers in the private sector in the Anglo-American world want forms of voice that will help them deal with problems cooperatively and improve their firm's performance. They want trade unions to cooperate in enlarging the surplus as well as protecting them from ill treatment. Whether unionized or not, many workers find that employer-initiated voice opportunities improve their working lives.

Given this, and differing management styles, unions need both to battle the bad employers and cooperate with the good employers, to use collective bargaining when it is the best mode for advancing worker interests and to use other tactics when they are more likely to succeed. They need to retain the old model where it is needed and to invent a new one. To return to the Darwinian metaphor we employed in the introduction, unions need variety in strategy if they are to fill enough new sustainable niches to reestablish their position as the preeminent employee institution in the economy.

There are two implications for management. One is that the experimentation with voice practices should continue. Smaller firms should do all they can to provide informal voice opportunities, while larger firms should provide multiple systems of voice—both direct and representative—to enhance trust, job satisfaction, and employee commitment. Beyond the workplace, employer lobbyists should think carefully about their stance toward voice regulation. A stance of endorsing variety in voice institutions, including both trade unionism and nonunion forms of representation, is much closer to what workers want and what will serve business well.

For their part, governments should encourage workers and firms to experiment with alternatives that best fit their circumstances rather than trying to box both sides into a single institutional frame. To enable workers to obtain the voice they want, the state must guarantee the right to union representation, which many workers want, and also give workers and management the right to establish nonunion forms of representative voice, where they seek that mode of voice regime. In both areas, the United States has much to learn from the experiences of the other major English-speaking countries.

References

Acemoglu, Daron, Simon Johnson, and James A. Robinson. 2001. "The Colonial Origins of Comparative Development: An Empirical Investigation." *American Economic Review* 91(5):1369–401.

Ackers, Peter, and Jonathan Payne. 1998. "British Trade Unions and Social Partnership: Rhetoric, Reality and Strategy." *International Journal of Human Resource Management* 9(4):529–50.

Adams, George W. 2004. *Canadian Labour Law.* 2nd ed. Aurora, Ont.: Canada Law Book.

Adema, Willem, and Maxime Ladaique. 2005. "Net Social Expenditure, 2005 Edition: More Comprehensive Measures of Social Support." OECD Social Employment and Migration Working Papers No. 29. Geneva: Organisation for Economic Co-operation and Development.

Airey, Colin, Jon Hales, Rosemary Hamilton, Christos Korvovessis, Anthony McKernan, and Susan Purdon. 1999. "The Workplace Employee Relations Survey (WERS) 1997–98: Technical Report." London: National Centre for Social Research.

Andrews, Kevin. 2005. *A New Workplace Relations System: A Plan for a Modern Workplace.* http://www.dewr.gov.au/ministersAndMediaCentre/andrews/documents/NewWork placeRelAccessed 11 August 2005.

Appelbaum, Eileen, Thomas Bailey, Peter Berg, and Arne L. Kalleberg. 2000. *Manufacturing Advantage: Why High-Performance Work Systems Pay Off.* Ithaca: Cornell University Press.

Australian Bureau of Statistics (ABS). 2001. *Census of Population and Housing 2001.* Canberra: Commonwealth of Australia.

———. 2006. *Employee Earnings, Benefits and Trade Union Membership August 2005.* Cat. No. 6310.0. Canberra: Commonwealth of Australia.

Australian Centre for Industrial Relations Research and Teaching (ACIRRT). 1999. *Australia at Work: Just Managing?* Sydney: Prentice-Hall.

———. 2002. *Australian Employees' Attitudes towards Unions.* Sydney: ACCIRT.

Australian Council of Trade Unions (ACTU). 1999. *Unions @ Work: The Challenge for Unions in Creating a JUST and FAIR Society.* Melbourne: ACTU.

———. 2003. *Future Strategies: Unions Working for a Fairer Australia.* Melbourne: ACTU.

Bain, George S. 1970. *The Growth of White Collar Unionism.* Oxford: Clarendon Press.

Bandura, Albert. 1997. *Self-Efficacy: The Exercise of Control.* New York: W. H. Freeman.

Barnard, Catherine, and Simon Deakin. 2000. "In Search of Coherence: Social Policy, the Single Market and Fundamental Rights." *Industrial Relations Journal* 31(4):331–45.

Beer, Michael. 1964. "Organizational Size and Job Satisfaction." *Academy of Management Journal* 7(1):34–45.

Benson, John. 2000. "Employee Voice in Union and Non-Union Australian Workplaces." *British Journal of Industrial Relations* 38(3):453–59.

Black, Melleny, Melody Guy, and Nathan McLellan. 2003. "Productivity in New Zealand 1988 to 2002." Working Paper 03/06. Wellington: New Zealand Treasury.

Block, Richard N., Karen Roberts, and R. Oliver Clarke. 2003. *Labor Standards in the United States and Canada.* Kalamazoo, Mich.: W. E. Upjohn Institute.

Botero, Juan, Simeon Djankov, Rafael La Porta, Florencio Lopez-de-Silanesa, and Andrei Shliefer. 2003. "The Regulation of Labor." NBER Working Paper 9756. Boston: National Bureau of Economic Research.

Boxall, Peter. 1993. "Management Strategy and the Employment Contracts Act 1991." In *Employment Contracts: New Zealand Experiences,* edited by Raymond Harbridge, 148–64. Wellington: Victoria University Press.

———. 1997. "Models of Employment and Labour Productivity in New Zealand: An Interpretation of Change since the Employment Contracts Act." *New Zealand Journal of Industrial Relations* 22(1): 22–36.

———. 2003. "New Zealand." In *The Handbook of Human Resource Management Policies and Practices in Asia-Pacific Economies,* vol. 2, edited by Michael Zanko and Matt Ngui, 228–84. Cheltenham: Edward Elgar.

Boxall, Peter, and Peter Haynes. 1997. "Strategy and Trade Union Effectiveness in a Neo-liberal Environment." *British Journal of Industrial Relations* 35(4):567–91.

Boxall, Peter, Keith Macky, and Erling Rasmussen. 2003. "Labour Turnover and Retention in New Zealand: The Causes and Consequences of Leaving and Staying With Employers." *Asia Pacific Journal of Human Resources* 41(2):195–214.

Boxall, Peter, and John Purcell. 2003. *Strategy and Human Resource Management.* Basingstoke: Palgrave Macmillan.

Briggs, Chris. 2004. "The Return of the Lockout in Australia: A Profile of the Lockouts since the Decentralisation of Bargaining." *Australian Bulletin of Labour* 30(2):101–12.

Bronfenbrenner, Kate. 2000. "Uneasy Terrain: The Impact of Capital Mobility on Workers, Wages, and Union Organizing." Commissioned research paper and supplement to *The U.S. Trade Deficit: Causes, Consequences, and Recommendations for Action.* Washington, D.C.: Trade Deficit Review Commission.

Bruce, Peter G. 1989. "Political Parties and Labor Legislation in Canada and the U.S." *Industrial Relations* 28(2):115–41.

Bryson, Alex. 2003. "Employee Desire for Unionization in Britain and Its Implications for Union Organizing." PSI Research Discussion Paper No. 12. London: Policy Studies Institute.

——. 2004. "Managerial Responsiveness to Union and Non-Union Worker Voice in Britain." *Industrial Relations* 43(1):213–41.

——. 2006. "Union Free-Riding in Britain and New Zealand." CEP Discussion Paper No. 713. London: Centre for Economic Performance, London School of Economics and Politics.

Bryson, Alex, and Richard B. Freeman. 2006. "Worker Needs and Voice in the US and the UK." NBER Working Paper. Boston: National Bureau of Economic Research.

Bryson, Alex, and Rafael Gomez. 2002. "Marching on Together? Recent Trends in Union Membership." In *British Social Attitudes: The 19th Report,* edited by Alison Park, John Curtice, Katarina Thomson, Lindsey Jarvis, and Catherine Bromley, 43–73. London: Sage.

——. 2003a. "Segmentation, Switching Costs and the Demand for Unionization in Britain." Centre for Economic Performance Discussion Paper No. 568. London: London School of Economics.

——. 2003b. "Buying Into Union Membership." In *Representing Workers: Union Recognition and Membership in Britain,* edited by Howard Gospel and Stephen Wood, 72–91. London: Routledge.

——. 2005. "Why Have Workers Stopped Joining Unions? Accounting for the Rise in Never-Membership in Britain." *British Journal of Industrial Relations* 43(1):67–92.

Bryson, Alex, Rafael Gomez, Morley Gunderson, and Noah M. Meltz. 2004. "Youth-Adult Differences in Demand for Unionization: Are American, British, and Canadian Workers All That Different?" *Journal of Labor Research* 16(1):155–67.

Bryson, Alex, Rafael Gomez, and Paul Willman. 2004. "The End of the Affair? The Decline in Employers' Propensity to Unionize." In *Union Organization and Activity,* edited by John Kelly and Paul Willman, 129–49. London: Routledge.

Buchanan, John, and Tanya Bretherton. 1999. "Experience of Young Adult Workers." In *Australia's Young Adults: The Deepening Divide,* edited by John Spearings. Sydney: Dusseldorp Skills Forum.

Buchanan, John, and Ron Callus. 1993. "Efficiency and Equity at Work: The Need for Labour Market Regulation in Australia." ACIRRT Working Paper No. 26. Sydney: University of Sydney.

Buhle, Paul. 1999. *Taking Care of Business: Samuel Gompers, George Meany, Lane Kirkland, and the Tragedy of American Labor.* New York: Monthly Review Press.

California Workplace Survey. 2002. http://sda.berkeley.edu:7502/archive.htm.

Callus, Ron, Jim Kitay, and Paul Sutcliffe. 1992. "Industrial Relations at Small Business Workplaces." *Small Business Review.* Canberra: Australian Government Publishing Service.

Campolieti, Michele, Rafael Gomez, and Morley Gunderson. 2004. "Have Canadian Workers Lost Their Voice?" Paper presented at Employee Voice and Influence in the Anglo-American World Research Workshop, Auckland University, 8–10 September 2004.

CBI. 2004. *Employment Trends Survey 2004: Measuring Flexibility in the Labour Market.* London: Confederation of British Industry.

Charlwood, Andy. 2002. "Why Do Non-Union Employees Want to Unionize? Evidence from Britain." *British Journal of Industrial Relations* 40(3):463–91.

——. 2003. "Willingness to Unionize Amongst Non-Union Workers." In *Representing Workers: Union Recognition and Membership in Britain,* edited by Howard Gospel and Stephen Wood, 51–71. London: Routledge.

——. 2004. "The New Generation of Trade Union Leaders and Prospects for Union Revitalization." *British Journal of Industrial Relations* 42(2):379–97.

Charlwood, Andy, and Peter Haynes. forthcoming 2008. "Union Membership Decline in New Zealand, 1990–2002." *Journal of Industrial Relations.*

Chor, Davin, and Richard B. Freeman. 2005. "The 2004 Global Labor Survey: Workplace Institutions and Practices around the World." NBER Working Paper 11598. Boston: National Bureau of Economic Research.

Coats, David. 2004. *Speaking Up! Voice, Industrial Democracy and Organisational Performance.* London: Work Foundation.

Colvin, M. 2006. "Both Sides Claim a Win in Cowra Abattoir Decision," Radio Broadcast, PM Program: Radio National, Australia, 7 July. www.abc.net.au/pm/content/2006/s1681629.htm

Commons, John R. 1934. *Institutional Economics.* New York: Macmillan.

Conway, Paul, and Adrian Orr. 2000. "The Process of Economic Growth in New Zealand." *Reserve Bank Bulletin* 63(1):4–20.

Cregan, Christina. 2005. "Can Organizing Work? An Inductive Analysis of Individual Attitudes towards Union Membership." *Industrial and Labor Relations Review* 58(2):282–305.

Creighton, Breen, and Andrew Stewart. 2000. *Labour Law: An Introduction.* 3rd ed. Sydney: Federation Press.

Crosby, Michael. 2005. *Power at Work: Rebuilding the Australian Union Movement.* Sydney: Federation Press.

Crouch, Colin. 1982. *Trade Unions: The Logic of Collective Action.* London: Fontana.

Cully, Mark, Stephen Woodland, Andrew O'Reilly, and Gill Dix. 1999. *Britain at Work: As Depicted by the 1998 Workplace Employee Relations Survey.* London: Routledge.

Cumming, Geoff. 2006. "Changing of the Guard." *New Zealand Herald,* 29 April, B7.

Dabscheck, Braham. 2006. "The Contract Regulation Club." *Economic and Labour Relations Review* 16(2):1–24.

Dark, Taylor E. 1999. "Decline: The 1995 Race for the AFL-CIO Presidency—American Federation of Labor and Congress of Industrial Organizations." *Labor History* 40(3):323–43.

D'Art, Daryl, and Thomas Turner. 2005. "Union Recognition and Partnership at Work: A New Legitimacy for Irish Trade Unions." *Industrial Relations Journal* 36(2):121–39.

Davis, Edward M., and Russell D. Lansbury. 1998. "Industrial Relations in Australia." In *International and Comparative Employment Relations,* edited by Greg J. Bamber and Russell D. Lansbury, 110–43. Sydney: Allen and Unwin.

Deeks, John, and Peter Boxall. 1989. *Labour Relations in New Zealand.* Auckland: Longman Paul.

Deery, Stephen, and Janet Walsh. 1999. "The Character of Individual Employment Arrangements in Australia: A Model of 'Hard' HRM." In *Employment Relations: Individualisation and Union Exclusion,* edited by Stephen Deery and Richard Mitchell, 115–29. Sydney: Federation Press.

Deom, Ester, and Jean Boivin. 2005. "Union-Management Relations in Quebec." In *Union-Management Relations in Canada,* 5th ed., edited by Morley Gunderson, Allen Ponak, and Daphne G. Taras, 486–520. Toronto: Pearson Education Canada.

Diamond, Wayne, and Richard B. Freeman. 2001. *What Workers Want from Workplace Organizations: A Report to the TUC's Promoting Trade Unionism Task Group.* London: Trades Union Congress.

———. 2002. "Will Unionism Prosper in Cyberspace? The Promise of the Internet for Employee Organization." *British Journal of Industrial Relations* 40(3):569–96.

Dickens, William. 1983. "The Effect of Company Campaigns on Certification Elections: Law and Reality Once Again." *Industrial and Labor Relations Review* 36(4):560–75.

DiMaggio, Paul J., and Walter W. Powell. 1983. "The Iron Cage Revisited: Institutional Isomorphism and Collective Rationality in Organizational Fields." *American Sociological Review* 48(2):147–60.

Dobbins, Tony. 2005a. "Growing Volume of Recognition Cases May Create 'Resource Logjam'." *Industrial Relations News* 31.

———. 2005b. "SIPTU Steps Up Its Organising Campaign." *Industrial Relations News* 38.

Donovan, Lord. 1968. *Report of the Royal Commission on Trade Unions and Employers' Associations, 1965–1968.* HMSO CMND 6323. London: Her Majesty's Stationery Office.

DTI. 2004. *High Performance Workplaces: The Role of Employee Involvement in the Modern Economy.* London: Department of Trade and Industry.

Ebbinghaus, Bernhard. 2002. "Trade Unions Changing Role: Membership Erosion, Organizational Reform, and Social Partnership in Europe." *Industrial Relations Journal* 33(5): 465–83.

Ebbinghaus, Bernhard, and Bernhard Kittel. 2005. "European Rigidity versus American Flexibility." *Work and Occupations* 32(2):163–95.

Eden, Genevieve. 1994. "Reinstatement in the Non-Union Sector: An Empirical Analysis." *Relations Industrielles* 49(1):87–101.

Elliott, Kimberly Ann, and Richard B. Freeman. 2003. *Can Labor Standards Improve under Globalization?* Washington, D.C.: Institute for International Economics.

European Commission. 2003. *Employment in Europe 2003: Recent Trends and Prospects.* Brussels: European Commission, Directorate-General for Employment and Social Affairs.

Farber, Henry S. 1989. "Trends in Worker Demand for Union Representation." *American Economic Review* 70(2):166–71.

———. 2001. "Notes on the Economics of Labor Unions." Working Paper No. 452. Princeton: Princeton University, Industrial Relations Section.

Farber, Henry S., and Alan B. Krueger. 1992. "Union Membership in the United States: The Decline Continues." NBER Working Papers 4216. Cambridge, Mass.: NBER.

———. 1993. "Union Membership in the United States: The Decline Continues." In *Employee Representation: Alternatives and Future Directions*, edited by Bruce E. Kaufman and Morris M. Kleiner, 105–34. Madison: Industrial Relations Research Association.

Farber, Henry S., and Bruce Western. 2002. "Ronald Reagan and the Politics of Declining Union Organization." *British Journal of Industrial Relations* 40(3):385–401.

Fine, Janice. 2003. "Non-Union, Low-Wage Workers Are Finding a Voice as Immigrant Workers Centers Grow." *Labor Notes* 293. http://www.labornotes.org/archives/2003/08/c.html.

Fiorito, Jack. 2003. "Union Organizing in the United States." In *Union Organizing: Campaigning for Trade Union Recognition*, edited by Gregor Gall, 191–210. London: Routledge.

Flanagan, Robert J. 2005. "Has Management Strangled U.S. Unions?" *Journal of Labor Research* 26(1):33–63.

Forsyth, Anthony, and Carolyn Sutherland. 2006. "From 'Uncharted Seas' to 'Stormy Waters': How Will Trade Unions Fare under the Work Choices Legislation?" *Economic and Labour Relations Review* 16(2):215–36.

Freeman, Anthony G. 1999. "ILO Labor Standards and U.S. Compliance." *Perspectives on Work* 3(1):28–31.

Freeman, Richard B. 1978. "Job Satisfaction as an Economic Variable." *American Economic Review* 68(2):135–41.

———. 1985. "Why Are Unions Faring Poorly in NLRB Representation Elections?" In *Challenges and Choices Facing American Labor,* edited by Thomas A. Kochan, 45–64. Cambridge: MIT Press.

———. 1998. "Spurts in Union Growth: Defining Moments and Social Processes." In *The Defining Moment: The Great Depression and the American Economy in the Twentieth Century,* edited by Michael D. Bordo, Claudia Goldin, and Eugene N. White, 265–96. Chicago: University of Chicago Press for NBER.

———. 2004. "Labor Representation and Participation around the World: One Way of Many." Paper presented at Industrial and Labor Relations Association Annual Meeting, San Diego, 3–5 January 2004.

———. 2005a. "From the Webbs to the Web: The Contribution of the Internet to Reviving Union Fortunes." NBER Working Paper 11298. Boston: National Bureau of Economic Research.

———. 2005b. "Labor Market Institutions without Blinders: The Debate over Flexibility and Labor Market Performance." NBER Working Paper 11286. Boston: National Bureau of Economic Research.

———. 2005c. *"What Do Unions Do?* The 2004 M-Brane Stringtwister Edition." *Journal of Labor Research* 26(4):641–68.

———. 2006. "In Search of the EU Social Dialogue Model." NBER Working Paper 12306. Boston: National Bureau of Economic Research.

Freeman, Richard B., and Joni Hersch. 2005. Introduction to *Emerging Labor Market Institutions for the Twenty-First Century,* edited by Freeman, Hersch, and Lawrence Mishel. Chicago: University of Chicago Press for NBER.

Freeman, Richard B., and James L. Medoff. 1984. *What Do Unions Do?* New York: Basic Books.

Freeman, Richard B., and Marit Rehavi. 2006. "Future Unionism Today: How Union Reps Use the Web." *Mimeo.* London: London School of Economics and Politics.

Freeman, Richard B., and Joel Rogers. 1999. *What Workers Want.* Ithaca: Cornell University Press.

———. 2002a. "Open Source Unionism: Beyond Exclusive Collective Bargaining." *WorkingUSA: Journal of Labor and Society* 5(4):8–40.

———. 2002b. "A Proposal to American Labor." *Nation* 274 (June 24): 18–24.

Frege, Carola M. 2002. "A Critical Assessment of the Theoretical and Empirical Research on German Works Councils." *British Journal of Industrial Relations* 40(2):221–48.

Frost, Ann C. 2000. "Union Involvement in Workplace Decision Making: Implications for Union Democracy." *Journal of Labor Research* 21(2):265–86.

———. 2001. "Reconceptualising Union Responses to Workplace Restructuring." *British Journal of Industrial Relations* 39(4):539–64.

Gallie, Duncan. 1996. "Trade Union Allegiance and Decline in British Urban Labour Markets. In *Trade Unionism in Recession,* edited by Duncan Gallie, Roger Penn, and Michael Rose, 140–74. Oxford: Oxford University Press.

Geary, John F. 1999. "The New Workplace: Change at Work in Ireland." *International Journal of Human Resource Management* 10(5):870–90.

Geary, John F., and William K. Roche. 2001. "Multinationals and Human Resource Practices in Ireland: A Rejection of the 'New Conformance Thesis.'" *International Journal of Human Resource Management* 12(1):109–27.

———. 2005. "The Future of Employee Information and Consultation in Ireland." In *Adding*

Value through Information and Consultation, edited by John Storey, 170–99. Basingstoke: Palgrave Macmillan.

Godard, John. 2004. "A Critical Assessment of the High-Performance Paradigm." *British Journal of Industrial Relations* 42(2):349–78.

Gomez, Raphael, and Morley Gunderson. 2004. "The Experience-Good Model of Union Membership." In *The Changing Role of Unions: New Forms of Representation,* edited by Phanindra V. Wunnava, 92–114. New York: M. E. Sharpe.

Gomez, Raphael, Morley Gunderson, and Noah M. Meltz. 2002. "Comparing Youth and Adult Desire for Unionization in Canada." *British Journal of Industrial Relations* 40(3): 521–42.

Gordon, M. E., J. W. Philbot, R. Burt, C. A. Thompson, and W. A. Spiller. 1980. "Commitment to the Union: Development of a Measure and an Examination of Its Correlates." *Journal of Applied Psychology* 65(4):479–99.

Goshal, Sumantra. 2005. "Bad Management Theories Are Destroying Good Management Practices." *Academy of Management Learning and Education* 4(1):75–91.

Gospel, Howard, and Andrew Pendleton. 2003. "Finance, Corporate Governance and the Management of Labour: A Conceptual and Comparative Analysis." *British Journal of Industrial Relations* 41(3):557–82.

Gospel, Howard, and Paul Willman. 2003a. "Dilemmas in Worker Representation: Information, Consultation and Negotiation." In *Representing Workers: Union Recognition and Membership in Britain,* edited by Howard Gospel and Stephen Wood, 144–165. London: Routledge.

——. 2003b. "High Performance Workplaces: The Role of Employee Involvement in a Modern Economy; Evidence on the EU Directive Establishing a General Framework for Informing and Consulting Employees." Discussion Paper 562. London: Centre for Economic Performance, London School of Economics.

——. 2005. "Changing Patterns of Employee Voice." In *Adding Value through Information and Consultation,* edited by John Storey, 126–44. Basingstoke: Palgrave Macmillan.

Grainger, Heidi. 2006. *Trade Union Membership 2005.* London: Department of Trade and Industry.

Greenhouse, Steven. 2004. "Labor Federation Looks beyond Unions." *New York Times,* 11 July.

Guest, David. 1995. "Human Resource Management, Trade Unions and Industrial Relations." In *Human Resource Management: A Critical Text,* edited by John Storey, 110–41. London: Routledge.

Gunderson, Morley, and Douglas Hyatt. 2005. "Union Impact on Compensation, Management and Productivity in the Organisation." In *Union–Management Relations in Canada,* 5th ed., edited by Gunderson, Allen Ponak, and Daphne G. Taras, 314–58. Toronto: Pearson Education Canada.

Gunderson, Morley, Allen Ponak, and Daphne Gottlieb Taras, eds. 2003. *Union–Management Relations in Canada.* 5th ed. Toronto: Pearson Education Canada.

Gunderson, Morley, and Andrew Sharpe. 1998. *Forging Business-Labour Partnerships: The Emergence of Sector Councils in Canada.* Toronto: University of Toronto Press.

Gwartney, James, and Robert Lawson. 2002. *Economic Freedom of the World: 2002 Annual Report.* Vancouver: Fraser Institute.

Gwartney, James, and Robert Lawson, with Erik Gartzke. 2005. *Economic Freedom of the World: 2005 Annual Report.* Vancouver: Fraser Institute.

Hancock, Keith. 1999. "Labour Market Deregulation in Australia." In *Reshaping the Labour Market: Regulation, Efficiency and Equality in Australia,* edited by Sue Richardson, 38–85. Cambridge: Cambridge University Press.

Harris Poll. 2005. "Negative Attitudes to Labor Unions Show Little Change in Past Decade, According to New Harris Poll." *Harris Poll* 68. http://www.harrisinteractive.com/harris _poll/index.asp?PID=598.

Haynes, Peter. 2005. "Filling the Vacuum? Non-Union Employee Voice in the Auckland Hotel Industry." *Employee Relations* 27(3):259–71.

Haynes, Peter, and Peter Boxall. 2004. "Free-Riding in New Zealand: Incidence, Motives and Policy Implications." *Labour and Industry* 15(2):47–63.

Haynes, Peter, Peter Boxall, and Keith Macky. 2003. *New Zealanders' Influence at Work: Report on the New Zealand Worker Representation and Participation Survey.* Auckland: University of Auckland Business School.

——. 2005. "Non-Union Voice and the Effectiveness of Joint Consultation in New Zealand." *Economic and Industrial Democracy* 26(2):229–56.

——. 2006. "Union Reach, the 'Representation Gap' and the Prospects for Unionism in New Zealand." *Journal of Industrial Relations* 48(2):193–216.

Haynes, Peter, Jack Vowles, and Peter Boxall. 2005. "Explaining the Younger-Older Worker Union Density Gap: Evidence from New Zealand." *British Journal of Industrial Relations* 43(1):93–116.

Heritage Foundation. 2005. *2005 Index of Economic Freedom.* Washington, D.C.: Heritage Foundation and *Wall Street Journal.* http://www.heritage.org/research/features/index/.

Higgins, Colman. 2005. "Congress Seeks Cash Backing from Unions in New Drive for Members." *Industrial Relations News* 26.

High Court of Australia. 2006. *State of New South Wales & Ors v Commonwealth (AKA Workplace Relations Challenge)* [2006]. HCA Trans 24.

Hirsch, Barry T., and David A. Macpherson. 2003. "Union Membership and Coverage Database from the Current Population Survey: Note." *Industrial and Labor Relations Review* 56(2):349–54, updated on http://www.trinity.edu/bhirsch/unionstats.

Holmstrom, Bengt, and Steven N. Kaplan. 2003. "The State of U.S. Corporate Governance: What's Right and What's Wrong?" NBER Working Paper 9613. Boston: National Bureau of Economic Research.

Howe, John. 2005. "Deregulation of Labour Relations in Australia: Toward Command and Control." Working Paper No. 34. Melbourne: Centre for Employment and Labour Relations Law, University of Melbourne.

Hyman, Richard. 2001. *Understanding European Trade Unionism: Between Market, Class and Society.* London: Sage.

——. 2003. "The Historical Evolution of British Industrial Relations." In *Industrial Relations: Theory and Practice,* edited by Paul Edwards, 37–57. Oxford: Blackwell.

Ichniowski, Casey, Thomas A. Kochan, David Levine, Craig Olson, and George Strauss. 1996. "What Works at Work: Overview and Assessment." *Industrial Relations* 35(3):299–333.

Industrial Democracy in Europe (IDE). 1981. *Industrial Democracy in Europe.* Oxford: Clarendon.

Jacoby, Sanford M. 2000. "Corporate Governance in Comparative Perspective: Prospects for Convergence." *Comparative Labor Law & Policy Journal* 22(1):5–32.

Jarley, Paul, and Nancy Johnson. 2003. "Unions as Social Capital." Paper presented at the

13th World Congress of the International Industrial Relations Association, Berlin, 8–12 September.

Jolls, Christine. 2005. "The Role and Functioning of Public-Interest Legal Organizations in the Enforcement of the Employment Laws." In *Emerging Labor Market Institutions for the Twenty-First Century,* edited by Richard B. Freeman, Joni Hersch, and Lawrence Mishel. Chicago: University of Chicago Press for NBER.

Jurgens, Ulrich, Katrin Naumann, and Joachim Rupp. 2000. "Shareholder Value in an Adverse Environment: The German Case." *Economy and Society* 29(1):54–79.

Katz, Harry C., Rosemary Batt, and Jeffrey H. Keefe. 2003. "The Revitalization of the CWA: Integrating Collective Bargaining, Political Action, and Organizing." *Industrial and Labor Relations Review* 56(4):573–89.

Kaufman, Bruce E. 1999. "Does the NLRA Constrain Employee Involvement and Participation Programs in Non-Union Companies? A Reassessment." *Yale Law and Policy Review* 17(2):729–811.

——. 2001. "The Employee Participation/Representation Gap: An Assessment and Proposed Solution." *University of Pennsylvania Journal of Labor and Employment Law* 3(3): 491–550

——. 2004. "Prospects for Union Growth in the United States in the Early 21st Century." In *Unions in the 21st Century: An International Perspective,* edited by Anil Verma and Thomas A. Kochan, 44–60. Basingstoke: Palgrave Macmillan.

Kaufman, Bruce E., and David I. Levine. 2000. "An Economic Analysis of Employee Representation." In *Nonunion Employee Representation: History, Contemporary Practice, and Policy,* edited by Kaufman and Daphne G. Taras, 149–75. Armonk, N.Y.: M. E. Sharpe.

Kaufman, Bruce E., and Daphne Gottlieb Taras. 2000. "Introduction." In *Nonunion Employee Representation: History, Contemporary Practice, and Policy,* edited by Kaufman and Taras, 3–20. Armonk, N.Y.: M. E. Sharpe.

Kelly, John. 2004. "Social Partnership Agreements in Britain: Labor Cooperation and Compliance." *Industrial Relations* 43(1):267–92.

Kenyon, Peter D., and Philip E. T. Lewis. 1992. "Trade Union Membership and the Accord." *Australian Economic Papers* 31(59):325–45.

Kersley, Barbara, Carmen Alpin, John Forth, Alex Bryson, Helen Bewley, Gill Dix, and Sarah Oxenbridge. 2005. *Inside the Workplace: First Findings from the 2004 Workplace Employment Relations Survey (WERS 2004).* London: DTI, ACAS, ESRC, PSI.

Kinnie, Nicholas, Sue Hutchinson, John Purcell, Bruce Rayton, and Juani Swart. 2005. "Satisfaction with HR Practices and Commitment to the Organisation: Why One Size Does Not Fit All." *Human Resource Management Journal* 15(4):9–29.

Kochan, Thomas A. 1979. "How American Workers View Labor Unions." *Monthly Labor Review* 102:23–31.

——. 2003. "A US Perspective on the Future of Trade Unions in Britain." In *Representing Workers: Union Recognition and Membership in Britain,* edited by Howard Gospel and Stephen Wood, 166–77. London: Routledge.

——. 2004. "Restoring Workers' Voice: A Call to Action." In *The Future of Labor Unions,* edited by Julius G. Getman and Ray Marshall, 47–70. Austin: Lyndon B. Johnson School of Public Affairs, University of Texas Press.

Kochan, Thomas A., Richard Locke, Paul Osterman, and Michael Piore. 2004. "Extended Networks: A Vision for the Next Generation Unions." In *Unions in the 21st Century: An*

International Perspective, edited by Anil Verma and Thomas A. Kochan, 30–43. Basingstoke: Palgrave Macmillan.

Kumar, Pradeep, and Gregor Murray. 2003. "Strategic Dilemma: The State of Union Renewal in Canada." In *Trade Union Renewal: A Comparative Study,* edited by Peter Fairbrother and Charlotte Yates, 200–220. New York: Continuum.

La Porta, Rafael, Florencio Lopez-de-Silanes, and Andrei Shleifer. 1999. "Corporate Ownership around the World." *Journal of Finance* 54(2):471–517.

La Porta, Rafael, Florencio Lopez-de-Silanes, Andrei Shleifer, and Robert Vishny. 1998. "Law and Finance." *Journal of Political Economy* 106(6):1113–55.

——. 1999. "The Quality of Government." *Journal of Law, Economics, and Organization* 15(1):222–79.

Leigh, Duane E. 1986. "Union Preferences, Job Satisfaction, and the Union-Voice Hypothesis." *Industrial Relations* 25(1):65–71.

Lerner, Stephen. 2002. "Three Steps to Reorganizing and Rebuilding the Labor Movement: Building New Strength and Unity for All Working Families." *Labor Notes* 285. http//www.labornotes.org/archives/2002/12/e.html.

LeRoy, Michael H. 1999. "Employee Participation in the New Millennium: Redefining a Labor Organization under Section 8(a)(2) of the NLRA." *Southern California Law Review* 72(6):1651–723.

——. 2004. "The Power to Create or Obstruct Employee Voice: How US Public Policy Skews Employer Preference for 'No Voice' Workplaces." *Socio-Economic Review* 4(2):311–9.

Lipset, Seymour Martin, and Noah M. Meltz. 1997. "Canadian and American Attitudes toward Work and Institutions." *Perspectives on Work* 1(3):14–20.

——. 2000. "Estimates of Non-Union Employee Representation in the United States and Canada: How Different Are the Two Countries?" In *Nonunion Employee Representation: History, Contemporary Practice, and Policy,* edited by Bruce E. Kaufman and Daphne G. Taras, 223–30. Armonk, N.Y.: M. E. Sharpe.

Lipset, Seymour Martin, and Noah M. Meltz, with Raphael Gomez and Ivan Katchanovski. 2004. *The Paradox of American Unionism: Why Americans Like Unions More Than Canadians But Join Much Less.* Ithaca: Cornell University Press.

Logan, John. 2002. "Consultants, Lawyers and the 'Union Free' Movement in the USA since the 1970s." *Industrial Relations Journal* 33(3):197–214.

Machin, Stephen. 2000. "Union Decline in Britain." *British Journal of Industrial Relations* 38(4):631–45.

Machin, Stephen, and Stephen Wood. 2005. "HRM as a Substitute for Trade Unions." *Industrial and Labor Relations Review* 58(2):201–19.

Macky, Keith, Peter Boxall, and Peter Haynes. 2005. "Predictors of Union Belonging and Joining Intentions in New Zealand." Mimeo. Department of Management and Employment Relations, University of Auckland.

Martins, Pedro S., and Pedro T. Pereira. 2004. "Does Education Reduce Wage Inequality? Quantile Regression Evidence from 16 Countries." *Labour Economics* 11:355–71.

McCallum, Ron. 1994. "Voluntary Trade Unionism in New South Wales: Timely Innovation or Backward Step?" *Australian Journal of Labour Law* 7(1):1–32.

McLennan, Kenneth. 2006. "A Management Perspective on *What Do Unions Do?*" In *"What Do Unions Do?" A Twenty-Year Perspective,* edited by James T. Bennett and Bruce E. Kaufman. New Brunswick, N.J.: Transaction.

McPhillips, David. 2005. "Employment Legislation in Canada." In *Union-Management Re-*

lations in Canada, 5th ed., edited by Morley Gunderson, Allen Ponak, and Daphne G. Taras, 211–33. Toronto: Pearson Education Canada.

Meldrum, Bill. 1980. *Managing Employee Involvement: Based on New Zealand Case Studies.* Wellington: New Zealand Employers Federation.

Millward, Neil, Alex Bryson, and John Forth. 2000. *All Change at Work: British Employment Relations 1980–1998, as Portrayed by the British Workplace Industrial Relations Survey Series.* London: Routledge.

Milton, Laurie P. 2003. "An Identity Perspective on the Propensity of High-Tech Talent to Unionize." *Journal of Labor Research* 24(1):31–53.

Murray, Gregor. 2005. "Unions: Membership, Structures, Actions and Challenges." In *Union-Management Relations in Canada,* 5th ed., edited by Morley Gunderson, Allen Ponak, and Daphne G. Taras, 79–116. Toronto: Pearson Education Canada.

Naughton, Richard. 1994. "The New Bargaining Regime under the Industrial Relations Reform Act." *Australian Journal of Labour Law* 7(2): 147–69.

Ochel, Wolfgang. 2001. "Collective Bargaining Coverage in the OECD from the 1960s to the 1990s." *CESifo Forum* 4 (2001):62–65.

O'Connell, Philip, Helen Russell, James Williams, and Sylvia Blackwell. 2003. "The Changing Workplace: A Survey of Employees' Views and Experiences." *Forum on the Workplace of the Future.* Research Series No. 2. Dublin: ESRI and NCPP.

OECD. 1997. *Employment Outlook.* Paris: OECD.

———. 1999. *Employment Outlook.* Paris: OECD.

———. 2004. *Employment Outlook.* Paris: OECD.

———. 2006. *OECD Factbook 2006, Economic, Environmental, and Social Statistics.* http://caliban.sourceoecd.org/vl=34238121/cl=29/nw=1/rpsv/factbook/about.h

O'Grady, John. 2000. "Joint Health and Safety Committees." In *Injury and the New World of Work,* edited by Terrence Sullivan, 162–97. Vancouver: UBC Press.

Olson, Mancur. 1965. *The Logic of Collective Action: Public Goods and the Theory of Groups.* Cambridge: Harvard University Press.

O'Neill, Stephen, Indra Kuruppu, and Barbara Harris. 2006. *Workplace Relations Reforms: A Chronology of Business, Community and Government Responses.* Canberra: Parliamentary Library. http://www.aph.gov.au/library/pubs/online/WorkplaceRelations.htm.

Osterman, Paul. 2003. *Gathering Power: The Future of Progressive Politics in America.* Boston: Beacon Press.

Palmer, Tom, Heidi Grainger, and Grant Fitzner. 2004. *Trade Union Membership 2003.* London: Department for Trade and Industry.

Partnership 2000 for Inclusion, Employment and Competitiveness. Department of the Taoiseach 1996. Dublin: Government of Ireland.

Payette, Suzanne. 2000. "What Is New in Workplace Innovation." *Workplace Gazette* 3(1): 110–19.

Peetz, David. 1998. *Unions in a Contrary World: The Future of the Australian Trade Union Movement.* Cambridge: Cambridge University Press.

———. 2002. "Decollectivist Strategies in Oceania." *Relations Industrielles* 57(2):252–81.

———. 2004. "Co-operative Identity, Social Capital, Altruism and Free-Riding in Australia and Canada." Paper presented to the International Colloquium on Citizenship at Work, Centre de recherche interuniversitaire sur la mondialisation et le travail (CRIMT), Montreal, 21–23 June.

Peetz, David, and Barbara Pocock. 2005. "Organising and Delegates: An Overview." In *Re-*

working Work: AIRAANZ 2005 Proceedings of the 19th Conference of the Association of Industrial Relations Academics of Australia and New Zealand, vol. 1, *Refereed Papers,* edited by Marian Baird, Rae Cooper, and Mark Westcott. Sydney: AIRAANZ.

Penney, Robert A. 2004. "Workers against Unions: Organizing and Anti-Union Counter-mobilizations." In *Rebuilding Labor: Organizing and Organizers in the New Union Movement,* edited by Ruth Milkman and Kim Voss, 88–113. Ithaca: Cornell University Press.

Peter D. Hart Research Associates Inc. 2001. Hart Poll, Study # 6221.

———. 2002. "Labor Day 2002." Survey of 900 adults nationwide, including oversample of 100 nonmanagerial workers conducted August 10–13, for AFL-CIO.

———. 2003. Hart Poll, Study #6923.

Pil, Frits K., and John Paul MacDuffie. 1996. "The Adoption of High-Involvement Work Practices." *Industrial Relations* 35:423–55.

Poole, Michael, Roger Mansfield, Julian Gould-Williams, and Priya Mendes. 2005. "British Managers' Attitudes and Behaviour in Industrial Relations: A Twenty-Year Study." *British Journal of Industrial Relations* 43(1):117–34.

Porter, Michael. 1992. "Capital Disadvantage: America's Failing Capital Investment System." *Harvard Business Review* 70(5):65–83.

Poterba, James M., and Lawrence H. Summers. 1995. "A Survey of U.S. Companies, Time Horizons, and Hurdle Rates." *Sloan Management Review* 37(1):43–53.

Premack, Steven L., and John E. Hunter. 1988. "Individual Unionization Decisions." *Psychological Bulletin* 103(2):223–34.

Price, Rachael F. 2004. "Cause for Celebration, Cause for Solicitude: Unions, the Internet and International Solidarity." Master's thesis in labor studies, University of Waikato, New Zealand.

Public Information Officer, High Court of Australia. 2006. "State of NSW v Commonwealth of Australia; State of WA v Commonwealth of Australia; State of SA v Commonwealth of Australia; State of Qld v Commonwealth of Australia; State of Victoria v Commonwealth of Australia; Australian Workers' Union & Another v Commonwealth of Australia, Unions NSW & Others v Commonwealth of Australia," High Court of Australia, 14 November. wc.d.

Purcell, John. 1995. "Ideology and the End of Institutional Industrial Relations: Evidence from the UK." In *Organised Industrial Relations in Europe: What Future?* edited by Colin Crouch and Franz Traxler, 101–19. Aldershot: Avebury.

Purcell, John, and Nicholas Kinnie. 2006. "HRM and Business Performance." In The *Oxford Handbook of Human Resource Management,* edited by Peter Boxall, John Purcell, and Patrick Wright. Oxford: Oxford University Press.

Pyman, Amanda. 2004. "The Impact of the Workplace Relations Act on Trade Union Effectiveness: An Exploratory Analysis." PhD thesis, Department of Management, Monash University, Melbourne.

Pyman, Amanda, Brian Cooper, Julian Teicher, and Peter Holland. 2006. "A Comparison of the Effectiveness of Employee Voice Arrangements in Australia." *Industrial Relations Journal* 37(5): 543–59.

Quinlan, Michael. 1998. "Industrial Relations Policy Developments 1977–1998: A Critical Review." *Journal of Australian Political Economy* 42:75–105.

Reid, Frank, Noah M. Meltz, and Raphael Gomez. 2005. "Social, Political and Economic Environments." In *Union-Management Relations in Canada,* 5th ed., edited by Morley Gunderson, Allen Ponak, and Daphne G. Taras, 142–74. Toronto: Pearson Education Canada.

Riddell, Chris. 2004. "Union Certification Success under Voting versus Card-Check Procedures: Evidence from British Columbia, 1978–1998." *Industrial and Labour Relations Review* 57(4):493–517.

Riddell, Chris, and Craig Riddell. 2004. "Changing Patterns of Unionisation: The North American Experience." In *Unions in the 21st Century: An International Perspective,* edited by Anil Verma and Thomas A. Kochan, 146–64. Basingstoke: Palgrave Macmillan.

Riddell, Craig. 1993. "Unionization in Canada and the United States: A Tale of Two Countries." In *Small Differences That Matter: Labor Markets and Income Maintenance in Canada and the United States,* edited by David Card and Richard B. Freeman, 109–48. Chicago: University of Chicago Press.

Roche, William K. 2001. "Accounting for the Trend in Trade Union Recognition in Ireland." *Industrial Relations Journal* 32(1):37–54.

Roche, William K., and Jacqueline Ashmore. 2002. "Irish Unions: Testing the Limits of Social Partnership." In *Changing Prospects for Trade Unionism: Comparisons between Six Countries,* edited by Peter Fairbrother and Gerard Griffin, 137–76. London: Continuum.

Roche, William K., and John F. Geary. 2000. "Collaborative Production and the Irish Boom: Work Organization, Partnership and Direct Involvement in Irish Workplaces." *Economic and Social Review* 31(1):1–36.

Roche, William K., and Joe Larragy. 1990. "Cyclical and Institutional Determinants of Annual Trade Union Growth and Decline in Ireland: Evidence from the DUES Data Series." *European Sociological Review* 6(1):49–72.

Rogers, Joel, and Wolfgang Streeck, eds. 1995. *Works Councils: Consultation, Representation, and Cooperation in Industrial Relations.* Chicago: University of Chicago Press.

Roth, Paul. 2001. "International Labour Organisation Conventions 87 and 98 and the Employment Relations Act." *New Zealand Journal of Employment Relations* 26(2):145–69.

Roy Morgan Research. 2005. "2.5 Million Australians Belong to a Trade Union—And a Further 1.5 Million Want to Join Them." Roy Morgan Research, Finding No. 3928, 17 November. http://www.roymorgan.com/news/polls/2005/3928/index.cfm?printversion=yes,12/06

Sako, Mari. 1998. "The Nature and Impact of Employee 'Voice' in the European Car Components Industry." *Human Resource Management Journal* 8(2):6–13.

Segelod, Esbjörn. 2000. "A Comparison of Managers' Perceptions of Short-termism in Sweden and the US." *International Journal of Production Economics* 63:243–54.

Shaw, M., and M. Schubert. 2006. "Push for Test Case on IR Laws," *The Age,* 5 April, Melbourne, Australia. www.theage.com.au/news/national/push-for-test-case-on-ir-laws/2006/04/04/1143916

Shleifer, Andrei, and Robert Vishny. 1990. "Equilibrium Short Horizons of Investors and Firms." *American Economic Review Papers and Proceedings* 80(2):148–53.

Sisson, Keith. 1993. "In Search of HRM." *British Journal of Industrial Relations* 31(2):201–10.

Sneade, A. 2001. "Trade union membership 1999–2000." *Labour Market Trends* September: 433–44.

Statistics New Zealand. 2003. *Key Statistics March 2003.* Wellington: Statistics New Zealand.

Stein, Jeremy. 1988. "Takeover Threats and Managerial Myopia." *Journal of Political Economy* 96(1):61–80.

——. 1989. "Efficient Capital Markets, Inefficient Firms: A Model of Myopic Corporate Behavior." *Quarterly Journal of Economics* 104(4):655–69.

Stewart, Andrew. 2006. "Work Choices in Overview: Big Bang or Slow Burn?" *Economic and Labour Relations Review* 16(2):25–50.

Streeck, Wolfgang. 1997. "Citizenship under Regime Competition: The Case of the 'European Works Councils.'" Jean Monnet Working Paper No. 9. New York: New York University School of Law.

Streeck, Wolfgang, and Anke Hassel. 2002. "Trade Unions as Political Actors." In *International Handbook of Trade Unions,* edited by John T. Addison and Claus Schnabel, 335–65. Cheltenham: Edward Elgar.

Strope, Leigh. 2004. "Labor's Fight for Its Future Takes to the Internet." *Albany Times Union,* July 6.

Taras, Daphne G. 1997a. "Why Non-Union Representation Is Legal in Canada." *Relations Industrielles/Industrial Relations* 52(4):761–80.

——. 1997b. "Collective Bargaining Regulation in Canada and the United States: Divergent Cultures, Divergent Outcomes." In *Government Regulation of the Employment Relationship,* edited by Bruce E. Kaufman, 295–342. Madison: Industrial Relations Research Association.

——. 2000. "Portrait of Nonunion Employee Representation in Canada: History, Law, and Contemporary Plans." In *Nonunion Employee Representation: History, Contemporary Practice, and Policy,* edited by Bruce E. Kaufman and Daphne G. Taras, 120–38. Armonk, N.Y.: M. E. Sharpe.

——. 2001. "Explaining Canadian–American Differences in Union Density." In *Proceedings of the 53rd Annual Meeting, Industrial Relations Research Association,* 153–62. Urbana-Champaign: Industrial Relations Research Association.

——. 2006. "Non-Union Representation and Employer Intent: How Canadian Courts and Labour Boards Determine the Legal Status of Nonunion Plans." *Socio-Economic Review* 4(2):321–36.

Teicher, Julian, and Richard Bryan. 2002. "The Australian State and the Global Economy." In *Employee Relations Management: Australia in a Global Context,* edited by Teicher, Peter Holland, and Richard Gough, 15–35. Sydney: Pearson Education Australia.

Teicher, Julian, Rob Lambert, and Anne O'Rourke. 2006. "Introduction: The Work Choices Act as the Triumph of Neoliberalism." In *WorkChoices: The New Industrial Relations Agenda,* edited by Teicher, Lambert, and O'Rourke. Sydney: Pearson Education Australia.

Terry, Michael. 2004. "'Partnership': A Serious Strategy for UK Trade Unions?" In *Unions in the 21st Century: An International Perspective,* edited by Anil Verma and Thomas A. Kochan, 205–19. Basingstoke: Palgrave Macmillan.

Thompson, Mark, and Allen Ponak. 2005. "The Management of Industrial Relations." In *Union-Management Relations in Canada,* 5th ed., edited by Morley Gunderson, Allen Ponak, and Daphne G. Taras, 414–46. Toronto: Pearson Education Canada.

The Treasury. 2004. *New Zealand Economic Growth: An Analysis of Performance and Policy.* Report to the Minister of Finance, April. Wellington: The Treasury.

Turner, H. A. "The Donovan Report." *Economic Journal* 79(313):1–10.

Turner, Lowell. 1998. *Fighting for Partnership: Labor and Politics in Unified Germany.* Ithaca: Cornell University Press.

Ulrich, David. 1996. *Human Resource Champions: The Next Agenda for Adding Value and Delivering Results.* Boston: Harvard Business School Press.

United States Bureau of the Census. 2005. *Statistical Abstract.* Washington, D.C.: U.S. Government Printing Office.

van Barneveld, Kristin. 2006. "Australian Workplace Agreements under Work Choices." *Economic and Labour Relations Review* 16(2):165–84.

Vandenberg, Robert J., Hettie A. Richardson, and Lorrina J. Eastman. 1999. "The Impact of High Involvement Work Processes on Organizational Effectiveness: A Second-Order Latent Variable Approach." *Group and Organization Management* 24(3):300–339.

van den Broek, Diane. 2003. "Recruitment Strategies and Union Exclusion in Two Australian Call Centres." *Relations Industrielles* 58(3):515–36.

Verma, Anil, and Daphne G. Taras. 2005. "Managing the High-Involvement Workplace." In *Union-Management Relations in Canada*, 5th ed., edited by Morley Gunderson, Allen Ponak, and Daphne G. Taras, 447–85. Toronto: Pearson Education Canada.

Visser, Jelle. 2000. "Trends in Unionisation and Collective Bargaining." Geneva: International Labour Office.

Waldegrave, Tony. 2004a. "Employee Experience of Employment Relationships under the Employment Relations Act 2000." In *Employment Relationships: New Zealand's Employment Relations Act*, edited by Erling Rasmussen, 145–58. Auckland: Auckland University Press.

——. 2004b. "Employment Relationship Management under the Employment Relations Act 2000." In *Employment Relationships: New Zealand's Employment Relations Act*, edited by Erling Rasmussen, 119–33. Auckland: Auckland University Press.

Wallace, Alfred Russell. 1858. "On the Tendency of Varieties to Depart Indefinitely from the Original Type. Instability of Varieties Supposed to Prove the Permanent Distinctness of Species." Written at Ternate, February 1858, presented by Charles Darwin at the Royal Society in 1858. http://www.zoo.uib.no/classics/varieties.html.

Walton, Richard E., and Robert B. McKersie. 1965. *A Behavioral Theory of Labor Negotiations*. New York: McGraw-Hill.

Weil, David. 2004. "Individual Rights and Collective Agents: The Role of Old and New Workplace Institutions in the Regulation of Labor Markets." In *Emerging Labor Market Institutions for the Twenty-First Century*, edited by Richard B. Freeman, Joni Hersch, and Lawrence Mishel, 13–44. Chicago: University of Chicago Press for NBER.

Whatman, Richard, Craig Armitage, and Richard Dunbar. 1994. "Labour Market Adjustment under the Employment Contracts Act." *New Zealand Journal of Industrial Relations* 19(1):53–73.

Wheeler, Hoyt N., and John A. McClendon. 1991. "The Individual Decision to Unionize." In *The State of the Unions*, edited by George Strauss, Daniel G. Gallagher, and Jack Fiorito, 47–83. Madison: Industrial Relations Research Association.

Willman, Paul. 2004. "Structuring Unions: The Administrative Rationality of Collective Action." In *Union Organization and Activity*, edited by John Kelly and Paul Willman, 73–88. London: Routledge.

Willman, Paul, and Alex Bryson. 2005. "Things Can Only Get Better: A Picture of Union Finances at the End of the 20th Century." Paper presented at the Society for the Advancement of Socio-Economics 17th Annual Meeting on Socio-Economics, Central European University and Corvinus University of Budapest, 30 June–2 July, 2005.

Willmott, Ben. 2006. "Information and Consultation: Apathy or Culture Change?" *Impact: Quarterly Update on CIPD Policy and Research* 15. London: Chartered Institute for Personnel and Development.

World Economic Forum. 2003. *Global Competitiveness Report 2003–2004*. Geneva: World Economic Forum.

Wyllie, Allan, and Justine Whitfield. 2003. *Site and Employee Surveys: Components of the Evaluation of the Employment Relations Act.* Auckland: Phoenix Research.

Yates, Charlotte. 2003. "The Revival of Industrial Unions in Canada: The Extension and Adaptation of Industrial Union Practices to the New Economy." In *Trade Union Renewal: A Comparative Study,* edited by Peter Fairbrother and Charlotte Yates, 221–43. New York: Continuum.

Zogby International. 2005. *The Attitudes and Opinions of Unionized and Non-Unionized Workers Employed in Various Sectors of the Economy toward Organized Labor.* Report to the Public Service Research Foundation. http://www.zogby.com/news/ReadNews.dbm ?ID=1011.

Contributors

Peter Boxall is Professor of Human Resource Management at the University of Auckland. He is coeditor with John Purcell and Patrick Wright of *The Oxford Handbook of Human Resource Management* (Oxford University Press, 2007) and coauthor with John Purcell of *Strategy and Human Resource Management* (Palgrave Macmillan, 2003).

Alex Bryson is Principal Research Fellow at the Policy Studies Institute, London, and Visiting Fellow at the Centre for Economic Performance, London School of Economics. He is coauthor of *Inside the Workplace: Findings From the 2004 Workplace Employment Relations Survey* (Routledge, 2006).

Michele Campolieti is Associate Professor in the Department of Management (Scarborough Campus) and at the Centre for Industrial Relations and Human Resources at the University of Toronto, and a research associate of the Canadian Labour Market and Skills Researcher Network. His research interests span econometrics, labor economics, and industrial relations.

Brian Cooper is Research Fellow in the Department of Management, Monash University, Victoria, Australia. His research interests include stress and coping, employee well-being, and applied statistical modeling.

Richard B. Freeman is Ascherman Professor of Economics at Harvard University, Codirector of the Labor and Worklife Program at the Harvard Law School, and Director of the Labor Studies Program at the National Bureau of Economic Research. He is also Senior Research Fellow in Labour Markets at the Centre for Economic Performance at the London School of Economics.

Ann Frost is Associate Professor in the Richard Ivey School of Business at the University of Western Ontario. Her research interests include workplace restructuring, dynamics in industrial relations, the high-performance workplace, and knowledge management in services.

John Geary is Professor of Industrial Relations and Human Resources and Director of Doctoral Studies at the College of Business and Law at University College Dublin. He is the coauthor with William Roche of *Partnership at Work: The Quest for Radical Organisational Change* (Routledge, 2006).

Konstantinos Georgiadis is a doctoral student at the University of Bath. His research interests include employee involvement, organizational change, differentiation strategies, labor negotiations, effects of training programs, and the limitations of quantitative methods in human resource management research.

Rafael Gomez is Lecturer in the Department of Management at the London School of Economics, Professor of Economics at Glendon College and a Visiting Professor of Management at Moscow State University. In 2006, he was awarded the Labor and Employment Relations Association's 2005 John T. Dunlop Outstanding Scholar Award for exceptional contributions to international and comparative labor and employment research.

Morley Gunderson holds the CIBC Chair in Youth Employment at the University of Toronto, where he is Professor at the Centre for Industrial Relations and the Department of Economics. In 2002, he was awarded the Industrial Relations Research Association Excellence in Education Award in Labour Economics and in 2003 the Gérard Dion Award for Outstanding Contributions to the Field of Industrial Relations.

Peter Haynes is Senior Lecturer at the University of Auckland and a former trade union official in the public sector. His research spans studies of worker representation and participation, union strategy, high-performance work systems, and service-sector human resource management.

Peter Holland is Senior Lecturer in Human Resource Management and Employee Relations in the Department of Management at Monash University, Victoria. His publications include *Employment Relations in Australia* (Pearson Education, 2002), co-edited with Julian Teicher and Richard Gough.

Thomas A. Kochan is the George Maverick Bunker Professor of Management at MIT's Sloan School of Management and Codirector of the MIT Workplace Center and of the Institute for Work and Employment Research. His recent books include *Restoring the American Dream: A Working Families' Agenda for America* (MIT Press, 2005).

Keith Macky is Senior Lecturer in Human Resource Management at the Department of Management and International Business, Massey University, Auckland. His research interests include high-involvement work practices, employee responses to organizational downsizing and restructuring, and employee retention strategies.

David Peetz is Professor of Industrial Relations at Griffith University, Brisbane. He is the author of *Unions in a Contrary World* (Cambridge University Press, 1998) and *Brave New Workplace: How Individual Contracts Are Changing Our Jobs* (Allen and Unwin, 2006).

John Purcell was formerly Professor of Human Resource Management at the University of Bath and is currently academic adviser to the Advisory, Conciliation and Arbitration Service (ACAS) and Deputy Chairman of Britain's Central Arbitration Committee, which deals with trade union recognition claims. He is co-author with Peter Boxall of *Strategy and Human Resource Management* (Palgrave Macmillan, 2003).

Amanda Pyman is Lecturer in Industrial Relations and Human Resource Management at the Kent Business School, University of Kent. Her research interests include employee voice, union strategy, campaigning and renewal under changing labor legislation, the labor market implications of internet recruitment, and privacy and surveillance in the workplace.

Julian Teicher is Professor and Head of the Department of Management and Director of the Graduate School of Business at Monash University, Victoria. His recent publications include *WorkChoices: the New Industrial Relations Agenda* (Pearson Education, 2006), co-edited with Rob Lambert and Anne O'Rourke.

Index